How to Prove There
Is a God

D1564459

Books by Mortimer Adler

Dialectic (1927) • *Music Appreciation* (1929) • *The Nature of Judicial Proof* (with Jerome Michael, 1931) • *Crime, Law, and Social Science* (with Jerome Michael, 1933) • *Diagrammatics* (with Maude Phelps Hutchins, 1935) • *Art and Prudence* (1937) • *What Man Has Made of Man* (1937) • *Saint Thomas and the Gentiles* (1938) • *How to Read a Book* (1940) • *The Philosophy and Science of Man* (1940) • *Problems for Thomists: The Problem of Species* (1940) • *Scholasticism and Politics* (as editor, 1940) • *A Dialectic of Morals* (1941) • *How to Think about War and Peace* (1944) • *A Syntopicon: An Index to The Great Ideas* (as editor, 2 volumes, 1952) • *Research on Freedom* (2 volumes, 1954) • *The Idea of Freedom* (volume 1, 1958) • *The Revolution in Education* (with Milton Mayer, 1958) • *The Capitalist Manifesto* (with Louis O. Kelso, 1958) • *The New Capitalists* (with Louis O. Kelso, 1961) • *Great Ideas from the Great Books* (1961) • *The Idea of Freedom* (volume 2, 1961) • *The Great Ideas Today* (as editor, with Robert Hutchins, 1961) • *Gateway to the Great Books* (as editor, 10 volumes, with Robert Hutchins, 1963) • (*The Conditions of Philosophy* (1965) • *The Difference of Man and the Difference It Makes* (1967) • *The Annals of America* (as editor, 21 volumes, 1968) • *The Time of Our Lives* (1970) • *The Common Sense of Politics* (1971) • *Propaedia* (as editor, 30 volumes, 1974) • *The American Testament* (with William Gorman, 1975) • *Some Questions about Language* (1976) • *Philosopher at Large* (1977) • *Reforming Education* (1977) • *Great Treasury of Western Thought* (as editor, with Charles Van Doren, 1977) • *Aristotle for Everybody* (1978) • *How to Think about God* (1980) • *Six Great Ideas* (1981) • *The Angels and Us* (1982) • (*The Paideia Proposal* (1982) • *How to Speak/How to Listen* (1983) • *Paideia Problems and Possibilities* (1983) • *A Vision of the Future* (1984) • *The Paideia Program* (with members of the Paideia Group, 1984) • *Ten Philosophical Mistakes* (1985) • *A Guidebook to Learning* (1986) • *We Hold These Truths* (1987) • *Intellect: Mind over Matter* (1990) • *Truth in Religion* (1990) • *Haves Without Have-Nots* (1991) • *Desires, Right, and Wrong* (1991) • *A Second Look in the Rearview Mirror* (1992) • *The Great Ideas* (1992) • *The Four Dimensions of Philosophy* (1993) • *Art, the Arts, and the Great Ideas* (1994) • *Adler's Philosophical Dictionary* (1995) • *How to Think about The Great Ideas* (2000) • *How to Prove There Is a God* (2011)

How to Prove There Is a God

Mortimer J. Adler's Writings and
Thoughts about God

Compiled and Edited by
Ken Dzugan

Senior Fellow and Archivist
Center for the Study of the Great Ideas

OPEN COURT
Chicago and La Salle, Illinois

To all the members of
the Center for the Study of The Great Ideas

To order books from Open Court, call toll-free 1-800-815-2280, or visit our website at www.opencourtbooks.com.

Open Court Publishing Company is a division of Carus Publishing Company.

First printing 2012

Library of Congress Cataloging-in-Publication Data

How to prove there is a God : Mortimer J. Adler's writings and thoughts about God / Mortimer J. Adler ; edited by Ken Dzugan.
  p. cm.
  Includes index.
  ISBN 978-0-8126-9689-9 (trade paper : alk. paper)
  1. Adler, Mortimer Jerome, 1902-2001. 2. God—Proof. 3. God (Christianity)
  I. Adler, Mortimer Jerome, 1902-2001. II. Dzugan, Ken.
  BT103.H69 2011
  202—dc23

                                        2011027765

Contents

Has Mortimer Adler Proved There Is a God?

This book presents some of the simplest and most direct statements of Mortimer Adler's argument for the existence of God. Some of what appears in this book has been completely unavailable to the public up till now, and the rest of it has been quite hard to track down.

Much of Dr. Adler's early work in this area might seem to take the form of arguing against the existence of God! But this is just because Dr. Adler wanted to show that some arguments which satisfied some people were not quite adequate. He wanted to closely examine several different arguments which he thought insufficient, though in some cases they contained excellent insights, in order to make adjustments to these arguments, and finally arrive at an argument which would be completely sound. He kept chiseling and polishing his argument from the 1940s until the 1970s. Eventually, he believed he had arrived at the perfectly sound argument he had been looking for.

Dr. Adler sometimes speaks of a 'leap of faith', but this doesn't mean he thought faith was required in order to show that God exists. Dr. Adler maintained that the existence of God as creator and sustainer of the Universe could be strictly demonstrated by pure philosophical argument, without any recourse to faith. Where a leap of faith was required was in making a connection between this God and the personal life of the believer—for after all, we can imagine that there might be a God who would not care about the plight of mere humans.

Dr. Adler worked in the tradition of philosophy known as Thomism, after St. Thomas Aquinas (1224–1274). Most Thomists are Catholics, but Dr. Adler was not a Catholic or even a Christian until late in his life. For most of his active life as a philosopher, he described himself as a pagan, and yet he contributed articles to Thomistic journals, including *The Thomist*. His frequent articles in the Thomistic tradition, along with his avowed paganism, earned Dr. Adler the nickname of "The Peeping Thomist."

St. Thomas Aquinas held that the existence of God could be proved by pure philosophical reasoning, without having to rely on faith, the Bible, or the Church. In a famous passage in his *Summa Theologica*, St. Thomas outlined five ways in which the existence of God might be proved, and these Five Ways have been the focus of intense interest and debate ever since:

ST. THOMAS AQUINAS'S FIVE WAYS

The First and more manifest Way is the argument from motion. It is certain, and evident to our senses, that in the world some things are in motion. Now whatever is in motion is put in motion by another, for nothing can be in motion except it is in potentiality to that towards which it is in motion; whereas a thing moves inasmuch as it is in act. For motion is nothing else than the reduction of something from potentiality to actuality. But nothing can be reduced from potentiality to actuality, except by something in a state of actuality. Thus that which is actually hot, as fire, makes wood, which is potentially hot, to be actually hot, and thereby moves and changes it. Now it is not possible that the same thing should be at once in actuality and potentiality in the same respect, but only in different respects. For what is actually hot cannot simultaneously be potentially hot; but it is simultaneously potentially cold. It is therefore impossible that in the same respect and in the same way a thing should be both mover and moved, i.e. that it should move itself. Therefore, whatever is in motion must be put in motion by another. If that by which it is put in motion be itself put in motion, then this also must needs be put in motion by another, and that by another again. But this cannot go on to infinity, because then there would be no first mover, and, consequently, no other mover; seeing that subsequent movers move only inasmuch as they are put in motion by the first mover; as the staff moves only because it is put in motion by the hand. Therefore it is necessary to arrive at a first mover, put in motion by no other; and this everyone understands to be God.

The Second Way is from the nature of the efficient cause. In the world of sense we find there is an order of efficient causes. There is no case known (neither is it, indeed, possible) in which a thing is found to be the efficient cause of itself; for so it would be prior to itself, which is impossible. Now in efficient causes it is not possible to go on to infinity, because in all efficient causes following in order, the first is the cause of the intermediate cause, and the intermediate is the cause of the ultimate cause, whether the intermediate cause be several, or only one. Now to take away the cause is to take away the effect. Therefore, if there be no first cause among efficient causes, there will be no ultimate, nor any intermediate cause. But if in efficient causes it is possible to go on to infinity, there will be no first efficient cause, neither will there be an ultimate effect, nor any intermediate efficient causes; all of which is plainly false. Therefore it is necessary to admit a first efficient cause, to which everyone gives the name of God.

The Third Way is taken from possibility and necessity, and runs thus. We find in nature things that are possible to be and not to be, since they are found to be generated, and to corrupt, and consequently, they are possible to be and not to be. But it is impossible for these always to exist, for that which is possible not to be at some time is not. Therefore, if everything is possible not to be, then at one time there could have been nothing in existence. Now if this were true, even now there would be nothing in existence, because that which does not exist only begins to exist by something already existing. Therefore, if at one time nothing was in existence, it would have been impossible for anything to have begun to exist; and thus even now nothing would be in existence—which is absurd. Therefore, not all beings are merely possible, but there must exist something the existence of which is necessary. But every necessary thing either has its necessity caused by another, or not. Now it is impossible to go on to infinity in necessary things which have their necessity caused by another, as has been already proved in regard to efficient causes. Therefore we cannot but postulate the existence of some being having of itself its own necessity, and not receiving it from another, but rather causing in others their necessity. This all men speak of as God.

The Fourth Way is taken from the gradation to be found in things. Among beings there are some more and some less good, true, noble and the like. But "more" and "less" are predicated of different things, according as they resemble in their different ways something which is the maximum, as a thing is said to be hotter according as it more nearly resembles that which is hottest; so that there is something which is truest, something best, something noblest and, consequently, something which is uttermost being; for those things that are greatest in truth are greatest in being, as it is written in Metaph. ii. Now the maximum in any genus is the cause of all in that genus; as fire, which is the maximum heat, is the cause of all hot things. Therefore there must also be something which is to all beings the cause of their being, goodness, and every other perfection; and this we call God.

The Fifth Way is taken from the governance of the world. We see that things which lack intelligence, such as natural bodies, act for an end, and this is evident from their acting always, or nearly always, in the same way, so as to obtain the best result. Hence it is plain that not fortuitously, but designedly, do they achieve their end. Now whatever lacks intelligence cannot move towards an end, unless it be directed by some being endowed with knowledge and intelligence; as the arrow is shot to its mark by the archer. Therefore some intelligent being exists by whom all natural things are directed to their end; and this being we call God. (From the *Summa Theologica* of St Thomas Aquinas)

St. Thomas did not think of these as fully worked-out rigorous proofs; they are brief indications of the lines such proofs might take. One obvious objection is that none of the Five Ways arrives at a complete conception of God. For instance, the "first mover" whose existence is supposedly demonstrated in the First Way might be some entity less than God as defined by Christians, Muslims, and Jews. St. Thomas was well aware of this limitation, and provided arguments that these entities were indeed God in another work, his *Summa Contra Gentiles*.

Dr. Adler maintained that some of these Five Ways were insufficient to prove God's existence, while some of them needed more work to arrive at a fully worked out and completely sound argument.

Dr. Adler's early writings on the existence of God are quite difficult, but as Dr. Adler got more experience, he also developed the skill of presenting his ideas in a more popular form. Parts I and II of this book show Adler explaining his ideas very clearly for a general audience. No prior knowledge of the subject is required to read Parts I and II. Part III comprises an article Adler wrote in 1943 on the existence of God, in which he raises various problems with traditional Thomistic arguments; a strongly worded attack on Dr. Adler's article by the more traditional Thomist, Herbert Thomas Schwartz; and then a much fuller and more detailed treatment of the question by Dr. Adler, including a vigorous response to every one of Schwartz's arguments. We can see here Mortimer Adler's respect for logical rigor, always prepared to abandon an argument if it wasn't good enough, even if it apparently yielded a conclusion he wanted to reach.

In the 1930s and 1940s Dr. Adler spoke and wrote about his increasing concern that academics were becoming far too specialized and were writing in ways that could only be understood by colleagues in the same field of study. Dr. Adler also realized that all the authors of the great books through the nineteenth century had written for the generally educated reader, not other specialists. And so in the 1940s Dr. Adler decided that in the future he would address his writing to the generally educated reader, not specialists.

Has Mortimer Adler proved that there is a God? You, the reader will have to decide this question for yourself, after reading Parts I and II of this book. Whatever you decide, you will certainly have an entertaining and absorbing experience and will learn something about God and about good and bad philosophical arguments.

—KEN DZUGAN
Senior Fellow and Archivist
Center for the Study of The Great Ideas

I

Adler's Case for God's Existence

1 How to Think about God's Existence

MORTIMER J. ADLER

Does God exist? Do you believe in God? These are questions that most people answer—affirmatively or negatively—without giving them much thought. Their answers stem from habits of belief or disbelief, from childhood conditioning, from emotional yearnings or aversions, but not from sustained reasoning or reflective thought.

REASON TO BELIEVE IN GOD?

Do we have reason to believe that God exists? Can reasons be given for our belief in God? These are questions that cannot be answered without a great deal of thought.

Philosophers have tried to answer them since Greek antiquity. From Plato and Aristotle right down to the present century, every philosopher of eminence has tried his hand at it—arguing not for or against God's existence, but for or against the reasonableness of the belief that there exists in reality a being that corresponds to our notion of God. And in our century, eminent scientists, toward the end of their lives, have had their say about it, too.

So far as thinking goes, it is not an easy matter. In fact, it is one of the most difficult problems to think clearly and cogently about. I have spent more than fifty years of my philosophical life thinking about how to think about God; and now, toward the end of it, I feel that I have at last found out how to come up with a solution that makes belief in God's existence reasonable—at least beyond a reasonable doubt.

Since I was a student at Columbia University in 1921, when I first read the "Treatise on God" in the *Summa Theologica* of St.

3

Thomas Aquinas, I have been fascinated by arguments for God's existence. If one likes to think, the two great subjects to put one's mind to work on are mathematical physics and speculative theology. And, in our century, the advances in physics and cosmology help us in our thinking about God. If the human mind can infer the existence of such imperceptible and even undetectible physical things as black holes, perhaps it can reach a bit further to infer the existence of a being that lies beyond the whole of physical reality.

For fifty years I have worked over the arguments for God's existence again and again, reading and re-reading the books of the great philosophers and theologians. But at every stage of my own intellectual development, I have found grave faults in what I thought earlier. I mistaught class after class of college students who, at various stages in my career, I tried to persuade that this or that argument did the trick, only to discover later that these arguments were full of holes and wouldn't stand up.

Once a student properly gave me my comeuppance. Conducting a seminar on Aquinas's "Treatise on God," I announced to the class that until I had succeeded in persuading every one present that Aquinas had demonstrated God's existence, I would not move on to other questions about God's nature and attributes. One by one they gave in—either from conviction or plain weariness—but one, Charles Adams, indomitably held out.

Finally, my colleague in the course, Professor Malcolm Sharp called a halt and suggested that, instead of sticking to my guns, I should tell the students about Aquinas's life. So I told them of this robust and remarkable medieval monk and scholar who churned out, in a career of less than twenty years, works of the highest intellectual quality, which would fill much more than a five-foot shelf. He did this without the convenience of a typewriter, electric lights, a decent library, and all the while traveling back and forth on muleback across the Alps from Paris to Rome.

When I finished, Charles Adams spoke up. "You should have told us all this about Aquinas to begin with," he said, "instead of wasting our time with those no-good arguments." When I asked him, "Why?" he replied: "Because, obviously, Aquinas could not have done all that without God's help!"

GOD BY THE LIGHT OF REASON

In the two score years since I gave up college teaching, I have delivered elaborate lectures about the proofs of God's existence to popular audiences all over the country. I mention this fact because the experience has taught me how widespread and intense is the popular interest in the subject.

Announce a lecture on the proof of God's existence and you get a standing-room only audience, even if, as happened once in Chicago, a Marilyn Monroe film is playing in the theater right next door. No other subject attracts as much attention or sustains it as well. When the lecture builds up to the statement of a proof, you can hear a pin drop in the hall.

Let me say one more thing about these popular audiences and the lectures I gave. The audiences included people who already believed in God by virtue of their religious faith. Their interest was in learning if reasons quite apart from faith, can support their belief. The audiences also included people who did not believe in God but were sufficiently open minded to be interested in learning whether thinking, totally unaided by faith, can produce reasons for belief. The lectures I gave tried to satisfy both parts of the audience by approaching the question of God's existence in the light of reason alone and without any help or guidance from religious faith.

In the course of the last forty years, the lecture got better and better, but never good enough. At least, it never satisfied me, even though it sometimes appeared to satisfy the audience. I knew better than they did that the thinking still fell short of its goal. Only in the last couple of years have I finally reached home. That is why I have at last published a book on the subject, *How to Think about God*, the writing of which I have been putting off for more than a quarter of a century.

A CLEAR IDEA OF GOD

To boil my best thinking about God down to its bare essentials, I will confine myself to the two steps one must take with one's mind. The first of these is to hold before one's mind the clearest notion one can form of God, so as to be able to use the word "God" with maximum precision. The second step is to formulate the question to which God is the one and only answer. There is a third step which I will mention before I close. Rather, I should say: there is a third phase of good thinking about God which consists in acknowledging a step which one's mind would like to take but which reason simply cannot manage.

What meaning do we give to the word "God"? What notion do we have in mind when we use that word? An eleventh-century archbishop of Canterbury, St. Anselm, discovered the way to answer that question. When we think about God, are we not thinking about a being than which no greater can be thought of? Thinking about God, must we not be thinking of the supreme being—the being Anselm so adroitly and precisely described by his formula: "the being than which we can think of no greater"?

Realizing that we must answer these questions affirmatively leads us to recognize other affirmations we are compelled to make. We must think of the supreme being as one that really exists, not just one that exists only in our minds.

As Anselm pointed out, if the God we are thinking of existed only in our minds and not in reality, then we would not be thinking of a truly supreme being. A million dollars that we have in the bank has more being and more power than a million dollars we may only have in our dreams of wealth. To exist in reality as well as in the mind is to have more and greater existence.

That is why we must think of the supreme being as having existence in reality. So far Anselm was completely right, and right he was also in insisting that the kind of real existence to be attributed to the supreme being must be one without beginning or end. His only error lay in supposing that from the fact that we *must think* of the supreme being as having real existence, it follows that the supreme being *must have* real existence. The second "must" simply does not follow from the first.

However, a number of other things do follow. The kind of real existence we must attribute to the supreme being is not only eternal or everlasting, but also one that does not depend upon the existence of anything else and is not limited by the power of anything else. In short, we must think of God, the supreme being, as independent and infinite. Nor would God be the being than which no greater can be thought of unless God must also be thought of as omnipotent and omniscient.

Asking the Right Question

With this notion of God before our minds, we are now prepared to take the second step in our thinking. That consists in asking the one right question to which the only answer is God. Many attempts have been made to find this question. Failure to find it has produced faulty arguments for God's existence.

The one right question is simply this: Why is there something rather than nothing? The undoubted existence of the world—the cosmos as a whole—provides us with the undeniable fact that something does exist. But there might have been nothing at all. So far as we know and understand the nature of the world, it does not have in itself a sufficient reason for its own existence. It is but one of many possible worlds that might have been. Actual world though it is, it might have been different in a large number of respects.

The clinching step in the reasoning comes next. Whatever might have been otherwise than it is, such as the world in which we live, might also not exist at all. In place of the world, there might just be nothing. Why, then, is there something rather than nothing?

The only answer to that question is the creative action of a supreme being whose omnipotence includes the power to do what only an infinite being can do—make something out of nothing, or prevent something that exists from ceasing to exist and being replaced by nothingness instead.

I have used the word "creative." In the strict meaning of that term, no finite being can be creative. Creation consists in making something *ex nihilo*, out of nothing. The strict synonym for "creation" is "ex-nihilation." Human beings produce many things, but they never exnihilate, because whatever they make, they make out of something rather than nothing.

Even if the world has always existed and never began, which so far as science and philosophy can tell may be the case, its present existence—its existence at this very moment and at every moment of its enduring existence—requires that it be preserved, kept from being replaced by nothingness. The only explanation of its preservation in existence is the "ex-nihilating" action of God.

FROM PHILOSOPHY TO FAITH

So far our philosophical thinking can carry us, but no further. The God we have found reason to believe in lacks one essential feature of the God who is worshipped in the three great religions of the West—an overflowing love for His creatures. The crucial defect of philosophical thinking about God is that it is not able to show us that the supreme being, whose creative action explains the world's existence, is also benevolently disposed toward mankind.

Failing that, reason cannot bridge and cross the chasm to the warm world in which there is love and friendship between God and man. The best thinking philosophy can do leaves us out in the cold.

Disappointed that philosophy can do no better in its thinking about God, people may be impelled to dismiss it with a shrug and a "Well, then, what of it?" That is a good question and there is a good answer to it.

The leap of faith that carries one across the chasm is not, as is generally supposed, a leap from no grounds for believing in God to the attainment of such belief.

Rather it is a leap from a reasonable belief in God's existence (the attainment of which is certainly a remarkable achievement of the human mind) to a belief that lies beyond all reason—belief in a just, merciful and loving God, and in His benevolent care and concern for man.

Philosophical thinking is not to be dismissed as futile because it cannot go the whole way in support of religious faith. On the contrary, it should be honored all the more for having acknowledged its limitations and making crystal clear the final step that only a leap of faith can take.

2 The God I Pray To (A Conversation)

MORTIMER J. ADLER

MORTIMER ADLER: Over there was Adler I with a lurking belief in God which had varying degrees of strength. It hasn't had the same vitality all through my life.

Then Adler II, pursuing rational grounds for affirming God's existence, having gotten nearer and nearer and finally getting there. Then seeing that getting there wasn't enough. What I could affirm by reason was the "God of the philosophers," to use Pascal's phrase, not the God of Abraham, Isaac, and Jacob.

I can't honestly say that I'm trying strictly as a philosopher to do this for those who are interested in God without any other light to guide them. While reason can't go all the way, I want to see how far reason can go. I want to go to the point where there is a chasm between what reason can establish without any guidance from grace or faith and what's left to accomplish by the light of faith.

EDWARD WAKIN: What was involved as the "pagan philosopher" moved from Adler I to Adler II?

MORTIMER ADLER: I started to read St. Thomas when I was eighteen years old and I taught him for many years. I thought the first article of religious faith by Aquinas would be the existence of God. Not at all. I was never so startled. He calls that a Preamble to Faith. In his treatise on faith, the first article is that God revealed himself to us. There would be no way of proving that. I know there is a lot of historical evidence on Christ, but obviously the nonbeliever can take the historical evidence and do something else with it. So that's really an act of belief, way beyond knowledge.

In the order of sacred theology—and Aquinas was writing sacred theology—the question of God's existence comes second,

9

after he has revealed himself. In my task, the question of God's existence comes at the very end. What must come first is what you mean by the word 'God'. Next come the steps of inference. Aquinas doesn't do that. As a sacred theologian, he doesn't have to.

All my life I have been dissatisfied with the proofs for God's existence. I've never stopped thinking about it. I have two giant files with folders and notes on God's existence. I've read almost every book in the field and have made notes and more notes. During the last thirty years, I've given many lectures on the subject and I think I finally found the *one* satisfying argument. And I'll tell you the two criteria of the argument.

In the first place, one must be satisfied with less than certitude. One needs to be satisfied with a lesser degree of proof—what is called "beyond a reasonable doubt" in a court of law. Not beyond a shadow of a doubt, but beyond reasonable doubt.

In the second place, you must look for the one question to which the only possible answer is God. There are many questions to which God is an answer, but there are other answers, too, for these questions. Here, one applies the fundamental rule of inference laid down by the great fourteenth-century philosopher, William of Occam. When asking if something exists, one asks if the answer is absolutely necessary. If it isn't, out comes Occam's proverbial razor and slash. You cut away the answer.

EDWARD WAKIN: Did you come to your conclusion all of a sudden like Saul on the road to Damascus?

MORTIMER ADLER: In the last two years I became convinced that I had found reasonable grounds for affirming God's existence.

EDWARD WAKIN: What of someone who already believes in God and revealed truth? What does Adler and his affirmation mean to believers?

MORTIMER ADLER: I think they should be interested to learn how far reason provides grounds for what they believe. Which would be better: To believe what is, in part at least, reasonable; or to believe what is totally contrary to reason? I think that two extremes are equally wrong—that of the rationalists who have no place for faith at all and the fideists who have no use for reason. I take a middle ground.

EDWARD WAKIN: Before we go any further, let's nail down your "reasonable affirmation of God's existence."

MORTIMER ADLER: As I said, you have to find the question to which there is no other answer. That question is *Why is there something rather than nothing?* Science can't answer that question. As an existentialist will tell you, the world exists without a sufficient reason for existing. Its only sufficient reason must lie in another, not in itself. What other? Answer: God. That's the argument: in a nutshell.

EDWARD WAKIN: That sounds like a familiar argument. What's new about saying that everything must have a cause, taking us back to a First Cause, God?

MORTIMER ADLER: By no means. As St. Thomas argued against Aristotle, you can't prove the world is everlasting and you can't prove that it ever began. Confronted with these alternatives, if you choose that the world began, you've already assumed the existence of God. That begs the question. You would be assuming that God exists, when that is precisely what he argued for. To avoid this error, we must proceed on the *assumption* of an everlasting cosmos a cosmos that has always existed,

EDWARD WAKIN: What is the next step in your argument for God's existence?

MORTIMER ADLER: The world exists. It continues to exist. But it is not the only possible cosmos. There is no compelling reason to think that the natural laws which govern the present cosmos are the only possible natural laws. Modern philosophers and scientists regard the world as a merely possible world. It could have been otherwise. That which can be otherwise is also capable of not existing absolutely.

That leads to the affirmation of God, not as creator but as preserver of the cosmos. God is the preservative cause of the continuing actual existence of what is a merely possible cosmos.

EDWARD WAKIN: How far does this argument take you in knowing about God?

MORTIMER ADLER: If reason enabled me to know everything about God, God would not have to reveal himself. The attributes

I have mentioned are metaphysical. They are not moral attributes. Reason alone can't make the bridge from an infinite, supreme being—which has existence in, through, and from itself—to a being that is just, merciful, providential, concerned, caring, benevolent, morally good. Earlier thinkers would say that the leap of faith consists in going from either no grounds or insufficient grounds for affirming God's existence to belief in God. I say that the leap of faith consists in going from sufficient grounds for affirming God's existence to belief in a God that is benevolent, just, merciful, and providential.

EDWARD WAKIN: So that is the point at which faith enters the picture?

MORTIMER ADLER: Belief itself is a God-given gift. You don't acquire it, though you can predispose yourself to receive it. The whole merit of believing—as St. Augustine wrote—is that it's a gratuitous act beyond reason's reach. If reason could prove everything, we wouldn't have any merit at all in believing.

EDWARD WAKIN: Can you foresee making the leap of faith yourself?

MORTIMER ADLER: That's a prediction I would not like to make.

EDWARD WAKIN: Then have you stopped at the point at which you affirmed God's existence?

MORTIMER ADLER: Not exactly. I wouldn't pray to the "God of the philosophers," and I pray to God in private.

EDWARD WAKIN: So you are praying to a moral God who really cares about you? The metaphysical God would not care about you and would not be listening?

MORTIMER ADLER: That's right, precisely.

EDWARD WAKIN: Before the emergence of Adler II who affirmed God's existence, did you pray?

MORTIMER ADLER: Yes, I did. I think I have all my life in one way or another believed in God.

EDWARD WAKIN: So you had belief in the belief?

MORTIMER ADLER: I had believed before I found the argument that satisfied me. The last sentence in my book says that

Pascal is right: "The heart has its reasons that reason does not know."

Philosophical theology cannot settle the dispute over whether God is indifferent to our fate or concerned with it. In our state of ignorance, the odds are fifty-fifty either way. Faced with this choice, the individual can resort to the reasoning involved in Pascal's wager. This reasoning led Pascal to believe in a God that promised eternal rewards and punishments, not merely according to our merits but also in accordance with his benevolent grace. (In Pascal's words: "If you win, you win everything; if you lose, you lose nothing.") How each person weighs the alternatives is not determined in the last analysis by reasoning alone, but by tendencies that rise from the deepest wellsprings of the human spirit.

EDWARD WAKIN: Where does this lead for you?

MORTIMER ADLER: I find it very difficult to believe in the immortality of the soul. Yet this is indispensable really to making an active commitment to the Jewish, the Moslem, or the Christian faith. Belief in God without belief in immortality of the soul is a curiously unsatisfactory belief. Can you see that?

EDWARD WAKIN: You are then depriving yourself of the benefits of belief.

MORTIMER ADLER: That's right. I suppose the next thing I ought to do is turn my attention to the immortality of the soul.

EDWARD WAKIN: You have written that, born a Jew, you have had little or no involvement in Jewish religious life, yet have contemplated becoming a Christian—a Catholic in your forties and an Episcopalian in your early sixties.

MORTIMER ADLER: I don't think anyone can give a perfectly rational answer to the question: Why are you *not* a Catholic? Why are you *not* an Episcopalian? The questions are beyond reason.

In my forties, I was devoted to Aquinas and my whole intellectual life was tied up with my engagement in Scholastic philosophy and with my Scholastic colleagues. I was warmed by the intellectual community and felt an urge to become one of them.

In my sixties, I married a second time and my wife and her family were Episcopal. We were married in the Episcopal Church with

the blessing of the bishop of California. Why didn't I take this up?
I don't know the answer to that question.

EDWARD WAKIN: That is confounding, you know.

MORTIMER ADLER: I know, but don't push me. As a final thing,
though, I would have much to say about why I pray to God—both
on my knees in church where I go with my wife and children and
when I'm lying in bed at night before I go to sleep. I think the
answer is that each of us finally is ultimately alone. And the only
one who is there is God—the Supreme Being whom one would
like to believe is concerned and caring.

EDWARD WAKIN: And if you were invited to deliver a sermon on
a Sunday morning to believers, what would be your basic message?

MORTIMER ADLER: I would say: Thank God for your belief and
thank philosophy for showing you that it is not absurd.

3 Adler Under Fire

MORTIMER J. ADLER, WILLIAM F. BUCKLEY, AND JEFF GREENFIELD

WILLIAM F. BUCKLEY: Mortimer Adler is a great many things, but indisputably the world's most dogged philosopher and probably that discipline's most exuberant philosopher. He cannot stand it that philosophers spend so much time talking to each other, and for that reason, early on in his career when he teamed up with President Robert Hutchins of the University of Chicago, he undertook no less a task than instructing the entire community disposed to read and to think, how to read and how to think.

He took his doctorate in psychology from the University of Columbia, notwithstanding that he never earned an undergraduate degree because he refused to take a test in swimming. He was attracted to the study of law, but before long he became in effect a student of everything, undertaking in due course the heroic task of editing the *Encyclopaedia Britannica's* version of the *Great Books* with its famous *Syntopicon*, often described as a Baedeker through the world of thought.

Throughout his hectic lifetime he has written books, and we are here to discuss his most recent book, *How to Think about God: A Guide for the 20th-Century Pagan.* It is a book that reaches a conclusion I shan't, out of perversity, divulge until the end of the program. I give you this hint, that he gives the lazy agnostic a rough time.

Our examiner today will be Mr. Jeff Greenfield, whom I'll introduce in due course.

I think we will begin by asking Dr. Adler to distinguish between sacred theology and philosophical theology.

MORTIMER ADLER: Sacred theology has its basic principles and articles of religious faith. It is reason undertaking to understand what faith instructs the mind with. Philosophical theology proceeds to think about God without any aid, direction or light from faith, using reason alone and the evidences of one's experience. It's a very much more difficult subject than sacred theology where one has given at the very beginning the basic articles of faith. Yet the question about God's existence: St. Thomas teaches us that the proposition that God exists is strictly not an article of faith alone, but a preamble to faith, that the first article of—at least of Christian faith—is that God has revealed himself to us. And that, philosophical theology, of course, proceeds without entirely.

WILLIAM F. BUCKLEY: Well, to accept revelation, Thomas says, is or is not an act of faith?

MORTIMER ADLER: It is.

WILLIAM F. BUCKLEY: It's not an act of reason?

MORTIMER ADLER: No, no. Entirely an act of faith.

WILLIAM F. BUCKLEY: In other words, sheer ratiocination would not do it.

MORTIMER ADLER: Would not do it.

WILLIAM F. BUCKLEY: Okay. Now, in your book, you, while recognizing St. Thomas and the sacred theologians of several religions, you point out to the reader that you are going to start on the premise that, in effect, nothing is known, but things are knowable.

MORTIMER ADLER: That's correct.

WILLIAM F. BUCKLEY: Yes, so in that sense you're an epistemological optimist. Now, you begin by reaching a very interesting conclusion which I would like to hear you dilate on, namely that it doesn't really matter whether there was a prime mover.

MORTIMER ADLER: That it seems to me is terribly important. That is, if one begins by assuming that the world started at some time—there was a time when there was nothing and the world began—

WILLIAM F. BUCKLEY: You're making a temporal point.

MORTIMER ADLER: That's right. A temporal point. —Then one has begged the question because one has assumed God's existence.

WILLIAM F. BUCKLEY: Why?

MORTIMER ADLER: Because if anything comes into existence out of nothing it needs a cause, and that cause has to be the—my phrase for that cause—

WILLIAM F. BUCKLEY: Exnihilation.

MORTIMER ADLER: —Exnihilation. And the word 'creation' means exnihilation. Hence—and St. Thomas is very clear about this—

WILLIAM F. BUCKLEY: Why can't that cause be chemical?

MORTIMER ADLER: Because all of our natural science, which I think is reliable, teaches us that the causes in nature do nothing but cause change. No, there is no natural cause that is the cause of existence or being.

I think I learned the fundamental truth that helped me write *How to Think about God* in one sentence in St. Thomas—not in the treatises on God but in the treatises on the divine government—in which St. Thomas says, "God is the proper cause of being." Only God causes being—not motion, not change, not the pattern of things. God—the only thing that God is exclusively the cause of is existence or being.

Therefore—and the other thing I learned from St. Thomas, which again helped me, curiously enough, though I'm proceeding without the light of faith—there are in the sacred theology of St. Thomas two great insights. One, this point about God being the exclusive cause of being. The other is that St. Thomas himself argues that only by faith does one hold that the world began. Obviously, faith takes the opening sentence of Genesis: "In the beginning, God created heaven and earth." Reason can neither prove that the world began nor that it didn't begin. I mean, with respect to the question—the cosmological question—of the world's having beginning, St. Thomas is completely agnostic, and I think quite rightly so.

WILLIAM F. BUCKLEY: Well, you say that, on the one hand, reason is not entitled to prefer one position over the other—

MORTIMER ADLER: Correct.

WILLIAM F. BUCKLEY: —but you say that science is tending to the big bang—

MORTIMER ADLER: But the big bang—The scientist is, of course, very—

WILLIAM F. BUCKLEY: But it's still a hypothesis.

MORTIMER ADLER: Well, the big bang theory is not a theory of the world's exnihilation. After all, something exploded. Something existed before the big bang happened. All that the big bang accounts for is the present shape of the universe, not its origin. So that I think the scientist—I think—is very loose in saying that was the beginning. That's not a beginning in any real sense of beginning. That's merely the emergence of the present shape of the cosmos.

So that one must—in order to prove God's existence without begging any questions—one must prove God's existence in terms of a world that is everlasting, without beginning and end—

WILLIAM F. BUCKLEY: Prove or deduce?

MORTIMER ADLER: I would prefer to say—I guess the word 'prove' is too strong. I think it is really a more modest claim than that. To establish the reasonableness of the belief in God's existence—

WILLIAM F. BUCKLEY: And the converse: the unreasonableness of disbelief.

MORTIMER ADLER: Yes, the opposite.—and do it with, in a sense, the jury's verdict of beyond a reasonable doubt—not beyond the shadow of a doubt, but beyond a reasonable doubt.

WILLIAM F. BUCKLEY: Well now, develop if you will, Dr. Adler, the importance in your analysis of leaving in abeyance the question of whether there was a beginning.

MORTIMER ADLER: The importance of it is to avoid doing something which is a logical error and would be begging the question. If one assumes, without proof, that the world had a beginning, one is in effect assuming God's existence. Therefore, in order not to make that illicit assumption, one must assume the contrary—make the hard problem for oneself of assuming an everlasting universe, a cosmos that had no beginning or end—and then say, given that cosmos, can we prove—can we infer—can we show the reasonableness of believing in God.

WILLIAM F. BUCKLEY: So in other words, what you do is take the more difficult of the two alternatives.

MORTIMER ADLER: That's right. The one against yourself.

WILLIAM F. BUCKLEY: That's right. And then proceed to argue from there.

MORTIMER ADLER: Precisely.

WILLIAM F. BUCKLEY: Okay. Now, having done that, you take us on in to the uniqueness of the word 'God', and I wonder whether in that particular section of your book you might be accused of a formal subjectivity.

MORTIMER ADLER: I think not. Here, by the way, I am most greatly indebted to that marvelous, extraordinary eleventh-century Archbishop of Canterbury, St. Anselm. Anselm said if you're going to think about God, your mind obliges you to think about a being than which no greater can be thought of. That's binding on the mind.

WILLIAM F. BUCKLEY: The ontological—

MORTIMER ADLER: No—we're not arguing for God's existence. This is an argument about what you must think when you think about God. It's called the ontological argument. What is fallacious is when we suppose that it proves God's existence. What Anselm is saying is you must think of God as that than which nothing greater can be thought of, namely the Supreme Being, and if you are thinking of a Supreme Being, you must think of that being as really existing, for if that being you're thinking of is only in your mind, it is not the Supreme Being because it is more and greater being to exist in reality as well as in the mind. Therefore, you must think of God as really existing. Furthermore, you must think of God as having an everlasting or enduring existence, not a transient existence—it doesn't come into being and pass away.

WILLIAM F. BUCKLEY: Are we talking about an attribute now, or something that's—

MORTIMER ADLER: Not an attribute—We are saying how we must think about—what notion it is we form—about God. If you think about God as the Supreme Being—as that than which nothing greater can be thought of—you must think of God as really existing, permanently or everlastingly in existence, and also as having an independent and unconditioned existence depending on nothing else for his existence and unconditioned by anything else. When you've done that, you've thought about the Supreme Being who is omnipotent and omniscient, unconditioned and independent. That is the notion of God that—

WILLIAM F. BUCKLEY: Now, would two people's notions of God if they followed your specifications differ, or must they, by definition, be identical?

MORTIMER ADLER: I think they—that is, what Anselm—at least what I take him to be saying—if one uses one's reason in thinking about God, one is obliged—one is necessitated—to affirm in one's notion of God these attributes: omnipotence, omniscience, real existence, everlasting, existence, unconditioned existence, independent existence.

WILLIAM F. BUCKLEY: Now—

MORTIMER ADLER: May I say, the error that is—You mentioned the ontological argument—

WILLIAM F. BUCKLEY: Yes.

MORTIMER ADLER: Anselm himself—I think he made an extraordinary discovery when he did that—then made the mistake of saying that because I must think of God as really existing, therefore God exists. That does not follow. That does not follow. But the ontological—so-called ontological—argument which is not a reasonable basis for believing in God's existence is absolutely controlling in how one must think about God's nature. And I think this reverses the order of sacred theology, because in sacred theology, St. Thomas proceeds from God's existence to God's nature, whereas in philosophical theology one proceeds from one's understanding of God's nature, as Anselm has done, to the question of God's existence. Unless one has this clear notion of God's nature—or a sufficiently clear notion—one can't even begin to ask whether in the world of reality there exists something that corresponds to that notion.

WILLIAM F. BUCKLEY: Well, but is the skeptic, even after reading

Anselm, not left with the suspicion that the perception of such a creature as God—

MORTIMER ADLER: I have to stop you.

WILLIAM F. BUCKLEY: Yes, I can't use "creature." You don't like the word 'creature'.

MORTIMER ADLER: Well, the creator can't be a creature.

WILLIAM F. BUCKLEY: That's right, that's right, that's right.—the perception of such an idea as God is an act of philosophical exertion that simply attempts to deal with infinity without defining it?

MORTIMER ADLER: Well, I'm glad you mentioned infinity because an unconditioned and independent existence is an unlimited existence and an infinite existence. I would again—I did mention—

WILLIAM F. BUCKLEY: Yes.

MORTIMER ADLER: —if one thinks about God as the Supreme Being that than which nothing greater can be thought of, one must think of an infinite being.

WILLIAM F. BUCKLEY: Yes.

MORTIMER ADLER: But this is simply saying—You see, what Anselm did by that extraordinary phrase—it's one of the most extraordinary acts of the mind: "God is that than which nothing greater can be thought of"—when you say that, what follows—an infinite existence, real existence, everlasting existence, omnipotence, omniscience, independent existence, unconditioned existence—that is the notion of God. Now the question remains, is there in reality a being corresponding to that notion? That's where the crux—where the argument begins.

WILLIAM F. BUCKLEY: Yes, and the ontological argument doesn't necessarily follow from the insight of Anselm.

MORTIMER ADLER: No.

WILLIAM F. BUCKLEY: There is no nexus. So this is your criticism of sacred theology: Reasoning from Anselm's insight on over to the ontological existence—

MORTIMER ADLER: Aquinas criticizes Anselm, not for doing what I said, but for doing the invalid thing of saying because I must think of God as really and necessarily existing, God does exist that way.

Curiously enough, Aquinas was acquainted with Anselm's argument as an argument for God's existence and rejected it as invalid, but he didn't do what I've just done. He didn't see what a remarkable contribution Anselm had made to the necessity of how we must think about God, not to the necessity of God's existence. And with that notion in mind, then the question opens up.

And the next step is a very simple one. It's almost like there's— Ask yourself, what question is there to which there is only one answer, namely God? What question can you ask to which no other answer can be given except God? For example, why does the world—the cosmos—have the shape it has at present? God is not the answer to that question because there are other answers possible. Maybe God is—but maybe, not necessarily. Why do things happen as they do? God is not the answer to that question, though God may be the answer, but not necessarily. Why do some men in life reap rich rewards and others suffer calamity? God is not the answer to that question.

WILLIAM F. BUCKLEY: Not necessarily.

MORTIMER ADLER: Not necessarily. There is only one question to which no other answer is possible, and that is, why is there something rather than nothing? Why is there something rather than nothing? Now, that at first looks simple, but—

WILLIAM F. BUCKLEY: Because someone is capable of exnihilation.

MORTIMER ADLER: The answer is, if the present world—the cosmos as it exists now, right now—is a merely possible cosmos, and everyone—I don't think anyone would say that the world could not be otherwise than it is—and what can be otherwise than it is also capable of not being at all. And if the present cosmos, being capable of being otherwise than it is, is also capable of not being at all, then at this very moment, unless something caused its existence in the sense of preventing it from being reduced to nothingness, nothingness would take its place. And so at this very instant and at every instant in time which the cosmos exists, without beginning or end, an exnihilating cause is operative. The act of God is required. Exnihilating, not in the sense of initiating the existence of the world, but preserving it in existence. I think I learn more from Question 104 of the *Summa Theologica* than any other, in which Thomas explains that God's preservation of the cosmos is creative.

WILLIAM F. BUCKLEY: Well now, explain why, inasmuch as it is a workaday piece of scientific knowledge, that matter cannot be destroyed; it merely changes its form.

MORTIMER ADLER: That's right.

WILLIAM F. BUCKLEY: So under the circumstances, annihilation is as difficult as exnihilation.

MORTIMER ADLER: Precisely. In that—

WILLIAM F. BUCKLEY: You can have entropy, but you still have matter.

MORTIMER ADLER: Right. Again, the third most remarkable sentence in the whole of the *Summa*—One was that God is the proper cause of being, the only cause of being. Two, that there is no way of proving that the world had either beginning or end. The third is—I was stunned by it when I first read it—God annihilates nothing.

WILLIAM F. BUCKLEY: Because He cannot?

MORTIMER ADLER: No. No. That's an act of will. That's free. But the point about that is in the whole of our science we've never seen anything annihilated. All change, I mean, is transformation. We talk about destruction. We talk about things being—We use the word "annihilated" loosely. We say, "That city was annihilated by a war." Not at all. It just reduced to rubble and ashes and dust. Nothing is annihilated, and so that since we have no experience of annihilation, we have no experience of exnihilation either. But at this very moment, since what is could be not—or not be—it needs a cause for its existence that it doesn't have in itself—

WILLIAM F. BUCKLEY: In other words, there has to be an agent of its being—

MORTIMER ADLER: Being.

WILLIAM F. BUCKLEY: —as also of its continuing to be.

MORTIMER ADLER: Well, it'd have to be—At every moment, there has to be an agent of its continuing to be—and its continuing to be is its existence—moment from, moment it exists.

WILLIAM F. BUCKLEY: Now, does that agent have to be intelligent?

MORTIMER ADLER: Well, I would say that this is probably the least, shall I say, rigorous part of the argument. If one says we must think of God as that than which nothing greater can be thought of, must we think of God as living as opposed to inert? This may be anthropomorphic reasoning, but it would seem to me to say that that which exists as a living organism has more being than that which is merely an inert piece of matter. Therefore, if God is that than which nothing greater can be thought of, we must think of God as being alive. Is an intelligent living organism—Does an intelligent being have more power and more being than a non-intelligent? The answer is yes. So I think the attribution of both life—ontologically understood, not unifically understood—the attribution of both life and intelligence to God follows, though not as easily as the attribution of existence.

WILLIAM F. BUCKLEY: Is it something that Anselm insisted on, or not?

MORTIMER ADLER: Yes.

WILLIAM F. BUCKLEY: It is.

MORTIMER ADLER: Yes.

WILLIAM F. BUCKLEY: But his insistence on that was, you would classify, as a theological deduction—

MORTIMER ADLER: No, I would, as a philosopher, without any aid from the light of faith, would say that what I've just said holds my mind. I am thinking as strictly as I can.

WILLIAM F. BUCKLEY: But you said it was less rigorous—

MORTIMER ADLER: Because it's—Someone may say, 'Well, when you say that to be alive and to be rational or be intelligent is better than not to be, aren't you being, shall I say, prejudicially human?' I think not. I say that about existence and infinity and unconditioned, I have no doubt. No one can possibly challenge me on that. I think I can defend—I say that a little more modestly—the proposition that to think of God as that than which nothing greater can be thought of, one must think of God as living and intelligent.

WILLIAM F. BUCKLEY: Now, the scrutiny given to the thought thus far by Immanuel Kant revealed what misgivings?

MORTIMER ADLER: Kant made a simple mistake. He said, dismissing Anselm's argument, that $100 in my pocket is no greater than $100 in my mind. I think that's just nonsense. A hundred dollars in my pocket will do things that $100 in my mind will not do. (*Laughter*) I can understand the error that he made. Existence is not an ordinary predicate—not an ordinary attribute. It's not like red or green or large or heavy or here or there. And he therefore thought that existence did not characterize anything. Perhaps it doesn't. Existence is not a characterizing term. But to say that that which exists in reality does not have more existence and more power than that which exists only in the mind is nonsense. And that's the error Kant made.

WILLIAM F. BUCKLEY: And what was the impact of that error on—

MORTIMER ADLER: It dismissed the ontological argument, and then Kant made another error that was understandable in his day and not today. One of the reasons why I thought that I could do something in this book in the twentieth century that could not be done by a philosophical theologian in any earlier century is that I can overcome Kant's chief objection to philosophical theology, which was that one cannot use concepts drawn from experience to deal with that which transcends experience. Now obviously, God transcends experience. And if you have to use only concepts drawn from experience, you can't, he said, legitimately, use them about God. In twentieth-century physics, we talk about certain elementary particles, we talk about the black holes. We are not using concepts drawn from experience. Those transcend experience.

WILLIAM F. BUCKLEY: And they're deduced.

MORTIMER ADLER: No. The modern logic of contemporary science calls those—it's very important—theoretical constructs, rather than empirical concepts. Now I say that God is not an empirical concept. We do not, shall I say, abstract it from any experiences. We abstract horse or chair or cow. But since we now know from the thinking in theoretical physics that one can take a theoretical concept and then, using—

WILLIAM F. BUCKLEY: And rely on it.

MORTIMER ADLER: Rely on it.—and show that there exists in reality something that corresponds to that theoretical concept using Ockham's very fundamental—Ockham is again very helpful here—he says you are entitled to infer—to establish the existence of a theoretical construct if nothing else will explain the phenomenon. Now when scientists say a meson exists—a meson is never perceptible—they're saying that theoretical construct of a meson or a neutrino or a black hole, which is not a concept drawn from experience, 'I infer the existence of that because without that theoretical construct I cannot explain the phenomenon that I do observe in the laboratory—the traces on the screen.'

So that what I'm saying is I've avoided Kant's objection, because I think if I'd thought of God as a—I don't have any—The point is, I have no definition of God. What I've done with Anselm is not a definition of God. What I've done is to construct a theoretical construct that my mind is compelled to make and then say—

WILLIAM F. BUCKLEY: There is no other explanation.

MORTIMER ADLER: That's right. Precisely it.

WILLIAM F. BUCKLEY: And now, did Kant linger over the notion of the theoretical construct or was physics not sufficiently advanced?

MORTIMER ADLER: That's precisely the point. He didn't have any conception of that. Kant was living in the age of Newtonian physics. Newtonian physics didn't need theoretical constructs. It is really modern cosmology and modern nuclear physics that I think emancipates us from Kant's strictures and makes it—I take courage in thinking about God from the kind of thinking physicists do about black holes.

WILLIAM F. BUCKLEY: Yes, yes.

MORTIMER ADLER: If they can do it, I can do it.

WILLIAM F. BUCKLEY: Right. Now, when the time comes to infuse your concept with attributes, what do you do?

MORTIMER ADLER: You have now touched the nerve of the—I think—the most difficult point in the book, which is in the epilogue, in which I talk about the chasm and the bridge. Again, let me rely on a great Christian thinker, Blaise Pascal, who said, "I am not interested in the God of the philosophers. I'm interested only in the God of Abraham, Isaac, and Jacob, of Moses and Jesus Christ." And he's right. The God of the philosophers is not a God to worship. What I've said so far, though I think I have given reason—good sound reason—to believe in God's existence, the God whose existence I've given reason for belief in has attributes that fall short of the attributes required of a God to worship and rely upon and love. I haven't proved that God is benevolent. That is not part of my reasoning and thinking about God. I have not shown that God cares for us and is concerned with us. I haven't shown that God's providence arranges things wisely and well. And all the things that I think are required for the life of the religious person—well, certainly charity, the love of God, being loved, love—Let's take just love for a moment—benevolence. There's nothing in, I think—

WILLIAM F. BUCKLEY: What about ensoulment?

MORTIMER ADLER: Well, ensoulment is life.

WILLIAM F. BUCKLEY: But since nothing can be annihilated, is there a commitment within the confines of your architecture to the endurance of the soul?

MORTIMER ADLER: Well, yes, but you've now—When you talk about the human soul and its immortality, you've gone way beyond my original premises now. Let me see if I can say it another way, Bill. What is the leap of faith which is required for religious life? Well, I think—In my judgment, one of the main contributions I've made in this book is to say it is not going from insufficient grounds for believing in God to belief in God. That's what most people think the leap of faith is—that you don't have enough grounds, so you have to add faith. I say—

WILLIAM F. BUCKLEY: You're saying there are plenty of grounds.

MORTIMER ADLER: There are plenty of grounds for believing in God's existence. The leap of faith is from believing in God's existence to believing in a benevolent God. That's the leap of faith, because there, I think, one goes beyond reason.

WILLIAM F. BUCKLEY: Let alone an anthropomorphic God.

MORTIMER ADLER: That's right. Well, I think that phrase is a misunderstanding of the meaning of 'person'. We are persons— Because the meaning of the word 'person' in both theology and philosophy and in Roman jurisprudence is a rational being with free will, and if one attributes mind and freedom to God—as I think one does when one talks about God's having intelligence being unconditioned independent—one is saying that God is a person—a person in that fundamental metaphysical meaning of person. If that's anthropomorphic, that's all right. I mean—

WILLIAM F. BUCKLEY: Well, of course, that's a great Christian assertion.

MORTIMER ADLER: Sure, sure.

WILLIAM F. BUCKLEY: So now we're—I don't want to lose our train of thought here. Here you are adducing Pascal who said, "I am really uninterested"—

MORTIMER ADLER: —in the God of the philosophers.

WILLIAM F. BUCKLEY: Yes. I'm uninterested in any proof that there is a God in the denatured sense in which Professor Adler deduces him. (*Laughter*) I want to know what role that God should play in my life, if any, and this depends on giving him a profile—

MORTIMER ADLER: Which requires that act of faith, that leap of faith that I said.

WILLIAM F. BUCKLEY: Now, is it a matter of—Is your refusal to discuss the Christian God in terms of—

MORTIMER ADLER: Or the Jewish God or the Muslim God—any one of those three.

WILLIAM F. BUCKLEY: —is that a terminological decision based on a decision not to mix empirical and speculative thought, or is it because you simply haven't gotten around to it?

Mortimer Adler: No. The subtitle of that book—the subtitle the publishers gave it—is *A Guide for the 20th Century Pagan.* I wanted to call it *An Introduction to Theology for the 20th Century Pagan.* And the reason I used the word "pagan" is that one of the definitions of 'pagan' in *Webster's Dictionary* is one who does not worship the God of Christians, Jews, and Muslims. Now those who worship obviously worship on the basis of faith, not on the basis of philosophical reason. So I wanted to stay within what could be said to pagans without any appeal to faith, and then say—what one can say to pagans without any appeal to faith is just this: It isn't entirely, shall I say, dismissible, because the God whose existence I have given reason to believe in has many traits in common with the God that is worshipped. Not all. Many.

Too, if the God of Abraham, Isaac, and Jacob were not infinite, not omnipotent, not omniscient, not alive, not intelligent, not the exnihilating creator, then the God of the philosophers and the God of Abraham, Isaac, and Jacob would be utterly different. But that's not so. They converge, but don't meet. That's the gap that Pascal was talking about—that chasm between the God of the philosophers—Now, he turned his back. Being of profoundly religious faith he had no need of the God of the philosophers.

I'm saying that I think persons of profound faith have some need to know that their faith is reasonable, though they go beyond what is reasonable. That is the answer to the agnostic. The person of profound faith still should be proud and happy to know that what he holds by faith has reasonable grounds even though what he holds by faith exceeds what one can say by reasonable grounds. That's the essence of what I'm trying to say.

William F. Buckley: In other words, the scaffolding is there—the intellectual scaffolding is there—and faith supplies, so to speak, the facade.

Mortimer Adler: It puts the flesh and blood on it.

William F. Buckley: The flesh and blood on it, yes. Now, in the case of Pascal, there was a conscious rejection of the challenge to bridge the two, was there not?

Mortimer Adler: He just was on the other—

William F. Buckley: The call of the faithful—

MORTIMER ADLER: He said, 'I'm on the other side of the chasm, and I don't care about their side at all', you see.

WILLIAM F. BUCKLEY: And what successor has attempted this chasm?

MORTIMER ADLER: I don't, you see—if I may be immodest a moment—In the modern world philosophers fall into two groups. They've either been pagans like Hume and the twentieth-century agnostic philosophers who argue that God's existence can't be proved, that God is an illegitimate notion, and there is no valid argument for God's existence. In other words, the philosophers who are purely philosophers and pagans have been adverse—negative. On the other hand, there are modern philosophers who are Christians and Jews who, in thinking about God and in arguing for God's existence, have allowed the light of faith to add to their philosophy what doesn't belong there. They have, shall I say, illegitimately introduced into their philosophical thought something that they borrowed from their faith.

WILLIAM F. BUCKLEY: And in that sense have become sacred theologians?

MORTIMER ADLER: That's right. And what I've tried to do—and I think I'm almost alone in this—is while standing with the pagans, in the sense that I allow no light of faith to intrude upon my thought, I've been positive rather than negative, affirmative rather than adverse. And I think that is a very important thing to achieve.

WILLIAM F. BUCKLEY: Yes, yes. Now can you account for the apparent lack of curiosity on the subject? It is, of course, the paramount question.

MORTIMER ADLER: Well, curiously enough, that's not my—

WILLIAM F. BUCKLEY: Why is it that so many people who are ostensibly educated have devoted so very little thought to this question? I doubt if the typical doctored teacher has ever heard of Anselm.

MORTIMER ADLER: Let's leave academics out for a moment.

WILLIAM F. BUCKLEY: Okay.

MORTIMER ADLER: My experience is the other way, Bill. In the last thirty years I have from time to time in various parts of the country given lectures on the existence of God, always to standing-room-only audiences. Last summer in Aspen, while I was writing this book, I announced three lectures and set them on a Wednesday, Thursday, and Friday afternoon at four o'clock—brilliantly sunny afternoons in June when the trout streams in the mountains and the golf course and the tennis courts were beckoning. I had filled—in fact I had to move from a smaller to a larger auditorium—and I had to repeat the lectures a second time to accommodate the—

WILLIAM F. BUCKLEY: That sounds like Abelard.

MORTIMER ADLER: Well, the interesting thing is that this is the most far—Academics may turn their backs on it, but I assure you that the populace in general is avid on this question.

WILLIAM F. BUCKLEY: Well then, let's examine the narrower question. Why are the academics insouciant?

MORTIMER ADLER: They have been—

WILLIAM F. BUCKLEY: Is it sloth? Fashion?

MORTIMER ADLER: No. I think they've been corrupted—I have to say they've been corrupted by modern thought. They've been corrupted by Hume and Kant and the whole line of doubters who have never understood the conditions of the argument and how to do it. I mean, the errors I've talked about are errors that pervade the academic mind, and so they think it's a closed book. And the philosophers whom they admire have argued that this is beyond reason's power to do—

WILLIAM F. BUCKLEY: They admire Aristotle, don't they?

MORTIMER ADLER: Not generally. (*laughing*) I wish they did. I wish they did. Not generally.

WILLIAM F. BUCKLEY: What was it that Kant meant when he referred to the difficulties that the agnostics had with the physico-teleological argument?

MORTIMER ADLER: Well, I think the argument from design—I think most of the arguments that have been given for God's existence are faulty. The reason behind my saying that is the inadequate or defective arguments come from asking the wrong questions. The questions I said—There are lots of questions to which God may be the answer but need not be.

WILLIAM F. BUCKLEY: Yes.

MORTIMER ADLER: When you build an argument in answer to a question to which God may be the answer but need not be, you've got a faulty or insufficient argument. You've got to find the question to which God is the only possible answer, and that is the question, 'Why is there something rather than nothing?' I think that's simple and clear.

WILLIAM F. BUCKLEY: Yes. And is there any reason why the natural curiosity of the academics does not turn to a more rigorous examination of this question? Is it something that they tend to fear because of its—

MORTIMER ADLER: Yes.

WILLIAM F. BUCKLEY: —awful abstruseness?

MORTIMER ADLER: I don't think it's so much that it's abstruse. In academic circles theology is an unfashionable subject, at least the kind of strict philosophical theology that I'm talking about. You'll recall in the 1960s that furor about the death of God. That the academics just lapped up. Of course, the most extraordinary thing is how that has completely disappeared. I have two shelves of books that have been dropped into nothingness—where they belong, as a matter of fact. (*laughter*)

WILLIAM F. BUCKLEY: Except that you can't annihilate them. (*Laughter*)

MORTIMER ADLER: Yes. (*laughing*)

WILLIAM F. BUCKLEY: And your point being that it was simply an intellectual fad.

MORTIMER ADLER: Yes.

WILLIAM F. BUCKLEY: Well now, is there a sign of any reversal? I remember Will Herberg was always talking about a reawakening of interest at all levels in religion. Do you see that happening? Will your book, for instance, engage the attention of the academic community?

MORTIMER ADLER: I'm hoping so. I'm pretty sure it will engage the attention of the general public because of my experience in lectures. I'm hoping—and this is a slender hope—that the clarity, and, I think, persuasiveness of the reasoning done there in the explanation of why Anselm's argument is wrong as an argument for the existence of God, the explanation why Kant's strictures now no longer hold—

WILLIAM F. BUCKLEY: Wrong, but heuristic.

MORTIMER ADLER: That's right—will prevail. And since my claims for natural theology are not exorbitant—I don't attempt to prove that I've given reason for believing in the Christian God or the Jewish God because, as I say, there's a leap there. I think the academic community would react very negatively if I—if anyone—claimed by reason and reason alone, one could establish a grounds for believing in the God worshipped and loved by religious Jews, Muslims, and Christians.

WILLIAM F. BUCKLEY: Well—

MORTIMER ADLER: I don't do that.

WILLIAM F. BUCKLEY: What you're saying is that you wouldn't undertake to do it, but—

MORTIMER ADLER: I don't think it can be done.

WILLIAM F. BUCKLEY: —but you—Well—

MORTIMER ADLER: I don't think it can be done.

WILLIAM F. BUCKLEY: Well, I think—I happen to think it can be done and has been done—people like C.S. Lewis and Chesterton—it seems to me that after reading them, I personally believe that it becomes unreasonable to suppose the opposite. There are arguments that are historical and empirical—for the reincarnation, for instance.

MORTIMER ADLER: Yes.

WILLIAM F. BUCKLEY: Now, your book is very philosophically meticulous in insisting that—in telling the reader—that you're not going to assert anything the proof of which is not made by the integrity of your own philosophical arguments.

MORTIMER ADLER: That's correct.

WILLIAM F. BUCKLEY: And, therefore, you hope that its discreet appeal will make it inoffensive to people who want to continue to refuse to make Pascal's leap.

MORTIMER ADLER: That's correct. I think that's a very good—I mean, that's a perfect statement of my intention. I hope I've succeeded in carrying it out.

WILLIAM F. BUCKLEY: I think you have. Mr. Jeff Greenfield is an author, television commentator, graduate of the Yale Law School. He has a book coming out in June, the title of which I forget.

JEFF GREENFIELD: It's *Playing to Win.*

WILLIAM F. BUCKLEY: *Playing to Win.* Sorry.

JEFF GREENFIELD: You can't deduce much theology from it. It's about politics. Dr. Adler, let me just see if we can clear some ground first. The proof that you think you make here is not a demonstration of a God with specific intentions toward man. Would that be correct?

MORTIMER ADLER: Right.

JEFF GREENFIELD: All right. So that much of the questions that have been raised in the past about what God's will is toward us is swept aside in this.

MORTIMER ADLER: Not swept aside. Swept aside is not quite right. I think it's one of the most important questions of all, but I can't reach them by reason alone.

JEFF GREENFIELD: So that there are a whole range of issues in which we are used to hearing God invoked about which you say, 'Not provable'. Yes?

MORTIMER ADLER: I—Could I—

JEFF GREENFIELD: Well, let me show you what I mean.

MORTIMER ADLER: Could I just remove that word 'provable', because as I said to Bill a little earlier, the word 'proof' is a mathematical word.

JEFF GREENFIELD: Fair enough.

MORTIMER ADLER: Let's say reasonable rather than proof.

JEFF GREENFIELD: Okay. But whether one should be celibate before marriage because God wants us to is not—

MORTIMER ADLER: Not within my domain.

JEFF GREENFIELD: Right. Okay. (*Laughter*) Whether God wants to ban the teaching of evolution—none of these things are in your domain. Okay.

MORTIMER ADLER: Interesting, but not in my domain.

JEFF GREENFIELD: Yes, I understand that. Not uninteresting. (*Laughter*) Indeed, what I think Mr. Buckley was after is a question which I would have thought was not in your domain either. Specifically, it is conceivable to imagine a God who created a universe in which man did not have a soul. No?

MORTIMER ADLER: It is conceivable for the universe to exist without man being in it.

JEFF GREENFIELD: Yes.

MORTIMER ADLER: It is conceivable for the universe to exist with man being in it without an immortal soul. If the word "soul" simply means to be alive, then all potatoes have souls—(*Laughter*)

JEFF GREENFIELD: Yes.

MORTIMER ADLER: —but the immortal soul is something else again.

JEFF GREENFIELD: Yes, that—

MORTIMER ADLER: That's right.

JEFF GREENFIELD: Okay. So I think it's just important to have brought this down to where—

MORTIMER ADLER: Absolutely. My whole effort is to minimalize my— You see, may I say, as I said to Mr. Buckley, natural theology has brought upon itself, I think, some adverse reactions because it's claimed too much.

JEFF GREENFIELD: Fair enough.

MORTIMER ADLER: I want to claim modestly only what I think can be done clearly.

JEFF GREENFIELD: Now I want to explore those modest claims in the light of what you may regard as an apposite analogy. Child psychologists tell us that in an early stage of development infants attribute to their parents all sorts of attributes which they later discover to be untrue. For example—I cannot tell you how they come to this conclusion—but child psychologists tell us that at a certain early stage of development infants believe that their parents can be made to appear and disappear by an act of will. In other words, the infant believes that their hunger brings the parent into existence.

MORTIMER ADLER: That's a power on the part of the infant, not an attribute of the parent.

JEFF GREENFIELD: Well, but it's what the infant— That's true. At any—That's right. But that comes after the stage when the infants believe their parents are sort of—I guess god-like is the only way I can put it. That is, they believe—

MORTIMER ADLER: I wish my children thought that of me. (*Laughter*)

JEFF GREENFIELD: That's a later stage. (*Laughter*) In infancy they tend to believe their parents dwell everywhere and are omnipotent because their needs are answered. What I'm— I guess; what I'm getting at— is whether it is conceivable that the questions that you are addressing—the questions about the nature of existence out of nothingness—is a concept that is so far beyond us that the conclusions that you draw might at some other date be invalidated.

MORTIMER ADLER: I don't think so. And I don't think so because you and I and everybody else uses the word 'exists' or 'is'—there's no commoner word in any language than the ontological predicate 'is' or 'is not'—you and I day in and day out say that is or that does not exist, and when we say something does not exist we are thinking of nothing in its place sometimes. So I think the concept of being and not being or existence and nothingness are, shall I say, part of the very heart of human thinking.

JEFF GREENFIELD: Well, but you see what interests me—

MORTIMER ADLER: And you can't think without it, so I don't think we'll go beyond it.

JEFF GREENFIELD: That's possible, but in a sense—and I don't think I'm using this word invidiously—there's almost a sort of arrogance in this sense: There was a time when people believed that if there were sunspots on the sun, that was impossible, and it was impossible because God would not create such a thing. That's why Galileo had to recant.

MORTIMER ADLER: That's superstitious thinking, yes.

JEFF GREENFIELD: Yes, but that's exactly my point. From our perspective it's superstitious. From that time period, it was a matter of demonstrable theology.

MORTIMER ADLER: Mr. Greenfield, I don't think that time is going to affect the line of difference between superstition and rational thought. Either— when I go through the argument that you've heard me go through with Mr. Buckley—

JEFF GREENFIELD: Right.

MORTIMER ADLER: —either your own mind—I can't appeal to anything but your own mind—either as you, hear that, your mind says, 'Yes, I can think'—If I say to you, 'Can you think of God as anything less than the Supreme Being?' Do you want to think of God—When you use the word 'god', do you want to think of an inferior being? A being than which there is a superior? I don't think you would use the word 'god' that way. I'm appealing to you—

WILLIAM F. BUCKLEY: He'd excogitate him out of existence.

MORTIMER ADLER: That's right. So that the steps I've asked you to take, I can only appeal to your reason or anybody's else's reason—

JEFF GREENFIELD: Well, you couldn't appeal to him at all if he were, say, a solipsist, could you?

MORTIMER ADLER: I wouldn't try.

WILLIAM F. BUCKLEY: Or even a nihilist.

MORTIMER ADLER: I wouldn't try. If he's a solipsist, I don't want to exist in his universe. (*laughing*)

JEFF GREENFIELD: Yes, but you know that—But, Mr. Buckley, you know the answer to that, where a woman ran up to Bertrand

Russell in his solipsist phase and said, "Thank God, I thought I was the only one." (*Laughter*) I'm not dealing with that. What I'm dealing with—

MORTIMER ADLER: I don't think he's a solipsist.

JEFF GREENFIELD: What I'm dealing with—

WILLIAM F. BUCKLEY: He's— As I understand it, he's saying, can't you, hypothetically, assume an intellectual state in which that which you accept as axiomatic is rejected.

JEFF GREENFIELD: Disproven. Is disproven.

MORTIMER ADLER: No.

WILLIAM F. BUCKLEY: And I think— The answer is, I can't either.

JEFF GREENFIELD: All right. So that— Okay, but that— The reason why I come at it from this viewpoint is because you've now—

MORTIMER ADLER: I'm arrogant to that extent.

JEFF GREENFIELD: Right. So that all the past mistakes that theologians have made—all the past errors by which people have deduced what must be—are not affected by your argument here. Is this correct?

MORTIMER ADLER: I think not. And by the way, the great theologians do not harbor any of that superstitious nonsense that you're attributing to children and popular—

JEFF GREENFIELD: No, but as I recall—

MORTIMER ADLER: No one has ever— The great theologians of the past are not superstitious—

JEFF GREENFIELD: As I recall, and I may be—

WILLIAM F. BUCKLEY: What about the great philosophers, though?

MORTIMER ADLER: They're not superstitious. I mean I think—

WILLIAM F. BUCKLEY: What about the notion that a tree makes no noise when it falls unless someone is there to hear it?

MORTIMER ADLER: That's a sophomore proposition that no great philosopher I think, ever really—

WILLIAM F. BUCKLEY: Didn't Berkeley believe that?

MORTIMER ADLER: Berkeley held the position that "esse est percipi"—'to be is to be perceived', and certainly there is this sense in which it is true: that the objects of our experience exist in our experience. Berkeley's further reasoning was that—

WILLIAM F. BUCKLEY: Is frivolous.

MORTIMER ADLER: Yes.

JEFF GREENFIELD: But I'm thinking—

MORTIMER ADLER: Berkeley's further reasoning was that what we—that we can't go beyond our experience to objects that exist outside our experience—to go beyond our experience is invalid.

JEFF GREENFIELD: I was thinking, for instance—and I may be misplacing the theologian—it's been a while—but that. St. Anselm begins by beseeching God to help him in his project.

MORTIMER ADLER: St. Anselm was a religious person—

JEFF GREENFIELD: Right. Now—

MORTIMER ADLER: —and he does—

WILLIAM F. BUCKLEY: That's why he was a saint. (*Laughter*)

MORTIMER ADLER: By the way, he begins the argument on his knees in prayer. There's no question about it.

JEFF GREENFIELD: That's what I mean. A modern day thinker—or a modern day person—looking at that is entitled to say—Well, it seems to me he may be in a different ballpark than you're in, obviously.

MORTIMER ADLER: No. But, you see, the interesting thing is, though I'm not a saint—

JEFF GREENFIELD: Not yet.

MORTIMER ADLER: No, and it would be unsaintly even to aspire to be a saint—

WILLIAM F. BUCKLEY: It's unsaintly to aspire to be a saint?

MORTIMER ADLER: (*laughing*) Yes.

JEFF GREENFIELD: Bill, can I ask you a question about this, because I—It seems to me that this must ultimately dissatisfy you, you know—the nature of coming to rest at this conclusion.

WILLIAM F. BUCKLEY: No. It doesn't dissatisfy me because it seems to me that it is by no means incorrect to take on a discrete task, and that is the philosophical task that Professor Adler has undertaken. The fact that his conclusions are compatible with my Christian faith is pleasing to me. Now, there remains the nexus which he undertakes not to supply.

MORTIMER ADLER: That's right.

WILLIAM F. BUCKLEY: But he does not deny that it is suppliable—

MORTIMER ADLER: That's right.

WILLIAM F. BUCKLEY: —though it would be with reference to a different philosophical vocabulary, a vocabulary that may or may not rest in part on faith and, to a certain extent, on reason and—

JEFF GREENFIELD: But you see what—

WILLIAM F. BUCKLEY: —empirical experience.

MORTIMER ADLER: There is a lovely little essay by Augustine entitled 'The Merit of Believing'. There is no merit in believing if believing doesn't go beyond what can be established by reason—

WILLIAM F. BUCKLEY: Right.

JEFF GREENFIELD: But isn't that—

WILLIAM F. BUCKLEY: Even as Yusuf said, only the man who believes can genuinely be tolerant.

MORTIMER ADLER: Correct.

JEFF GREENFIELD: But isn't— Aren't you now back—

WILLIAM F. BUCKLEY: But if he doesn't believe, there's nothing to be intolerant about.

MORTIMER ADLER: Correct.

JEFF GREENFIELD: Aren't you now at the barrier that so many people in today's world face, which is you can prove or— I'm sorry. You can—

MORTIMER ADLER: Argue and give reasonable grounds.

JEFF GREENFIELD: —bring us to this conclusion, but at the point when it begins to make a difference in our lives, it doesn't help much. In other words, the old—you might call them sophomoric notions—the questions that a bright eighteen-year-old begins to ask: 'If God exists, why does he permit X?' These things aren't answered at all in this.

MORTIMER ADLER: You are entitled to say, after you've read my book, 'What of it?'

JEFF GREENFIELD: Yes. That's what I mean.

MORTIMER ADLER: And I'm going to answer that question, because I think it's a good question, and I think there's a good answer to it.

What of it? The negative answer: It will not solve the questions that are the crucial questions in your life. The questions of whether God is to be sought in prayer for help and you ought to rely on God's grace for your virtues. What it does, though, is to say this: If I do believe in God religiously, am I entirely in a world of unreason? Have I exercised a faith that is—

WILLIAM F. BUCKLEY: Childlike.

MORTIMER ADLER: —childlike. There are two medieval maxims I'd like to state in Latin first. Tertullian said, "Credo nisi absurdum est"—'I believe even if it's absurd'; then went on to say, "Credo quia absurdum est"—'I believe because it is absurd'. I think that's wrong. I think to say that I believe because it is absurd—even though it's absurd it's all right—but it need not be absurd. What I believe can have an insufficient ground reason, and so it is—I think the what of it is to know what that leap of faith is.

JEFF GREENFIELD: Okay.

WILLIAM F. BUCKLEY: And nobody likes to be intellectually infra dig.

MORTIMER ADLER: That's right, that's right.

WILLIAM F. BUCKLEY: That's a very important point.

JEFF GREENFIELD: I think the area that I'm thinking of—very quickly, if we have the time for it—is that— to turn on the evening news the other night in New York and see a funeral service for a mother and her five children who were killed in a fire, and to hear the minister say, "God looked down from heaven and said, 'I need these people'." I mean, that is almost obscene, isn't it, in the sense there is—

WILLIAM F. BUCKLEY: No, I don't think it's obscene at all.

JEFF GREENFIELD: All right. I will assert it. To me that is an obscene notion, and one that I would assume that—I can't draw any comfort—

WILLIAM F. BUCKLEY: Well, I think you should use a more precise word than 'obscene'.

MORTIMER ADLER: Yes. 'Obscene' isn't the right word.

JEFF GREENFIELD: Well, I think I meant it as—

MORTIMER ADLER: 'Gratuitous'—

WILLIAM F. BUCKLEY: Or 'profane'.

JEFF GREENFIELD: 'Offensive'?

WILLIAM F. BUCKLEY: Profane.

JEFF GREENFIELD: Offensive?

WILLIAM F. BUCKLEY: Oh well, yes, anything can be offensive.

MORTIMER ADLER: You do really have to be tolerant of what happens in funeral oratory. I mean, after all, the minister—the priest—

WILLIAM F. BUCKLEY: Lapidarian inscriptions are not written on the—

MORTIMER ADLER: —is trying to comfort the grieving.

JEFF GREENFIELD: But what I'm saying is that the kind of question that occurs to someone in the face of that tragedy and then to be told that it's God's will is nothing with which you are concerned in your exercise.

MORTIMER ADLER: I cannot say that, you see. I mean, I think the important thing to know is how far philosophy will take you. Let me put it another way. Philosophy at its best produces a shell into which faith can be poured; but it's a shell, and that shell is nothing to depend upon for one's, shall I say, the direction of one's life. But without that shell, faith is without foundation in anything that belongs to reason in the world of our experience.

JEFF GREENFIELD: But if the faith into which you are pouring, the shell—

MORTIMER ADLER: No, not— The shell into which you are pouring the faith.

JEFF GREENFIELD: I'm sorry. It's the faith which you are pouring into the shell—wrong preposition—is as difficult to maintain, given the real world, with or without that shell, then what is the purpose as it affects us? Just to give a foundation for a general notion that God can exist?

MORTIMER ADLER: I would say, pointing to my friend here, Bill Buckley, that he lives in the same real world you do. He knows how horrible it is, in many respects, how irrational and brutal, and I don't think it weakens his faith. I don't see any signs, and I don't see why it should weaken his faith. The inscrutability of God's providence— We are not— Milton's efforts to justify the ways of God to man are not proper, I think. We shouldn't try to do that. We should— If we have faith in God's love and benevolence, we must try to understand that this difficult world in which we live is still within God's providence. The man of faith can do that. I don't think he's disturbed by it. As a philosopher I can't explain it, and I'm not called upon—I mean, as a philosopher, I cannot move into the realm in which the questions—

WILLIAM F. BUCKLEY: That's right.

MORTIMER ADLER: That's right. But I don't see why that defect—to admit that defect—is a very important thing—to admit that deficiency—

JEFF GREENFIELD: Because my assumption is the reason why people crowd lecture halls to hear lectures about God is less a philosophical exercise than a search—

MORTIMER ADLER: You're quite right.

JEFF GREENFIELD: —for some kind of faith or comfort in the cold world.

MORTIMER ADLER: You're quite right. I think I've cheated them. I think they come hoping for more than I'm going to give them. On the other hand, they don't castigate me for that. Though they expected more, they are, I think, pleased to have the little I can give.

WILLIAM F. BUCKLEY: Well, they also go to you as to a virtuoso, so there's that which is a pleasing note on which to end the hour. Thank you, very much, Dr. Adler—

MORTIMER ADLER: Thank you.

WILLIAM F. BUCKLEY: —the author of *How to Think about God*; Mr. Greenfield; ladies and gentlemen of Georgetown.

II

A Debate about God and Science

4 The Guiding Hand of God in the Universe

OWEN GINGERICH

A remarkable fact I learned not long ago is that all the gold mined in historical times would fill a cube only fifty-five feet on each side. I can imagine it outside my window, dwarfing my neighbor's house but not larger than a modest office building. Now contrast this with iron. Six hours of steel production in the United States would fill this same cube. In other words, iron is enormously more abundant than gold.

If, sixty years ago, you had asked a physicist why iron is ten million times more abundant than gold, or why oxygen is twenty times more abundant than iron, he would probably have considered you a pest. It would have been like asking why the sun appears half a degree wide in the sky, or why a naked-eye supernova occurred in 1604. Kepler asked questions like that, but most people considered him a little odd.

Today if you ask a physicist why iron is ten million times more abundant than gold, or a hundred million times more abundant than uranium, he would no longer tell you to get lost. Instead, you would find an astonishing story about giant cauldrons in the interiors of stars where the elements are cooked up in an esoteric witches' brew. This modern alchemy is one of the impressive achievements of astrophysics in the past several decades.

Physicists now believe that fifteen billion years ago—give or take a few billion years—the basic building blocks of atoms were formed in the first moment of a mighty explosion called the Big Bang. From the pure energy of that initial blast came nuclear particles, including protons and electrons—the makings of hydrogen, the lightest and by far the most abundant element. Protons smashed into protons to form heavy hydrogen and helium, helium

47

being the second heaviest and second most abundant element. But the universe expanded so quickly that before elements like carbon or oxygen could form, the incredible density of that primordial cosmic egg had abated, and the collisions became too few to produce any appreciable amounts of the higher elements—elements that are vital to life and to our being here today.

My purpose here is not to give a course in stellar evolution but to present some reflections on natural theology. But as a preamble, let me briefly sketch how stars spend their lives, in order to explain where elements like carbon and oxygen come from. Most of the time stars shine by converting hydrogen into helium. But when the available hydrogen has been exhausted, the core of the star pulls together under the irresistible tug of gravity, the temperature increases, and now the formerly inert helium becomes a fuel, fusing into carbon and later into oxygen. If the star is massive enough, a long sequence of higher elements will be generated.

Eventually, however, there comes a place in the periodic table where the atoms no longer yield up nuclear energy for powering the star, but instead, they *demand* energy. This happens when the chain has gone about a quarter of the way through the list of elements, approaching the element iron. When the star has burned the atoms to this point, it swiftly falls into bankruptcy, and the star is about to become a supernova. Gravity resumes its inexorable grasp, and within seconds the core of the star collapses, squashing the electrons and protons into a dense sphere of neutrons. On the rebound, the neutrons irradiate the lighter atoms, and in a colossal overshoot they build up the heavier elements, including the gold and uranium. From the cosmic debris come the building blocks for future stars and planets, and even for you and me. We are, in a sense, all recycled cosmic wastes, the children of supernovae.

Early in this century, after the work of Darwin, which emphasized the fitness of organisms for their various environments, the Harvard chemist L.J. Henderson wrote a fascinating book entitled *The Fitness of the Environment,* which pointed out that the organisms themselves would not exist except for certain properties of matter. He argued for the uniqueness of carbon as the chemical basis of life, and everything we have learned since then, from the nature of the hydrogen bond to the structure of DNA, reinforces his argument. But today it is possible to go still further and to probe the origin of carbon itself, through its synthesis deep inside evolving stars.

Carbon is the fourth most common atom in our galaxy, after hydrogen, helium, and oxygen. A carbon nucleus can be made by merging three helium nuclei, but a triple collision is tolerably rare. It would be easier if two helium nuclei would stick together to form beryllium, but beryllium is not very stable. Nevertheless, sometimes before the two helium nuclei can come unstuck, a third helium nucleus strikes home, and a carbon nucleus results. And here the details of the internal energy levels of the carbon nucleus become interesting: it turns out that there is precisely the right resonance within the carbon that helps this process along.

Let me digress a bit about resonance. As you tune your radio, there are certain frequencies where the circuit has just the right resonance and you lock onto a station. The internal structure of an atomic nucleus is something like that, with specific energy or resonance levels. If two nuclear fragments collide with a resulting energy that just matches a resonance level, they will tend to stick and form a stable nucleus. Behold! Cosmic alchemy will occur!

In the carbon atom, the resonance just happens to match the combined energy of the beryllium atom and a colliding helium nucleus. Without it, there would be relatively few carbon atoms. Similarly, the internal details of the oxygen nucleus play a critical role. Oxygen can be formed by combining helium and carbon nuclei, but the corresponding resonance level in the oxygen nucleus is half a percent too low for the combination to stay together easily. Had the resonance level in the carbon been four percent lower, there would be essentially no carbon. Had that level in the oxygen been only half a percent higher, virtually all of the carbon would have been converted to oxygen. Without that carbon abundance, neither you nor I would be here.

I am told that Fred Hoyle, who together with Willy Fowler found this remarkable nuclear arrangement, has said that nothing has shaken his atheism as much as this discovery. Occasionally Hoyle and I have sat down to discuss one or another astronomical or historical point, but I have never had enough nerve to ask him if his atheism had really been shaken by finding the nuclear resonance structure of carbon and oxygen. However, the answer came rather clearly in an issue of the Cal Tech alumni magazine, where he wrote:

> Would you not say to yourself, "Some supercalculating intellect must have designed the properties of the carbon atom, otherwise the chance of my finding such an atom through the blind forces of nature would be utterly minuscule." Of course you would. . . . A common sense interpretation of the facts suggests that a superintellect has monkeyed with physics, as well as with chemistry and biology, and that there are no blind forces worth speaking about in nature. The numbers one calculates from the facts seem to me so overwhelming as to put this conclusion almost beyond question.[1]

Now Sir Fred and I differ about lots of things, but on this we agree: the picture of the universe is far more satisfying if we accept the designing hand of a superintelligence. Hoyle might feel a little uncomfortable to be classified as a natural theologian or a modern-day William Paley, but natural theology is, in fact, the central subject of this essay—a topic that I'm slowly spiraling in on. Here I need to delve a little more deeply into this example of the age-old argument of design.

Not long ago I used the carbon and oxygen resonance in a lecture at a university in the Midwest, and in the question period I was interrogated by a philosopher who wanted to know if I could quantify the argument by Bayesian probabilities. Now I'll confess that, at the time, I hadn't a clue that Bayesian statistics meant evaluating a proposition on the basis of an original probability and new relevant evidence. But even knowing how to handle that would hardly have enabled me to perform a convincing calculation, that is, a probability so overwhelming as to be tantamount to a proof that superintelligent design was involved in the placement of the resonance levels.

Clearly my petitioner was daring me to convince him, despite the fact that I had already proclaimed that arguments from design are in the eyes of the beholder and simply can't be construed as proofs to convince skeptics. Furthermore, in posing his question he had already pointed out the quicksands of using numerology to prove the existence of divine order in the cosmos. So I hasten to dampen any notion that I intend the resonance levels in carbon and oxygen nuclei to prove the existence of God.

---

[1] "The Universe: Past and Present Reflections," *Engineering and Science* (November 1981), pp. 8–12, esp. p. 12.

Even Paley, with his famous watch and his conclusion that it pointed to the existence of a watchmaker, said that "My opinion of Astronomy has always been, that it is not the best medium through which to prove the agency of an intelligent Creator; but that, this being proved, it shows, beyond all other sciences, the magnificence of his operations."[2]

In fact, I am personally inclined to find more impressive hints of design in the biological realm. As Walt Whitman proclaimed, "a leaf of grass is no less than the journey-work of the stars."[3] I would go still farther and assert that stellar evolution is child's play compared to the complexity of DNA in grass or mice. Whitman goes on, musing that,

> the tree-toad is a chef-d'oeuvre for the highest,
> And the running blackberry would adorn the parlors of heaven,
> And the narrowest hinge in my hand puts to scorn all machinery,
> And the cow crunching with depress'd head surpasses any statue,
> And a mouse is miracle enough to stagger sextillions of infidels.

Even Hoyle, by his allusion to the biology, seems to agree that the formation of, say, DNA, is so improbable as to require a superintelligence. Such biochemical arguments were popularized about forty years ago by Lecomte du Noüy in his book *Human Destiny*. Lecomte du Noüy estimated the probability of forming a two-thousand-atom protein as something like one part in 10^{321}. He wrote: "Events which, even when we admit very numerous experiments, reactions, or shakings per second, *need an infinitely longer time than the estimated duration of the earth in order to have one chance, on an average, to manifest themselves can, it would seem, be considered as impossible in the human sense.*"[4]

Lecomte du Noüy went on to say, "To study the most interesting phenomena, namely Life and eventually Man, we are, therefore, forced to call on an anti-chance, as Eddington called it; a 'cheater'

---

[2] William Paley, *Natural Theology or Evidences of the Existence and Attributes of the Deity* (Edinburgh, 1816), Chapter 22, p. 287.

[3] Walt Whitman, "Song of Myself," stanza 31, in *Leaves of Grass* (1891–92 edition).

[4] *Human Destiny* (New York, 1947), p. 35.

who systematically violates the laws of large numbers, the statistical laws which deny any individuality to the particles considered."[5]

There are many who place their faith in the roulette of chance, and they will find Lecomte du Noüy and Hoyle an aggravation to their fervently held assumptions about the meaninglessness of the universe. But there seem to be just enough evidences of design in the universe that those who accept as their credo faith in what has recently been called the Blind Watchmaker have had to give the existence of these evidences a name, the Anthropic Principle. Ironically, the Anthropic Principle was invented by several Princeton physicists with just the opposite intention, to highlight some of the remarkable properties of the universe that seem so well tuned to human existence. For example, had the original energy of the Big Bang explosion been less, the universe would have fallen back onto itself long before there had been time to build the elements required for life and to produce from them intelligent, sentient beings. Had the energy been more, it's quite possible that the density would have dropped too swiftly for stars and galaxies to form. As Goldilocks said at the little bear's bowl, "This porridge is just right."

Nowadays, however, another team has taken over the Anthropic Principle, scientists who wish to deny the role of design. Briefly stated, they have turned the argument on its head. Rather than accepting that we are here because of a deliberate supernatural design, they claim that the universe simply must be this way because we are here; had the universe been otherwise, we would not be here to observe ourselves, and that is that. Such is almost precisely the view enunciated by Stephen W. Hawking in his inaugural lecture as Lucasian Professor at Cambridge University—an illustrious chair once held by Newton—and a view of nature repeated by Hawking in his best-selling *A Brief History of Time.*[6] As I said, I am doubtful that you can convert a skeptic by the argument from design, and the discussions of the Anthropic Principle seem to prove the point.

Although it's unlikely that natural theology can offer proofs for the existence of God, I hasten to point out that surprisingly little in science itself is accepted by 'proof'. Let's take Newtonian

[5] Ibid., p. 38.
[6] Stephen W. Hawking, *A Brief History of Time* (New York, 1988), p. 125.

mechanics as an example. Newton had no proof that the earth moved, or that the sun was the center of the planetary system. Yet, without that assumption, his system didn't make much sense. What he had was an elaborate and highly successful scheme of both explanation and prediction, and most people had no trouble believing it, but what they were accepting as truth was a grand scheme whose validity rested on its coherency, not on any proof. Thus, when a convincing stellar parallax was measured in 1838, or when Foucault swung his famous pendulum at 2:00 A.M. on Wednesday morning, January 8th, 1851, these supposed proofs of the revolution and of the rotation of the earth did not produce a sudden, newfound acceptance of the heliocentric cosmology. The battle had long since been won by a persuasiveness that rested not on proof but on coherency.

Indeed, in science I find the idea of 'belief' somewhat curious. A few years ago I conducted a workshop for a rather diverse group of Christians, and I asked, "Can a theist believe in evolution?" Let me stop here and put in a footnote. Jehovah's Witnesses have sent me any number of copies of a book provocatively entitled *Life— How Did It Get Here? By Evolution or by Creation?* In replying to the donors, I point out that the question gives the wrong choice, and that it would be better to ask, "By chance or by design?" since it's entirely reasonable to accept both creation and evolution. I shall return to this point later, but first, back to the workshop question on whether a theist can believe in evolution.

I got a variety of responses, but it didn't occur to any of them to challenge what it might mean to '*believe*' in evolution. Does that mean to have faith in evolution in a religious sense? I have heard one leading paleontologist announce himself as a "devout evolutionist" when asked his faith, and I guess that is a possibility. But when pressed, most scientists would, I think, claim only that they accept evolution as a working hypothesis. In everyday, nonphilosophical usage, most people, scientists included, would say they believe in the results of science and that they believe the results of science to be true. Yet, and this is the anomalous part, most scientists would be mildly offended at the thought that their beliefs constituted an act of faith in a largely unproved but intricate system of coherencies.

Two autumns ago I heard a most extraordinary lecture about the mind and the brain viewed completely mechanistically, presented by a scientist with supreme confidence that his approach could explain everything. Afterward, on the way out, a thoughtful listener remarked to the somewhat startled speaker, "That was wonderful—in twenty years I have never met such a man of faith." She referred, of course, to his unshakable confidence that his extrapolations gave all the answers.

Now if we understand that science's great success has been in the production of a remarkably coherent view of nature rather than in an intricately dovetailed set of proofs, then I would argue that natural theology can also have a legitimate place in human understanding even if it falls short of proof. What is needed is a consistent and coherent worldview and, at least for some of us, the universe is easier to comprehend if we assume that it has both purpose and design, even if this cannot be proved with a tight logical deduction.

Nevertheless, there has been a persistent criticism that arguments from design will cause scientific investigators to give up too easily. If the resonance levels of carbon and oxygen are seen as a miracle of creation, would a Christian physicist try to understand more deeply why, from the mechanistic view of physics, the levels are that way and not in some other configuration? Might it not be potentially detrimental to the faith to explain a miracle? We must therefore surely ask, "Dare a scientist believe in design?"

There is, I shall argue, no contradiction between holding a staunch belief in supernatural design and being a creative scientist, and perhaps no one illustrates this point better than the seventeenth-century astronomer Kepler. Perhaps that is why he is one of my favorite characters in the entire history of science.

Kepler was nearly finished with the Lutheran theological curriculum at the University of Tübingen when he was more or less ordered by the Duke, who had supported him with a scholarship, to become a provincial mathematics and astronomy teacher in far-off Austria. It was as if a Harvard senior, a likely candidate for a summa in philosophy, was abruptly told in November to pack up and head for a position as math teacher in a high school in Guam. Kepler left the university under protest, claiming that there was no evidence that he even had any talent for astronomy. In fact, he was a straight A student except in astronomy, where he got an A-.

In Graz, Kepler put his mind to the heavens and soon began asking remarkable questions about the design of the universe.

Why are there just six planets? Why are they spaced the way they are? Why do they have the speeds they have? To ask why there were just six planets meant that Kepler was already a Copernican, so that he counted the earth as a planet, but not the sun and moon. The geocentrists, on the other hand, named the sun and moon as well as the five naked-eye planets to reach the mystical number of seven. One of the principal reasons Kepler was a Copernican arose from his deeply-held belief that the sun-centered arrangement reflected the divine design of the cosmos: The sun at the center was the image of God, the outer surface of the star-studded heavenly sphere was the image of Christ, and the intermediate planetary space represented the Holy Spirit. These were not ephemeral notions of his student years but a constant obsession that inspired and drove him through his entire life.[7]

Writing to a favorite correspondent, Herwart von Hohenburg, he said, "Copernicus piously exclaimed, 'So vast, without any question, is the Divine handiwork of the Almighty Creator.' But wow! It's quite refreshing to consider that we ought not to feel so astonished at the huge extent of the heavens as at the smallness of us human beings. Yet we must not infer that bigness is of special importance; otherwise the crocodile or elephant would be closer to God's heart than man."[8] And to his teacher Michael Maestlin back in Tübingen he wrote, "For a long time I wanted to be a theologian; for a long time I was restless. Now, however, behold how through my effort God is being celebrated in astronomy!"[9]

But Kepler did not stay long in Graz; the Counter-Reformation swept in, and the Protestant teachers were given until sundown to leave. Then, and throughout his life, he yearned for the call to Tübingen, but it never came. His theological views were suspect; among other things, a faculty committee specifically criticized him for believing that Calvinists should be considered Christian brothers.

---

[7] See, for example, his *Epitome of Copernican Astronomy* (1618) (*GBWW* I: 16, 85354; II: 15, 853–54).

[8] December 16th, 1598, *Johannes Kepler Gesammelte Werke*, 13, no. 107, pp. 144–158; my translation based on the one by Carola Baumgardt, *Johannes Kepler: Life and Letters* (New York, 1951), pp. 48–49.

[9] October 3rd, 1595, *Johannes Kepler Gesammelte Werke*, 13, no. 23, pp. 256–57; from Gerald Holton, "Johannes Kepler's Universe: Its Physics and Metaphysics," *American Journal of Physics* 24 (1956), pp. 340–51, esp. p. 351.

Instead of returning to his alma mater, Kepler turned the other direction, to Prague, where he became associated with the great observational astronomer Tycho Brahe. Their stormy direct inter-action lasted only ten months, but it was a critical encounter, for it gave Kepler's work a new direction and provided him with the crit-ical observations needed to find the elliptic path of Mars. This dis-covery and another, the so-called law of areas, are chronicled in his *Astronomia nova* (*GIT* 1983, 307–341), truly the New Astronomy. In its introduction he defended his Copernicanism from the point of view that the heavens declare the glory of God:

> I implore my reader [he writes] not to forget the divine goodness con-ferred on mankind, and which the psalmist urges him especially to consider. When he has returned from church and entered on the study of astronomy, may he praise and glorify the wisdom and great-ness of the creator. . . . Let him not only extol the bounty of God in the preservation of living creatures of all kinds by the strength and stability of the Earth, but also let him acknowledge the wisdom of the creator in its motion, so abstruse, so admirable.
>
> If someone is so dumb that he cannot grasp the science of astron-omy, or so weak that he cannot believe Copernicus without offending his piety, I advise him to mind his own business, to quit this worldly pursuit, to stay at home and cultivate his own garden, and when he turns his eyes toward the visible heavens (the only way he sees them), let him with his whole heart pour forth praise and gratitude to God the creator. Let him assure himself that he is serving God no less than the astronomer to whom God has granted the privilege of seeing more clearly with the eyes of the mind. (*GIT* 1983, 321-22)[10]

A detailed study of Kepler's life reveals an evolution of ideas on a number of topics, such as whether planets have 'souls' that guide them. He had grown up in an age when philosophers still attrib-uted heavenly motions in part to the individual intelligences of the planets, and in his youthful *Mysterium cosmographicum*, published while he was still in Graz, he endorsed the idea of animate souls as moving intelligences of the planets. But by the time of his mature work he could flatly state that, "I deny that the celestial movements are the work of mind" (*GBWW* I: 16, 933; II: 15, 933). However, on

---

[10] Slightly abridged and modified from my translation in *The Great Ideas Today* (1983).

his views of God as a geometer and of a universe filled with God's geometric designs he was unwavering.

Kepler's life and works provide central evidence that an individual can be both a creative scientist and a believer in divine design in the universe, and that indeed the very motivation for the scientific research can stem from a desire to trace God's handiwork. As Kepler put it in his ecstatic introduction to his *Harmonice mundi* of 1619, "The die is cast—I am writing the book—to be read now or by posterity it matters not. It can wait a century for a reader, as God himself waited six thousand years for a witness."[11]

Near the end of the same book Kepler cast his credo in the form of a psalm of praise and a prayer:

> I give Thee thanks, O Lord Creator, because I have delighted in thy handiwork and I have exulted in the works of thy hands. Behold! now, I have completed the work of my profession, having used as much of the ability as Thou halt given me; I have made manifest the glory of thy works, insofar as the narrows of my mind could grasp its infinity. If I have been allured into brashness by the wonderful beauty of thy works, or if I have loved my own glory among men, while advancing in work destined for thy glory, gently and mercifully pardon me: and finally, deign graciously to cause that these demonstrations may lead to thy glory and to the salvation of souls, and nowhere be an obstacle to that. Amen.[12]

I shall return to Kepler, but for now I realize that a single sterling example may not be convincing that belief in design is always innocent in guiding a scientist. For example, critics can easily point to Newton, who felt that God was continually adjusting the planetary system to keep the gravitational perturbations from throwing it out of kilter. In Query 31 of his *Opticks*, he refers to the irregularities that arise in the motions of planets because of the disturbing influence of the other planets, and he suggests that these irregularities will increase "till this system wants a reformation" (*GBWW* I: 34,

---

[11] Introduction to *Harmonice mundi, Johannes Kepler Gesammelte Werke*, 6, no. 290, p. 69 (*GBWW* I: 16, 1050; II: 15, 1050).

[12] End of Book V, Chapter 9, of *Harmonice mundi, Johannes Kepler Gesammelte Werke*, 6, no. 362; my translation is based on the ones by Charles Glenn Wallis (GBWW I: 16, 1050; II: 15, 1050) and by Eric J. Aiton, forthcoming, American Philosophical Society.

542; II: 32, 542). Leibniz, in a biting critique, commented that according to such a doctrine, "God Almighty wants to wind up his watch from time to time; . . . he is even obliged to clean it now and then by an extraordinary concourse. . . . I hold that this is a very mean notion of the wisdom and power of God."[13]

There's an interesting sequel to this Newton-Leibniz controversy. One actor is William Herschel, the discoverer of the planet Uranus and the man whose huge telescope, and the view of the heavens through it, inspired Haydn to write "The Heavens Are Telling." Herschel explored questions such as how one kind of nebula might evolve into another over long periods of time. His ideas challenged the French mathematical astronomer Pierre Simon Laplace to think about the formation of the solar system from a swirling nebula, something Laplace called the nebular hypothesis. Eventually, in 1802, Herschel made a trip to Paris to visit Laplace, and on 8th August the two of them called on the emperor Napoleon.

Napoleon was intrigued by the nebular hypothesis but felt Laplace had left something out. "Where is God in your proposal?" Napoleon asked. "Ah," replied Laplace, "I have no need for that hypothesis." Down through the centuries this has seemed like an arrogant and atheistic remark; in fact Laplace was just doing his science, saying that his own system of the planets, unlike Newton's, did not require a divine hand to keep things in order.

Some people feel threatened by a way of looking at the universe that does not explicitly require the hand of God. But it doesn't mean the universe is actually like that, just that science generally has no other way of working, because science can't cope with miracles. Science is, by its very nature, an attempt to find automatic, mechanistic explanations of the universe. Science isn't anti-God or atheistic, it's just neutral in the way it goes about explaining things. In the context, Laplace was being a good scientist, though I can't help feeling he was pretty arrogant as well, and he actually was a militant atheist.

Was Laplace being a better scientist than Newton because he didn't need design and the hand of God in his explanation? I think there is no doubt that Laplace's science superseded

---

[13] "Mr. Leibniz's First Paper, November, 1715," in H.G. Alexander, *The Leibniz-Clarke Correspondence* (Manchester, 1956), p. 11.

Newton's, but it's debatable that Newton's acceptance of a Deity made him the poorer scientist (see the discussion of Newton, *GIT*, 1992 pp. 96–169).

Nevertheless, chance as opposed to design has been raised to such a level of scientific orthodoxy that some of our contemporaries forget that this is just a tactic of science, an assumption, and not a guaranteed principle of reality. Few, however, have enunciated the mechanistic credo so stridently as the evolutionary biologist and historian of science William B. Provine, who has recently written,

> When [Darwin] deduced the theory of natural selection to explain the adaptations in which he had previously seen the handiwork of God, Darwin knew that he was committing cultural murder. He understood immediately that if natural selection explained adaptations, and evolution by descent were true, then the argument from design was dead and all that went with it, namely the existence of a personal god, free will, life after death, immutable moral laws, and ultimate meaning in life. The immediate reactions to Darwin's *On the Origin of Species* exhibit, in addition to favorable and admiring responses from a relatively few scientists, an understandable fear and disgust that has never disappeared from Western culture.[14]

Provine, in defending the gospel of meaninglessness, goes on to say that if modern evolutionary biology is true, then lofty desires such as divinely inspired moral laws and some kind of ultimate meaning in life are hopeless. I'm not sure why Professor Provine has such fear and loathing of design, but apparently, despite the examples of Kepler and Newton, he is still afraid that the arguments from design may block the march of science, and such a view is perhaps not totally unfounded. Let me explain.

Several years ago I participated in a remarkable conference of theists and atheists in Dallas. One session considered the origin of life, and a group of Christian biochemists argued that the historical record was nonscientific since it was impossible to perform scientific experiments on history. Furthermore, they amassed considerable evidence that the current scenarios of the chemical evolution of life were untenable. One of the atheists aligned against them, Professor Clifford Matthews from the

---

[14] *First Things* 6 (October 1990), p. 23.

University of Chicago, conceded that their criticisms had considerable validity. Calling their book on *The Mystery of Life's Origin*[15] brilliant, he summarized their arguments with respect to the standard picture of chemical evolution as saying, "1. the evidence is weak, 2. the premises are wrong, and 3. the whole thing is impossible."

As someone fully convinced in the existence of a superintelligence and a Divine Creator, I soon found myself in the somewhat anomalous position that to me, the atheists' approach was much more interesting than the theists'. That particular group of Christian biochemists had concluded that ordinary science didn't work in such a historical situation, that is, with respect to the origin of life, and they attempted to delineate some alternative "origin science" in which the explicit guiding hand of God could make possible what was otherwise beyond any probability. The reason I admired the atheist biochemists so much was that they hadn't given up. They were still proposing ingenious avenues whereby catalytic effects in the chemistry made the events far more likely. "Let us not flee to a supernaturalistic explanation," they said, "let us not retreat from the laboratory."

Now it might be that the chemistry of life's origins is forever beyond human comprehension, but I see no way to establish that scientifically. Therefore it seems to me to be part of science to keep trying, even if ultimately there is no accessible answer.

Am I contradicting myself to say, on the one hand, that the resonance levels in carbon and oxygen point to a superintelligent design and, on the other hand, that science must continue to search for underlying reasons why the resonance levels are that way and not some other way? I think not, for even if it is shown that those levels had to be the way they are because of some fundamental, invariable reason, there is still the miracle of design that led it to be so, choice or not. Therefore, I see no reason that an appreciation of the astonishing details of design should prevent us from trying to search further into their underlying causes. Hence I'm not prepared to concede that arguments from design are necessarily contra-scientific in their nature.

---

[15] Charles B. Thaxton, Walter L. Bradley, and Roger L. Olsen, *The Mystery of Life's Origin: Reassessing Current Theories* (New York, 1984).

Perhaps part of Provine's outrage came because he was responding to Phillip Johnson, Professor of Law at Berkeley, who is an articulate legal champion of the right to believe in God as Creator and a critic of an evolutionary process running entirely by chance. Earlier I mentioned the incredible odds calculated by Lecomte du Noüy against the chance formation of a protein molecule. Since we do have proteins, and since a mechanistic science has been highly successful, the overwhelming reaction has just been to ignore Lecomte du Noüy, since he is so obviously wrong. But is he? For science to overcome the odds, it is necessary for us to postulate catalysts and unknown pathways to make the formation of life from inert matter enormously easier, and it is of course precisely such pathways that are the challenge for science to find. But is not the existence of such pathways also evidence of design? And are they not inevitable? That is what materialists such as Provine do not want to hear, but as Hoyle says, the numbers one calculates put the matter beyond question.

So, while I differ from those Christian biochemists who postulate some new kind of "origin science," I do think a science totally devoid of the idea of design may be in danger of running into a blank wall. And this brings me to ask again, "Is natural theology and the idea of design a threat to science?" and I answer no, perhaps design might even be a necessary ingredient in science. In fact, I think it's the other way around—rather than natural theology being a threat to science, using design in science may be a threat to natural theology. If natural theology weds its arguments to particular scientific insights as evidences of design and arguments for a deity, it always runs the risk of having the ground cut out from under it.

Let me illustrate the danger by turning to what I call Hawking's Query. One of the great accomplishments of twentieth-century astronomy has been the explication of the expanding universe, and the idea that everything began in an indescribable explosion, the so-called Big Bang. "There is no way to express that explosion," writes the poet Robinson Jeffers.

All that exists
Roars into flame, the tortured fragments rush away from
each other into all the sky, new universes

Jewel the black breast of night; and far off the outer nebulae
like charging spearmen again
Invade emptiness.[16]

This is a thrilling scenario, and its essential framework, of everything springing forth from that blinding flash, bears a striking resonance with those succinct words of Genesis 1:3: "And God said,
'Let there be light'." Who could have guessed even a hundred
years ago, not to mention two or three thousand years ago, that a
scientific picture would emerge with electromagnetic radiation as
the starting point of creation!

But in fact, if we accept that moment of blazing glory as the
whole work of the Creator, we are on rather thin ice. Scientific theories, especially cosmological views, are notoriously subject to
change, and cosmologists have taken it as a special challenge to
eliminate the singularity of the beginning zero point when space
and time do not yet exist. And thus Professor Hawking, treating time
as one of the dimensions of the curved space-time in that opening
sequence, claims to have made a coordinate transformation that
eliminates the origin. In *A Brief History of Time*, Hawking writes:

> The idea that space and time may form a closed surface without
> boundary also has profound implications for the role of God in the
> affairs of the universe. With the success of scientific theories in
> describing events, most people have come to believe that God allows
> the universe to evolve according to a set of laws and does not inter-
> vene in the universe to break these laws. However, the laws do not tell
> us what the universe should have looked like when it started—it
> would still be up to God to wind up the clockwork and choose how to
> start it off. So long as the universe had a beginning, we could suppose
> it had a creator. But if the universe is really completely self-contained,
> having no boundary or edge, it would have neither beginning nor
> end: it would simply be. What place, then, for a creator?[17]

From a Christian perspective, the answer to Hawking's Query is
that God is more than the omnipotence who, in some other space-
time dimension, decides when to push the mighty ON switch. A few

---

[16] Used by permission from Robinson Jeffers, "The Great Explosion," in *The Beginning and End* (New York, 1963), p. 3.

[17] *A Brief History of Time*, pp. 140–41.

years ago I had the opportunity to discuss these ideas with Freeman Dyson, one of the most thoughtful physicists of our day. "You worry too much about Hawking," he assured me. "And actually it's rather silly to think of God's role in creation as just sitting up there on a platform and pushing the switch." Indeed, creation is a far broader concept than just the moment of the Big Bang. God is the Creator in the much larger sense of designer and intender of the universe, the powerful Creator with a plan and an intention for the existence of the entire universe. The very structures of the universe itself, the rules of its operation, its continued maintenance, these are the more important aspects of creation. Even Hawking has some notion of this, for near the end of his book he asks, "What is it that breathes fire into the equations and makes a universe for them to describe? The usual approach of science of constructing a mathematical model cannot answer the questions of why there should be a universe for the model to describe. Why does the universe go to all the bother of existing?"[18] Indeed, this is one of the most profound, and perhaps unanswerable, theological questions.

In reflecting on natural theology I have attempted to delineate a place for design both in the world of science and in the world of theology. As Kepler described astrology, the stars impel, but they do not compel.[19] There is persuasion here, but no proof. However, even in the hands of secular philosophers the modern mythologies of the heavens, the beginnings and endings implied in the Big Bang, give hints of ultimate realities beyond the universe itself. Milton Munitz, in his closely argued book, *Cosmic Understanding*,[20] declares that our cosmology leads logically to the idea of a transcendence beyond time and space, giving the lie to the notion that the cosmos is all there is, or was, or ever will be.

Yet ultimately natural theology is unsatisfying. With the eyes of faith the heavens declare the glory of God, but of what kind of God? Simply a God of very large numbers.[21] And this brings me to Kepler's query, to Kepler's Anguish. In 1613 he wrote:

---

[18] Ibid., p. 174.

[19] Kepler elaborates this idea in Book IV, Chapter 7, of his *Harmonice mundi* (1619).

[20] Milton K. Munitz, *Cosmic Understanding: Philosophy and Science of the Universe* (Princeton, 1986).

[21] From John Turkevitch, quoted in Diogenes Allen, *Quest* (New York, 1990), p. xiv.

There is nothing I want to find out and long to know with greater urgency than this: can I find God, whom I can almost grasp with my own hands in looking at the universe, also in myself?[22]

Munitz, in coming to the concept of transcendence, describes it as unknowable, which is somewhat paradoxical, since if the transcendence is unknowable then we cannot know that it is unknowable. Could the unknowable have revealed itself? Logic is defied by the idea that the unknowable might have communicated to us, but coherence is not. For me, it makes sense to suppose that the super-intelligence, the transcendence, the "ground of being" in Paul Tillich's formulation, has revealed itself through prophets in all ages, and supremely in the life of Jesus Christ.

As this essay draws to a close, I have obviously opened up a completely new vista that I don't have space to address: while natural theology could allow Kepler almost to grasp God with his own hands in looking at the universe, where is the equivalent to finding God within ourselves? Is it not within the moral precepts revealed in the sacrificial life of Christ? Can we be good without God? That was a question thoughtfully and provocatively raised in the *Atlantic Monthly* a few years ago,[23] and it deserves our attention. I suspect that the answer is deeply tangled with one of the most profound of Hawking's queries: Why does the universe go to all the bother of existing? Perhaps that part of the transcendence will lie forever beyond the narrows of our minds.

---

[22] Kepler to an unidentified nobleman, October 23rd, 1613, *Johannes Kepler Gesammelte Werke*, 17, no. 669, pp. 20–22; translation from Baumgardt, *Johannes Kepler: Life and Letters*, pp. 114–15.

[23] Glenn Tinder, "Can We Be Good Without God?" *Atlantic Monthly* (December 1989), pp. 69–85.

5 God, Chance, and Natural Theology

MORTIMER J. ADLER

1. INTRODUCTION

The preceding excellent essay by Professor Owen Gingerich was delivered at the Center of Theological Inquiry at Princeton. Its title refers to Kepler, a sixteenth-century astronomer, and Stephen Hawking, a twentieth-century cosmologist, both of whom make copious references to God, but only one of whom was a person of Christian religious faith.

In the title Professor Gingerich gave his essay, he added: "Reflections on Natural Theology." In that essay, he set forth scientific reasons for supporting the arguments of certain Christian natural theologians against chance and in favor of design in the natural processes of cosmological development and in biological evolution.

I mention all these things because in the first place, I think natural theology, as it has been developed in the nineteenth century, following Bishop William Paley in modern times, is not sound philosophically. It should be regarded as Christian apologetics, which is the use of reason to defend the truths of the Christian religion and to reconcile Christian faith with scientific knowledge. The truths of Christian faith are much more clearly and competently presented in dogmatic or sacred theology, as that was formulated in the great Summas of the Middle Ages.

Philosophical theology, which must never be confused, as it so often is, with natural theology, is strictly a branch of philosophy, and totally apart from any religious faith. As I have made clear in my recently republished book, entitled *How to Think about God*, it is theology written by pagans for pagans who are similarly deprived;

that is, by and for persons without any religious faith. The theology in Book Lambda of Aristotle's *Metaphysics* is philosophical theology as thus defined; it is defective in its conception of God, as will be pointed out presently.[1]

In the second place, I think that the argument for design that is presented by Aquinas in his fifth argument for the existence of the God in whom Christians believe is an unsound teleological argument, unsound because it is based on Aristotle's error of attributing the operation of final causes to the processes of natural motions or actions, whereas they properly belong only in the production of human works of art. This erroneous argument is later presented in Paley's *Natural Theology, or Evidences of the Existence and Attributes of the Deity* (1816), in which the watchmaker's design of the timepiece he makes is proposed as the model in terms of which we should think of God's relation to the universe he creates. The creator is not an artist making an artifact; the created universe is not a work of art.

In the third place, as I have shown in *How to Think about God*, the presence of chance in the universe, both in cosmological developments and in biological evolution, lies at the heart of an indispensable premise in the only sound philosophical argument for the existence of God.

That argument, occurring in philosophical theology, not in Christian apologetics, does not prove the existence of the God in whom Christians believe, whom they worship, and to whom they pray; but most, though not all, of the properties attributed to the God that Pascal calls the God of the philosophers are identical with the properties attributed to the God of Abraham, Isaac, and Jacob and the God of the Christian religion, as well as of Islam.

This, as I pointed out above, cannot be said of the God of Aristotle's *Metaphysics*, who is a prime mover and a final cause, but not the sole creative cause, or "exnihilator," of a universe that did not come into existence with the Big Bang, but pre-existed the Big Bang.

---

[1] *The Summa contra Gentiles* by Aquinas does not replicate the *Summa Theologica*, nor is it a work in philosophical theology. It is, strictly speaking, a work of Christian apologetics, written to persuade the Jews and Moors in Spain of the truth of the Christian religion.

In the fourth place, it is necessary to point out that according to sacred, dogmatic Christian theologians, there is no incompatibility between the existence of an omnipotent and omniscient God, eternally (that is, timelessly) existing, and the presence of chance occurrences in natural process and human acts of free choice, acts which those physicists, who are both materialists and determinists, deny because they cannot explain them in terms of their understanding of the causal and statistical laws of their science.

In the fifth place, what has just been said requires me to call attention to Hawking's serious errors in his *A Brief History of Time*, which Professor Gingerich fails to criticize. The Lucasian professor of physics at Cambridge University, holding Newton's chair, is undoubtedly a great physicist and cosmologist, but his understanding of God and creation is woefully deficient. He is philosophically naive and theologically ignorant, both with respect to sacred theology and with respect to philosophical theology, while at the same time referring to God and to God's mind frequently in his book, a book in which, for reasons I will point out, his own principles should prevent him from ever mentioning God.

Furthermore, if the Big Bang were the exnihilation of the cosmos studied by physicists, there would be no need for proof of the existence of God. On the contrary, any philosophically sound argument for the existence of God, in order to avoid begging the question, must assume that the physical cosmos had no beginning.

Both Aquinas and Kant give philosophically sound arguments showing that neither of these two assumptions—a beginning for the cosmos and of time, on the one hand, and an everlasting cosmos without a beginning or end in time, on the other hand—can be proved. Unless we accept the second hypothesis we cannot avoid begging the question. Hence, any sound philosophical argument for the existence of God must include the assumption that time and the cosmos are everlasting, i.e., have no beginning or end.

Hawking could have avoided the error of supposing that time had a beginning with the Big Bang if he had distinguished time as it is measured by physicists from time that is not measurable by physicists.

Here let me call attention to the error made in quantum mechanics of thinking that its uncertainties with respect to subatomic motions indicate an indeterminacy in nature or reality rather than indeterminability by us, caused by the intrusive action of our measurements. This is combined with the error made by some theoretical physicists, such as Arthur Holly Compton at the University of Chicago, the error of thinking that quantum indeterminacy in reality may help to explain human free choice. This is philosophical nonsense, no worse of course than the philosophical nonsense in Hawking's popular book.

In the sections to follow, I will amplify—and in the course of doing so, undoubtedly repeat—what I have just briefly outlined: first, with respect to sacred theology, philosophical theology, and natural theology, or Christian apologetics; second, with respect to the philosophical unsoundness of the teleological argument for God's existence, and the misconception of God as an artist like the watchmaker; third, with respect to the reason why I say that chance in cosmological developments and in biological evolution lies at the heart of the one sound philosophical argument for the existence of God; and here also why that argument must assume everlasting time and a cosmos without beginning or end; fourth, why there is no incompatibility between the eternal existence of an omnipotent and omniscient God and the occurrence of chance events and human free choice in time; and fifth, with respect to the central error to be found in Hawking's *A Brief History of Time*, an error shared by many other great physicists in the twentieth century, the error of saying that what cannot be measured by physicists does not exist in reality.

2. THE DOMAIN OF THEOLOGY

Theology began in Greek antiquity, in Book X of Plato's *Laws* and in Book Lambda of Aristotle's *Metaphysics*. Both Plato and Aristotle were pagan philosophers without any faith in the Olympian polytheism of Greek mythology and, of course, unenlightened by the divine revelation in which the Jews believed, and later the Christians and the Muslims.

Aristotle regarded theology as the highest grade of human knowledge, the highest level of abstraction reached by metaphysics, or what later came to be called *philosophia prima*. Let us call this discipline "philosophical theology" to avoid its confusion with what in modern times came to be miscalled "natural theology."

Aristotle's cosmology viewed the physical cosmos as a universe eternally (i.e., everlastingly) in motion. For him, the word eternal as applied to the world did not refer to the timeless and the immutable but to the everlasting and forever in time.

Aristotle never asked the existential question: What caused the everlasting cosmos in motion to exist? He asked instead: What caused the everlasting cosmos to be forever in motion? His answer to that question was: God, the prime mover, but not as the prime efficient cause from which the motion in the world first sprang as an effect, rather as the ultimate final cause, the object of desire which everlastingly motivated the observed changes in the cosmos.

Aristotle's philosophical theology contains an error that is also present in his physics; i.e., the error of attributing final causes to natural changes or motions. This error improperly attributes to natural processes the same teleology that is properly attributed to works of human art.

There is no doubt at all that final causes operate in human artistic production. The carpenter who makes a chair is not only its efficient cause, as the wood out of which it is made is its material cause, but the carpenter also has in his mind a formal cause (the design of the chair to be made) and a final cause—the purpose for which the chair, when made, will be used. In natural processes, there are only three causes—material, formal, and efficient—but no final cause. Teleology is not present in nature as it is in art.

The other work of purely philosophical theology in antiquity is to be found in the *Enneads* of Plotinus. It represents the flowering of neo-Platonic philosophy in the Hellenistic period. In the centuries of the Middle Ages there is one other work, written by a Christian—Anselm, the archbishop of Canterbury. The first three chapters of the *Proslogium* (GIT, 1969, pp. 316–343), containing an argument that has been called "the ontological argument for God's existence," does not employ any article of Christian faith. It could have been written by a pagan and it was intended for pagans—the fools that Anselm is trying to argue against when they deny God's existence. Anselm wrote other works, such as *Cur Deus Homo?*, which could only have been written by a person of profound Christian faith.

I shall explain later why the so-called ontological argument fails as a proof of God's existence. It was dismissed by Aquinas and later by Kant as a flawed proof. I will give better reasons than they gave for dismissing it. But the reasoning in those first three chapters of the *Proslogium* must be retained in any well-constructed philosophical theology as an explanation of how we must think about God as the one supernatural Supreme Being, who should be thought of as necessarily existing, i.e., as a being incapable of not existing.

With this one exception in the Christian Middle Ages, a new type of theological writing emerged with authors in the Patristic period, notably Augustine and Chrysostom, who were Platonists; and in the later Middle Ages with Albert the Great, Aquinas, and Duns Scotus, who were Aristotelians.[2] These were all persons of religious faith—Christian, Jewish, and Muslim. Their theology should be called "sacred dogmatic theology" because its first principles were articles of religious faith, based on interpretations of Sacred Scripture.

Strictly speaking, with the one exception aforementioned of Anselm's *Proslogium*, there was no purely philosophical theology in the centuries from the first to the seventeenth. As I have already pointed out, the *Summa contra Gentiles* written by Aquinas was not a work in sacred dogmatic theology. It reveals itself to us plainly as a work in Christian apologetics, written by Aquinas for the purpose of persuading the Jews and Moors in Spain of the truth of the Christian religion.

Purely philosophical theology does not appear in early modern times with the *Meditations* of Descartes and the *Theodicy* of Gottfried Wilhelm Leibniz. They wrote philosophically as apologists for their Christian faith. The exception is the *Ethics* of Spinoza. That is a work in purely philosophical theology. Its pantheism and its denial of a God who created the cosmos were so obviously contradictory of the Jewish faith that it was condemned by the rabbis of Amsterdam as heretical, and Spinoza himself was excommunicated.

Other works of Christian apologetics should be mentioned here. In antiquity there was a work by Boethius entitled *On the Catholic Faith*. In early modern times there were Pascal's *Pensées* and Locke's *The Reasonableness of Christianity*. In the nineteenth century

---

[2] For the sake of brevity, I will deal only with Christian authors in this period. An expanded account would, of course, include Jewish authors, such as Maimonides, and Muslim authors, such as Avicenna.

there was Cardinal John Henry Newman's *Grammar of Assent.* None of these authors would have mistakenly thought of their works as being in the category of "natural theology."

So far as I know, that mistaken denomination of a work in Christian apologetics begins in the nineteenth century with Bishop Paley's book entitled *Natural Theology, or Evidences of the Existence and Attributes of the Deity* (1816). Clearly, this was not a work in philosophical theology, written by a pagan. Clearly, it was a work in Christian apologetics, and a poor one at that, as I will point out later.

Works written by Christians for Christians or for nonbelievers are clearly not works in philosophical theology, and just as clearly they are not works in sacred dogmatic theology. They do not represent faith seeking understanding. Instead they represent faith offering reasons for the truth of its beliefs.

I have already suggested the epithet "Christian apologetics" as the correct denomination of such works to replace "natural theology," a term which came into use only in the nineteenth century. A very recent book written by John Polkinghorne, chaplain of Trinity Hall, Cambridge University, and entitled *Science and Creation* (1989) has an opening chapter entitled "Natural Theology." While still retaining that denomination, Polkinghorne's book is a fine work in Christian apologetics, not a work in philosophical theology. It is of great interest to us because of its explicit repudiation of the erroneous denials of chance and contingency in Bishop Paley's *Natural Theology.* I will quote the relevant passages from Polkinghorne's book in a later section of this essay.

3. THE CENTRAL ERROR IN MODERN CHRISTIAN APOLOGETICS

In the domain of theology, there are only three alternative categories of work: philosophical theology, dogmatic theology, and Christian or Jewish or Muslim apologetics. What has very recently come to be called "natural theology" is not a fourth alternative, for it is nothing but Christian apologetics.

In the light of what has just been said, one exception must be noted. A great Christian theologian, Aquinas was also a brilliant Aristotelian philosopher. In the *Summa Theologica* of Aquinas there are many philosophical insights that he might not have formulated had he been merely a pagan disciple of Aristotle. However, these insights are not derived from or dependent on any article of Christian faith. For that reason, they can be regarded as contributions to philosophical theology, even though they are not the work of a pagan mind.

I wish to call attention to one such insight because it is pivotal to the proof of God's existence as that is formulated in purely philosophical theology. It is the insight that being or existence is the *proper* effort of God. The italicized word "proper" signifies that God and God alone is the cause of being or existence. In the causation of being, he is not the first cause, because there are no second or other causes. All other causes, all of them natural causes, are causes of becoming or perishing. Only what is being itself can cause existent entities to exist. Such causation is supernatural. It does not occur in nature.

When God is understood not only as the Supreme Being but also as the creator (or exnihilator) of the cosmos, he must also be understood as a supernatural being and as a supernatural cause.

This involves a philosophical analysis of causation that makes a sharp distinction between the causation of being and the causation of becoming. That goes along with the differentiation between the operation of final causes in the processes of becoming that are productions of human art and the nonoperation of such causes in the phenomena of becoming that are natural processes.

The insight about God as the sole cause of being is unlike the proposition that the perfection of God as the Supreme Being includes moral as well as ontological perfection. Anselm's purely philosophical argument is that the Supreme Being—a being than which no greater can be thought—entails all the ontological perfections. Only a person of Christian (or Jewish or Muslim) faith would add God's moral perfection. That additional affirmation is an article of religious faith in a loving and benevolent God. It is totally beyond the reach of reason or purely philosophical thought.

If we put together these two contributions to purely philosophical theology made by Anselm and Aquinas we should be able to see the radical difference between the God of Aristotle (only a prime mover and only a final cause) and the God of Anselm and

Aquinas (a creator *ex nihilo* of the cosmos). Understanding that difference should help us to realize the inappropriateness of using Aristotelian arguments in the five ways advanced by Aquinas in Question 2, Article 3, of his *Summa Theologica* (GBWW I: 19, 12–14; II: 19, 12–14).

Any logically valid argument for the existence of God must choose one of two assumptions: either the world and time had a beginning, or they always existed and never came into being out of nothing. Neither of these two assumptions can be proved true on rational grounds, as Aquinas and later Kant argued. The first assumption is an article of Jewish, Christian, and Muslim faith. But to make that assumption in purely philosophical theology begs the question, for if we assume that the cosmos and time came into being out of nothing, we are also assuming that it was created *ex nihilo*, and that God as creator (exnihilator) exists, which was the proposition to be proved. Hence, to avoid begging the question, any purely philosophical proof of God's existence must assume that the world and time always existed and exists everlastingly. In other words, only if we assume that the world and time never began or came into being out of nothing, do we have a genuine problem of proving God's existence as the preservative, not origi-native, cause of the existence of the cosmos at every moment of its existence.

The chief error that I am concerned to expose in many works of modern Christian apologetics is the error of supposing that in order to defend Christian faith they must show that there is noth-ing contingent in cosmic processes and in biology and evolution; in other words, that nothing happens by chance or coincidence. Instead it is thought necessary to assert that everything happens according to a fully worked out design in the mind of God.

The underlying root of this error is an inadequate analysis of the processes of becoming. (1) If God created the cosmos, that is exnihilation—bringing the cosmos into existence out of nothing. (2) Biologica procreation is a mode of becoming, one in which no cause of being operates. (3) Artistic production, or human mak-ing, is unlike both exnihilation and biological procreation.

When this threefold differentiation is fully understood, it will be seen that Bishop Paley's profound error was to regard God's cre-ation of the cosmos as like a watchmaker's production of a time-piece. That is not only a false analogy but grossly anthropomorphic.

The cosmos is not a work of art on God's part any more than it is a work of procreation.

On the contrary, the cosmos is something other than the mechanism of a clock, all of whose motions are necessitated by the design imposed upon it by its human artificer. God is not the divine artificer, and the cosmos is not a work of divine art. Moreover, if nothing happened by chance and there was nothing contingent in the cosmos, no valid proof of God's existence could be philosophically constructed. I will explain why this is so in the next section.

4. A Sound A Posteriori Argument: From a Radically Contingent Cosmos to an Exnihilating Deity

Concepts are abstracted from sense-experience. They are all empirically derived. Hence we cannot have a concept of God. But not all the notions with which the intellect operates in thinking are concepts. There are, in addition, theoretical constructs, fictions of the mind that in the Middle Ages were called *entia rationis*. As in physics black holes and neutrinos are theoretical constructs, so in theology God is a theoretical construct.

Since all concepts are empirically derived, they do not raise question about the existence of their objects. The concept of dog or cow is abstracted from perceptual instances of dogs and cows, and so we do not ask whether what we have in mind when we use the word 'dog' or 'cow' actually exists.

But when we are dealing with theoretical constructs in mathematical physics or in theology, the question of existence is inescapable. Do black holes really exist? Do neutrinos? Does that which we have in mind when we use the word 'God' exist in reality?

Anselm mistakenly thought that because we cannot think of God as nonexisting while thinking of him as the Supreme Being, therefore God exists. The *non sequitur* is obvious. Anselm has instructed us about how to formulate a theoretical construct for the proper name 'God', but the question still remains whether what we have in mind with that theoretical construct is only a fiction of the mind or a really existent being—an *ens reale*, not just an *ens rationis*. On the other hand, a unicorn is a fiction of the mind that, so far as all the evidence goes, is just that. There are no perceptual instances of unicorns and no proof that they exist, even if not perceived.

With respect to theoretical constructs, the rule of inference by William of Ockham operates in theology in the same way that it operates in physical science. Ockham's rule—and razor—is that unless the existence of what is signified by our theoretical constructs is indispensable to explain observed phenomena or existences, the theoretical construct being thus tested is merely a fiction of the mind. Ockham's razor cuts out all unnecessary entities. It prevents us from committing the fallacy of reification—of adding to the world of real existences by positing entities that we have no reason to think exist. Ockham's rule is a principle of parsimony.

When we have the theoretical construct of God in our mind, even a God that is thought of as necessarily existing, we have to give reasons for positing the existence of the entity named. Since we cannot affirm the existence of God *a priori* by saying that God's existence is self-evident because we must think of the Supreme Being as necessarily existing, only an *a posteriori* argument for God's existence is valid. It is reasoning from the nature of the cosmos to the existence of God. Obeying Ockham's rule, we can posit the real existence of God, of whom we have a theoretical construct in our mind, because the existence of God is necessary to explain the existence of the cosmos.

The only valid argument for the existence of God is thus the inverse of the *a priori* ontological argument. It is reasoning from the nature of the cosmos to God, not from the nature of God to God's existence. The crucial point in this *a posteriori* argument is the radical contingency of the cosmos. Let me now explain how that is different from merely superficial contingency.

We usually think of the physical entities that come into being at one time and perish at another as contingent beings. If they existed necessarily, they could not come into being at one time and perish at another. But they are only superficially contingent. They do not come into being out of nothing, and when they perish, they do not pass into nothingness.

Biological progenitors cause the becoming of their progeny. They can cease to be and cease to function as causes while their progeny continue in being. When their progeny die as the result of the counteracting causes that operate against the inertia of being that has kept them alive, their perishing is merely a transformation of their matter—dust and ashes and skeletal bones instead of a living organism. The living organism has been replaced by matter in other forms, not by sheer nothingness. In contrast to such superficial contingency, we find radical contingency in the cosmos as a whole. Unless the cosmos were caused to exist at every moment of its existence, it would be replaced by the absolute void of nothingness.

How do we know that the cosmos is radically contingent? We know that all living organisms are superficially contingent because we know that they come into being at one time and perish at another. As pointed out earlier, in order to avoid begging the question, we must assume that the cosmos has everlasting existence, without a beginning or an end in time. What reason, then, do we have for thinking that this everlasting cosmos is radically contingent and in need of a cause of its existence?

Were this everlasting cosmos a necessary rather than a radically contingent existence—if it were incapable of not existing—we would have no ground for positing the existence of an exnihilating deity as the cause of its existence. Only if the cosmos is capable, at every moment of its existence, of not existing at all, would we have to posit the existence of a cause of its being, a cause that exnihilates it or preserves it from passing into nothingness.

The three crucial premises in the valid a posteriori argument for God's existence are as follows:

God and God alone causes being or existence. All natural causes are causes of becoming or perishing.

What does not exist necessarily and does not have the ground of its existence in itself needs a cause of its existence in another being at every moment of its existence.

Whatever is capable of being otherwise (because it involves events that happen by chance or free choice) is also capable of not being at all and so needs a cause of its existence at every moment of its existence.

In the light of Ockham's rule, we are, therefore, justified in positing (or affirming) the existence of a supernatural Supreme Being as the exnihilating cause of the existence of the cosmos, which would cease to exist if it were not thus creatively caused.

Still one question remains: What grounds do we have for thinking that the cosmos could be otherwise—that its processes involve chance or coincidence? That is a question of fact, which we will deal with in the next section. Suffice it to say here that if we find an affirmative answer to that question tenable, then the *a posteriori* argument is grounded in facts about the cosmos.

That school in modern Christian apologetics, which follows Bishop Paley in viewing the cosmos as if it were a work of art designed by a divine artificer, denies that anything happens by chance in the cosmos and so denies its radical contingency.

5. CREATION, CONTINGENCY, AND CHANCE

Whether or not contingency and chance exist in the cosmos is a question of scientifically discoverable fact. It is not a question to be answered by arguing that chance and contingency in the cosmos are incompatible with Christian faith in a morally perfect God who created the cosmos as an act of benevolent love.

Before we turn to the answer given by twentieth-century natural science, let us consider the relevance of certain questions about creation that were asked in the Middle Ages in sacred dogmatic theology. In his *Summa Theologica* Thomas Aquinas asks the question whether God could have created other universes than this particular cosmos, and even whether he could have created a better one than this. Aquinas rejects a negative answer to the first question on the ground that a negative answer would entail the denial of God's freedom in the act of creation. Creation is an act of God's free choice, not something necessitated by God's nature.

That this actual cosmos is only one of a number of possible universes is a mark of its radical contingency, if it is true that whatever can be otherwise is capable of not being at all. The truth of that proposition is not self-evident, but I think it is true beyond a reasonable doubt, if not beyond the shadow of a doubt.

The Christian faith that God created man in his own image by giving human beings immaterial intellects and, with that, also free will is a further indication that in the course of human affairs the totally unpredictable is present. The power of free choice is the power to choose otherwise at any moment, no matter how one does in fact choose at that moment; it is also the power not to

choose at all. The course of human history would be quite otherwise if human beings, exercising free will, had chosen it to be so.

The paleontological discoveries of Harvard professor Stephen
Jay Gould provide us with ample scientific evidence of chance at
work in the course of biological evolution. Twentieth-century par-
ticle physics and its cosmology, as influenced by the general theory
of relativity, provide similar evidence of chance at work in the eighteen billion years since the Big Bang; and the Big Bang itself,
which is not the exnihilation of the cosmos, is itself an unpredictable event.

The doctrine of the miscalled "natural theology," beginning
with Paley and coming down to our own day, represents poorly
conceived Christian apologetics that has its intellectual background in Newtonian classical mechanics. It is inconsistent with
the scientific facts discovered, and scientific theories formulated,
in the twentieth century.

I have earlier referred to a book of Polkinghorne, *Science and
Creation* (1989). It is a work of Christian apologetics, not a work in
pagan philosophical theology. It is written by a person of Christian
faith who is also a mathematical physicist. Polkinghorne is not
alone. His book includes a bibliography of other works in twentieth-century Christian apologetics that tend to confirm the views
that he himself advances.

For Polkinghorne, there is no incompatibility whatsoever
between the presence of chance, randomness, and contingency in
the cosmos and God's creation of it. Let me quote a few passages
from his book.

> The way that an element of randomness is seen to create openness to
> the future assigns a more positive role to chance in the process of the
> world than is acknowledged by those like Monod who see its opera-
> tion as destructive of all significance. . . .

> This chapter has portrayed a world whose processes can assemble
> complexity within a decaying environment and where random events
> can prove to be the originators of pattern. Such a world is a world of
> orderliness but not of clockwork regularity, of potentiality without
> predictability, endowed with an assurance of development but with a
> certain openness as to its actual form. It is inevitably a world with
> ragged edges, where order and disorder interlace each other and
> where the exploration of possibility by chance will lead not only to the

evolution of systems of increasing complexity, endowed with new possibilities, but also to the evolution of systems imperfectly formed and malfunctioning. The former superior entities will earn the epithet "successful" by their survival in the competition for constituent resources; the latter inferior entities will disappear from the evolving scene. It is just such a world that we live in. . . .

In other words, God chose a world in which chance has a role to play, thereby both being responsible for the consequences accruing and also accepting limitation of his power to control. . . .

Yet the order and disorder which intertwine in the process of the world show that the universe upheld by the divine Word is not a clear cold cosmos whose history is the inevitable unfolding of an invulnerable plan. It is a world kept in being by the divine Juggler rather than by the divine Structural Engineer, a world whose precarious process speaks of the free gift of Love. We are accustomed to think of the vulnerability accepted by the Word in the incarnation, a vulnerability potentially present in the baby lying in the manger and realized to the full in the man hanging on the cross. What is there revealed of the divine in the human life of Jesus is also to be discerned in the cosmic story of creation.

To this I would only add that Polkinghorne explicitly rejects what he regards as the outmoded as well as erroneous Christian apologetics of Paley and the anthropomorphic image of God as analogous to a watchmaker, producing a mechanical work of art that is intelligible to an extent that the cosmos known to twentieth-century physics and biology is not.

6. THEORETICAL PHYSICS AND PHILOSOPHICAL THEOLOGY

A few Christian apologists in the twentieth century, such as Polkinghorne, are knowledgeable in the field of twentieth-century theoretical physics. But, with the possible exception of Heisenberg, few if any twentieth-century theoretical physicists manifest any competence in philosophy and appear to be totally ignorant of philosophical theology.

One would not expect them to be persons of Christian faith or apologists for Christianity, but one would expect them to be silent about matters beyond their ken. They should at least be aware of the limitations of theoretical physics and not make unfounded remarks on the basis of their knowledge of that limited subject.

Einstein was a great theoretical physicist and great human being, but not a wise man. The possession of wisdom depends to some extent on clear philosophical thought. Einstein once said that what was not measurable by physicists was of no interest to them, or had no meaning for them; he also said (in his attack on quantum indeterminacy) that God, a being not measurable by physicists, does not throw dice. He said that he did not believe in a "personal" God, using the word personal as if it meant the same thing as anthropomorphic. Man is a person because he is in the image of God, not the reverse. In theology, the word person signifies a being with intellect and free will.

Hawking is a great theoretical physicist, both in quantum mechanics and in cosmology. But his philosophical naïveté and his ignorance of philosophical theology fills his *A Brief History of Time* with unfounded assertions, verging on impudence. Where Einstein had said that what is not measurable by physicists is of no interest to them, Hawking flatly asserts that what is not measurable by physicists does not exist—has no reality whatsoever.

With respect to time, that amounts to the denial of psychological time which is not measurable by physicists, and also to everlasting time—time before the Big Bang—which physics cannot measure. Hawking does not know that both Aquinas and Kant had shown that we cannot rationally establish that time is either finite or infinite. When he treats the Big Bang as if it were the beginning of time, not just the beginning of measurable time, he shows his ignorance of God as cause of being and of creation as an act of exnihilation, which the Big Bang is not.

Furthermore, Hawking's book is filled with references to God and to the mind of God, both not measurable by physicists, and so nonexistent by Hawking's own assertion about what has and what lacks reality. To discourse seriously about a nonexistent being without explicitly confessing that one is being fanciful or poetical is, in my judgment, impudence on the author's part.

Most theoretical physicists are guilty of the same fault when, in quantum theory, they fail to distinguish between a measurable indeterminacy and the epistemic indeterminability of what is in reality determinate. The indeterminacy discovered by physical measurements of subatomic phenomena simply tells us that we cannot know the definite position and velocity of an electron at one instant of time. It does not tell us that the electron, at any instant of time, does not have a definite position and velocity. They, too, convert what is not measurable by them into the unreal and the nonexistent. The definite position and velocity of the electron at any moment of time is not measurable because of the intrusive effect of the measurements themselves, though this effect may not itself be discernible.

In view of the ever-increasing specialization in all fields of learning, and therefore in higher education, we probably cannot look forward to a future in which theoretical physicists will also be persons who have sufficient grounding in philosophy and in philosophical theology, in order to avoid their making unfounded assertions about matters beyond their field of specialization. But they should at least be aware of their limited knowledge and be silent about matters beyond it.

On the other hand, we should also expect Christian apologists in the twentieth century to be aware of what has been discovered in this century about the physical cosmos and about biological evolution. Only thus will they avoid the errors of their predecessors in modern times who lived in a universe that was described by Newtonian classical mechanics, which we now realize is insufficient to describe the universe we have since been able to discern.

6 Gingerich Replies to Adler

OWEN GINGERICH

Mortimer Adler's essay springs in part from his earlier book *How to Think about God*. I was deeply intrigued as I read his book, for it was as compelling as a medieval mystery story, tightly logical and filled with excitement as flaws in past arguments by Aquinas and Anselm were systematically exposed. Finally, after a careful exposition of God's attributes as immaterial, immutable, necessary, uncaused, and infinite, he brings forth his conclusion that such a God indeed exists.

Much as I admire Adler's *tour de force*, I feel obliged to point out that our essays are based on fundamentally different approaches— his on logic, mine on rhetoric. In the twelfth century, logic and rhetoric were equally esteemed components of the medieval curriculum. In some pursuits logic was more suitable, whereas in others, such as ethics, rhetoric led the way. In the following century, the time of Thomas Aquinas, logic began to gain the ascendancy. Today, common opinion places logic on a pedestal, while "mere rhetoric" is a term of opprobrium. Likewise, "apologetics" has a decidedly negative ring to it. Here I shall argue that, contrary to the popular connotations of these words, rhetoric is the more relevant.

In a none-too-subtle (and rhetorical!) tone, Adler has quickly relegated natural theology to "Christian apologetics." (He ignores the fact that the first ninety-five percent of my essay, while being unabashedly theistic in its grounding, is not specifically Christian at all; it could equally apply to Jewish or Muslim theism.) Trying to redefine the contemporary usage of "natural theology" is a bit like Alice's Humpty-Dumpty saying that words mean just what he chooses them to mean. I would go along with physicist-priest John Polkinghorne (whose work Adler cites quite approvingly) and would define natural theology as "the search for God through the exercise of reason and the inspection of the world." Polkinghorne adds that this is "not an optional extra, for indulgence by the scientifically inclined, but rather it is an indispensable part of scientific inquiry."

Although I respect and admire Adler's severely philosophical rationale, I feel it isn't fully relevant to the question at hand. Adler's book, as well as his essay, is self-confessedly written by a pagan for pagans. The God he describes is not the God anyone would worship. Perhaps the distinguished Swiss theologian Karl Barth overstated it when he said, "This absolute and supreme being, the ultimate and most profound, this 'thing in itself,' has nothing to do with God." But neither Fred Hoyle's "superintelligence," Milton Munitz's "unknowable transcendence," nor the God of the Big Bang describes much about the God of consciousness, of conscience, or of creativity, that is, about the God of the great monotheistic religions.

While Adler has brilliantly demonstrated both the power and limitations of philosophical inquiry, logic has rather little to say about what we actually believe, whether it is in science or in theology. As Pascal said (in the closing quotation from Adler's *How to Think About God*), "the heart has its reasons that reason does not know" (GBWW I: 33, 222; II: 30, 222).

When Galileo began to argue for the heliocentric cosmology, it was his Ptolemaic opponent, Cardinal Bellarmino, who had logic on his side. Bellarmino could correctly point out that Galileo had no logical proof that the Earth moved. What Galileo could persuasively show was a series of examples that were more coherent, and somehow more reasonably understood, if one accepted a sun-centered cosmos. His argument was rhetorical, and it won the day.

Hence one of the themes of my essay: we have no proof from nature for the existence of God, no logical demonstration, but we do have pointers in the natural world—rhetorical pointers, if you will—toward the reasonableness of God's existence. This, then, is the appropriate arena for natural theology today, and it is not all that different from our system of beliefs as to what is found in natural science itself.

When I argued in my essay that the proper question is "design or chance?" rather than "creation or evolution?" I came dangerously close to what Adler has pointed out as the chief error of modern Christian apologetics. I certainly had not intended to argue that there is nothing contingent in the evolutionary process, or that nothing happens by chance. In fact, according to Alfred North Whitehead, one of the great ideas of the Judeo-Christian heritage that provided a fertile philosophical ground for the rise of modern science was the notion of God's freedom, and hence the contingency of nature. Since God could have made the universe in many different ways, the argument runs, it behooves the scientist to undertake the experiments to find out which way in fact describes the universe. The Princeton philosopher Diogenes Allen had already drawn my attention to the distinction between design and purpose, and probably I should have given more emphasis to the latter concept. A world ordered to God's purposes could be achieved in any number of ways, not merely by one pre-ordained design.

I suppose it is the insinuation of a causal uniqueness in design (which I did not intend) that launched Adler's attack on much modern natural theology on the grounds that it is based on Newtonian mechanics rather than on the scientific theories of the twentieth century. What I find curious is the extent to which Adler seems unwittingly to have fallen into the same error. He criticizes Stephen Hawking for treating the Big Bang "as if it were the beginning of time, not just the beginning of measurable time." But what is unmeasurable time? I suppose it is something like the unicorn, an *ens rationis.* All of Newtonian mechanics is based on the notion of an absolute, independent existence of time, even though a thinker like Augustine had long ago clearly stated that "There is no time before the world began," because "time does not exist without some movement and transition" (GBWW 1: 18, 325; II: 16, 378). The twentieth-century theory of relativity shows clearly how the march of time depends on its measurement, and the Newtonian notion of time like an ever-flowing stream, independent of the material world, is just as antiquated as Immanuel Kant's claim concerning the natural uniqueness of Euclidean three-dimensional geometry (GBWW I: 42, 24–26; II: 39, 24–26).

For Adler, acceptance of the Big Bang as the beginning of the universe and the beginning of time is tantamount to saying that God exists, and hence it begs the philosophical question. Natural theology's legitimate "inspection of the world" (in Polkinghorne's definition) undercuts the uniqueness of Adler's philosophical theology, which may perhaps explain his resistance to it. If I may indulge in a speculation, I suspect that here is the Achilles' heel through which some future philosopher will dissect Mortimer Adler's carefully crafted construction.

7 New Developments in Science Strengthen Adler's Argument for God's Existence

JOHN CRAMER

ADLER'S COSMOLOGICAL ARGUMENT

In 1980, Mortimer J. Adler published an interesting little book titled *How to Think about God.*[1] He subtitled it *A Guide for the 20th-century Pagan* and immediately appended a footnote to the subtitle defining a pagan as someone who does not worship the God of Christians, Jews, or Muslims. In the book, Adler critiqued traditional proofs for the existence of God as a springboard for presenting his own variation of the argument from contingency.

The philosophical asides on the French existentialists, the errors of Immanuel Kant, and the fads of theological and philosophical thought alone make the book enjoyable and worthwhile reading. The main argument, however, is of considerable interest in its own right. Moreover, many relevant developments have occurred since the publication of the book that, I believe, strengthen his case. Therefore, it seems appropriate to reconsider and extend his arguments and considerations.

The first move Adler makes is to discount the possibility that the cosmos had an absolute beginning. He does not argue the cosmos has existed forever; he explicitly assumes so. The reason for this move is that if the universe truly had an absolute beginning, it was made from nothing. In Adler's words, it was "exnihilated." But, an exnihilated cosmos implies ". . . that God, the exnihilator, exists."[2] Therefore, Adler is compelled to assume an eternal universe to avoid creating a circular argument for the existence of God.

---

[1] New York: Macmillan, 1980.
[2] Ibid., p. 38.

Starting with an eternal cosmos, Adler also rejects attempts to argue for the existence of a first cause of the cosmos, which would, of course, soon turn out to be God. With a universe stretching back into an infinite past, an infinite series of causes without *terminus* is just as possible as the eternal universe he has just assumed.

The basic premises of his argument derive from the traditional argument for the existence of God based on the existence of contingent entities (which Adler calls "the best traditional argument"). He lists these premises as follows:

1. The existence of an effect that requires the operation of a coexistent cause implies the coexistence of that cause.

2. Whatever exists either does or does not need a cause of its existence at every moment of its existence; that is, while it endures, from the moment of its coming to be to the moment of its passing away.

3. A contingent being is one that needs a cause of its continuing existence at every moment of its endurance in existence.

4. No contingent being causes the continuing existence of any other contingent being.

5. Contingent beings exist in this world and endure, or continue in existence, from the moment of their coming to be to the moment of their passing away.[3]

If these premises are true, it then follows that a noncontingent being must exist that continues the existence of those contingent beings we most certainly know exist. That is, a necessary being exists and holds all else in existence. The necessary being can only be the supreme being, God.

However, Adler judges the third premise probably false and the traditional argument for the existence of God from contingency a failure. The judgment is based on the observation that the contingency we observe in the universe is superficial, involving only transformations. Radical contingency, involving exnihilation and annihilation of entities, if it occurred, would call for a different conclusion. Adler also judges the third premise false because it is

---

[3] Ibid., pp. 116–19.

plausible that contingent beings, once generated, can indeed continue to exist on their own until some cause proves their contingency by causing them to cease to exist. Adler cites the way the inertia of an object continues the motion of the object and suggests an "inertia of being" may exist to continue existence and falsify the third premise.

Taken together, these ideas show that it is reasonable to reject the argument from contingency. That is, the argument does not lead inexorably to the conclusion that God exists. It might be true but one is not compelled to accept it. Rejection is intellectually respectable.

At this point, Adler recasts the argument. While he regards the third premise as implausible concerning particular entities in the universe, it might be true of the universe as a whole. The entire universe might be radically contingent though no part of it is radically contingent. What is true of the whole is not always true of the parts. For example, the set of all counting numbers is infinite but no one counting number is infinite. Adler argues that the cosmos as a whole is radically contingent.

The argument has two steps. He first notes that the present universe is only one of many possible universes. The long standing discussions among cosmologists about the type of universe we live in are ample evidence of the plausibility of this step. If cosmologists have not reached a conclusion, then the question is open and the possibility of other universes is a reasonable consideration. Do not misunderstand here. Adler needs only the *logical possibility* that the universe might have been other than it is. Physical actualization of the possibility is irrelevant to the force of the argument. Indeed, the *existence* of other universes confuses the argument by confusing the meaning of the term *universe*. Granted that the present universe is not the only possible universe, it then follows that the present universe has only *possible* existence; it does not have *necessary* existence.

The second step is to note that whatever might be otherwise might not exist at all. Anything that necessarily exists must be exactly what it is; it cannot be other than what it is. The converse is also true then—whatever can be otherwise does not exist necessarily and must be able to not exist. However, for the cosmos to cease to exist, it must be annihilated and not merely transformed.

Another way of arriving at the same conclusion is to rely on the principle of sufficient reason. Anything that exists does so because there is sufficient reason for it to do so. The cause that is the sufficient reason may reside either in the thing or in something else but the cause must exist. For a merely possible entity, the sufficient reason cannot reside in the entity but must reside in another. If the universe is merely possible, then the sufficient reason for its existence resides not in the universe but elsewhere. But the universe is all of the physical reality so the merely possible existence of the universe points "outside" the universe to the existence of a nonphysical reality.

Adler concludes then that, by the previous premises, there exists a necessary supreme being so that the universe stays in existence. God must be there to sustain the universe even if the universe is eternal. Beginning by rejecting belief in a creating God, Adler finds evidence of a sustaining God. The existence of a sustaining God, however, then becomes grounds for asserting the creating activity also. Thus, the idea of a created universe with a beginning (and, likely too, an end) now becomes more plausible than the idea of an eternal universe.

Adler regards his argument as showing *beyond reasonable doubt* that God exists. He does not claim *certainty* for the argument.

CRITIQUES AND COMMENTARY FROM PHYSICS

Physical science forms a significant background to the argument. At one point, Adler defends theology against the complaint that it deals with things beyond or outside the reach of common experience or observation by noting that most of modern physics also deals with theoretical constructs rather than empirical concepts.

A more important use of physical ideas occurs when Adler rejects the premise that for a contingent being to continue to exist requires the continuous action of a sustaining cause. Adler thinks something like "inertia of being" might plausibly be expected to continue the existence of contingent beings just as the inertia of a body keeps the body in motion (or at rest) without the continuous action of any cause. That is, he takes inertia to be inherent in the nature of a body, independent of the existence or action of other bodies. He is encouraged by that to suppose existence might also be inherent in a contingent object; independent of external causes.

Inertia is the only imaginable example of an inherent agent of perpetuation. Lacking this example, there would be no encouragement to think being might be self-continued. In fact, by Ockham's Razor, inventing an "inertia of being" might be an indefensible proliferation of entities. Since Ernst Mach is often said to have thought that the inertia of bodies is caused by distant bodies in the universe, deeper inquiry into the inherentness of inertia seems in order. An inertia caused by distant bodies can hardly be inherent or self-caused. It might be that Adler is mistaken, that the concept of inertia does not, after all, cast doubt on the third premise and the traditional proof from contingency.

It is true enough that classical, Newtonian inertia is inherent in an object. In fact, Newton frequently called it *vis insita*, the innate force. The modern view is not so clear. Leibniz, and then, most forcefully, Ernst Mach, insisted that motion is relative. As a consequence, Mach believed, inertial effects cannot be detected but for the existence of other bodies external to the body whose inertia is to be observed. Einstein attempted to incorporate Mach's ideas into his General Theory of Relativity. Taking Einstein as an authority, the modern physicist may not be so confident that inertia is inherent in an object.

Much as I would like to reconstitute the argument from contingency by seeing inertia as externally caused, I do not understand Mach to be denying the inherence of inertia. What Mach actually said on the subject is carefully, even cautiously, stated. I do not think he would describe distant objects as the *cause* of inertia. I think he would say they are the *measure* of inertia. In 1912 and at the end of his life, in response to his critics he said, for example, "I have remained . . . the only one who insists upon referring the law of inertia to the Earth, and in the case of motions of great spatial and temporal extent, to the fixed stars."[4] Notice he speaks of *the law of inertia* rather than of *inertia* itself. Notice too his lack of dogmatism about which reference frame is preferred, the Earth or the stars. It seems to me his primary concern was always focused on the problem of how motion was to be detected and measured. He categorically rejected absolute space and time but was uncertain exactly what was the best replacement for them.

---

[4] Ernst Mach, *The Science of Mechanics*, sixth edition (La Salle: Open Court, 1989), pp. 336–37.

Nevertheless, there are good reasons why people have understood Mach to be suggesting distant matter as a cause of inertia. Mach was a monist given to asserting the unity of the All, to arguing that everything affects everything else. Also, at several points in his discussions of Newtonian mechanics, Mach notes that we cannot be certain the inertia of a body is not affected by adjacent or distant matter. His remarks are plainly intended to tempt readers into wondering if such a causative interaction is possible. He is, however, always careful to avoid committing himself to the reality of an interaction. Mach was also known to think that it should some day be possible to explain both inertial motion and accelerated motion with the same concepts or same theory. If we think of accelerated motion as caused by external agents, then it seems that inertial motion would be externally caused also.

Though Einstein's efforts at incorporating Mach's ideas into relativity theory are generally judged to have succeeded only partially, the interest the great man showed in them has kept them alive as subjects of discussion to the present day. Perhaps that is because Einstein anointed them with the title, "The Mach Principle."

In Special Relativity, the increase in inertial mass above the rest mass of an object depends on the speed of the object. Consequently, at least part of the mass of an object is relative. Therefore, at least one part of the inertia of a body is not completely inherent to the object. In General Relativity, inertia acts to continue motion on a geodesic of space-time. Far from massive bodies, that is still a straight line despite the actual measured value of the mass. But the straight line (and this is Mach's main point) is defined with reference to the distant masses. Thus, our ability to see that the motion is continued is relative to those distant masses.

These considerations suggest how difficult it can be to decide whether a quantity is inherent in an object. It is not at all obvious that inertia is inherent in a body. One usual way of quantifying inertia (inertial mass) is to have a component that is externally determined, the relativistic mass increment. If inertia is not certainly inherent, perhaps the continuing of existence is not inherent either. Thus, the plausibility of the traditional argument may be stronger than Adler allowed.

My own view of the matter is that talk of distant matter causing inertia is wide of the mark. If one considers two small, uncharged objects moving in opposite directions near each other, seeing both motions as caused by distant objects quickly leads to trouble. Neglecting the very weak gravitational interaction, we have only distant matter as a cause of their linear motion if, tempted by Mach, we assume inertia is not inherent. But then we are faced with a single cause that produces exactly opposite effects. What sort of cause produces opposite effects simultaneously? Now add a third and a fourth object in arbitrary directions. Add as many as you like. What sort of single cause can produce an enormous and unpredictable range of effects? Is it a cause in any recognized physical sense? It would seem much more parsimonious to retain the Newtonian idea of an inherent inertia, altered, of course, by the relativity of measurements, than to countenance this type of causality.

We must remember that Adler's prime support for supposing that the continuing existence of an object might not require the continuous action of an agent was based on the fact that the motion of an object continues without the continuous action of an agent. To be sure, inertia of motion is logically distinct from inertia of existence. However, when one suggests the existence of until now an unknown property, inertia of existence, the case for the new property is strengthened by the suggestion that it is not wholly unique but is similar to something already known and accepted. That was Adler's purpose in referencing inertia of motion. Also, if it appears that the new property is truly unique, the case for its existence is accordingly weakened. Thus, a review of ideas about inertia weakens Adler's objections to the traditional cosmological argument.

CRITIQUES AND COMMENTARY FROM COSMOLOGY

Astrophysics and cosmology also bear on Adler's argument. Adler believes that "to affirm . . . that the world or cosmos had an absolute beginning—that it was exnihilated at an initial instant—would be tantamount to affirming the existence of God, the world's exnihilator."[5] Because he is attempting a secular proof for the existence of God, he feels constrained to posit an eternally

---

[5] Ibid., p. 38.

existent cosmos. He carefully explains that this position is not inconsistent with the Big Bang theory of the cosmos.

Adler has obviously read with careful attention the literature of modern cosmology. From this effort he feels safe in concluding that "the Big Bang theory does not posit an absolute beginning of the cosmos—a coming into being out of nothing—but only an initial event in the development of the cosmos. . . ."[6] That is, the present cosmos is not understood to have come into existence out of nothing. Something pre-existed the present cosmos. The Big Bang theory does not necessarily entail exnihilation of the universe and only exnihilation of the universe implies an exnihilator.

However, Adler overlooked a most interesting development. In 1973, Edward Tryon made a suggestion[7] that seems obvious in retrospect. Noting that the gravitational energy of the universe is necessarily negative, Tryon speculated that the negative gravitational energy might be enough to cancel the positive energies of motion and mass. In short, he suggested the total energy of the universe be zero.

Defending the idea, Tryon did a very short calculation to show the plausibility of the idea and suggested such an event be a variation of the familiar vacuum fluctuations that are ". . . utterly commonplace."[8] Of course, the familiar vacuum fluctuations are very small scale, creating electrons, positrons, or photons for a very short period. Tryon noted that the duration of a fluctuation is limited by the Heisenberg uncertainty. Then he used that fact as an argument in favor of a universe of *zero* total energy! Tryon explicitly invoked the Anthropic Principle as a defense, saying that the fact that we are here to observe the universe implies there has been such a large-scale fluctuation as he supposes.

These defenses are feeble. The common vacuum fluctuations are not and have not been thought of as events with zero energy. In fact, their energy is large enough to limit the lifetime of the fluctuations to unobservably short durations. By this and by its enormous scale, the zero energy universe differs from a vacuum fluctuation. The zero-energy universe shares no feature with vac-

---

[6] Ibid., p. 33.

[7] Edward P. Tryon, "Is the Universe a Vacuum Fluctuation?", *Nature* 246:5433 (14th December, 1973), pp. 396–97.

[8] Ibid., p. 397.

uum fluctuations save its origin from a vacuum. In short, nothing but a desperate wish for nonuniqueness supports identifying the zero-energy universe with a vacuum fluctuation.

Invoking the disputed Anthropic Principle is an even poorer defense. To show the absurdity of the principle, Richard Swinburne has told a fable about a man placed before a firing squad of twelve sharpshooters each of whom fires twelve shots. All 144 shots miss! The man laughs and remarks that it is no surprise they all missed since he is still around to be noticing it![9] Swinburne points out that the remark is fatuous; the 144 misses require further investigation. That we are here to think about it in no way explains the mystery of a zero-energy universe.

Tryon's idea has received a great deal of attention. Efforts have been made to find a reasonable, physical mechanism for causing this peculiar type of vacuum fluctuation to occur. Versions of the inflationary big bang theory have adapted to a zero energy universe, though multiple universes may arise to complicate the situation. The important point is that a zero-energy universe is now considered almost certainly correct.

The zero-energy universe affects arguments for the existence of God. One hears arguments like this. If the universe has zero total energy, then, assuming conservation of energy, the universe came from and amounts to nothing. The universe was and continues to be exnihilated. But, since the universe is everything physical and material, it must have been caused to arise by something beyond or outside itself. The universe must have been exnihilated by an exnihilator, by God.

This line of argument is too hasty and runs to a conclusion quite unacceptable to most modern cosmologists who, not surprisingly, go to great lengths to avoid encouraging it. One way to avoid it is to claim that current physics fails near the Singularity of the Big Bang. The point is that the material density and gravitational fields associated with the Singularity are so far beyond those for which current physics has been tested that we cannot be sure that current physics applies to the singularity. Furthermore, current theories predict "nonphysical" properties like an infinite density for the Singularity. Presumably, the Singularity makes sense

---

[9] "Argument from the Fine-Tuning of the Universe," in John Leslie, ed., *Physical Cosmology and Philosophy* (New York: Macmillan, 1990), p. 165.

within another, naturalistic, framework and there is no need to think there might be something supernatural about the Singularity and the origin of the universe.

Another possibility arises quite naturally out of the inflationary scenario into which the zero energy universe seems to fit. The universe we see, in this scheme, is not the entire universe; not everything there is. Only a part of everything there is had inflated into the bubble we think of as our universe. And it is only this bubble that has zero energy. As to the rest of everything that is, it is forever beyond reach because the expansion puts the other universes beyond the reach of light signals. This is a wildly speculative idea out on the very edge of what may be considered proper science. If Karl Popper is right that only falsifiable ideas belong to science, a forever unknowable and unobservable universe does not belong in science. The idea also means one must be very careful using the word *universe* because here it is plural and means less than "everything there is."

These responses are not notably satisfactory. The reason they are preferred by cosmologists is obvious. Bad as they are, they are preferable to believing God exists.

A final, major point of contact with cosmology appears in Adler's argument that the continued existence of the cosmos requires the continual action of a preserving agent. The first step in the argument is a conclusion drawn from cosmology; ". . . the cosmos which now exists is only one of many possible universes that might have existed in the infinite past, and that might still exist in the infinite future."[10] This picture is consistent with his decision to posit an eternal cosmos.

The next and crucial step is to say that "whatever might have been otherwise in shape or structure is something that also might not exist at all."[11] But "whatever can be otherwise than it is can simply not be at all."[12] Thus, we are led to the primary conclusion of Adler's effort. If the cosmos at every moment has the potential to not be (that is, to annihilate), then at every moment it must be caused to exist. The cause of this continual exnihilation is God, the continual exnihilator, whose existence as an initial exnihilator Adler took such care to avoid positing. Adler then immediately

---

[10] Adler, p. 143.
[11] Ibid., p. 144.
[12] Ibid., p. 144.

notes that there is no longer any need to avoid believing in an initial exnihilator.

Modern cosmology must be judged to be supportive of Adler's argument to the extent that it seriously countenances the possibility of many types of universe. Ironically, the significant degree of enthusiasm in current cosmology for other worlds arises from exactly the opposite intent. Most of the advocates of the existence (or possible existence) of other worlds—other parts of the universe—are very clearly motivated to deny the uniqueness of this part of the universe. They want to avoid explaining that uniqueness and readily perceive that the possibility of other worlds conveniently obscures that uniqueness.

There are many serious versions of many worlds theories. An early one, the Everett many-worlds theory, was derived not from cosmology but from an effort to understand quantum theory. A more recent one is J. Richard Gott's inflationary model of our universe as one of many inflated bubbles. Whether any of these is true is not particularly important. What is important is that the variety and present health of these ideas makes plain that there is no reason now to suppose the whole universe is *necessarily* what it is. The consensus of cosmologists is that the universe out there has the contingency Adler needs for his argument.

A notable dissenter from the consensus is Stephen Hawking. Much of his recent work has focused on the possibility of a universe without boundaries. His well-known popular book, *A Brief History of Time*, describes this idea and, more importantly, gives us a better sense of his underlying metaphysical opinions than do his more formal writings. The theory grows out of attempts to combine quantum theory with general relativity and is partially motivated by the general desire for simplicity. An unbounded universe is simpler because no boundary conditions are required to explain it. Boundary conditions and the basic physical laws are the main unspecified features of most cosmological theories.

At first, Hawking is careful to note that the theory is only a proposal that "cannot be deduced from some other principle. Like any other scientific theory, it may initially be put forward for aesthetic or metaphysical reasons, but the real test is whether it makes predictions that agree with observation."[13] Hawking showed that

---

[13] *A Brief History of Time* (New York: Bantam, 1988), pp. 136–37.

simplified versions of this idea predict the observed uniformity of the background radiation and an inflationary stage of expansion with enough non-uniformity left over to explain the present degree of structure in the universe.

The significance of the theory for our purposes is that Hawking does not stop there. He goes on to say, "So long as the universe had a beginning, we could suppose it had a creator. But if the universe is really completely self-contained, having no boundary or edge, it would have neither beginning nor end: it would simply be. What place, then, for a creator?"[14]

The force of his question comes from the fact that the universe he envisions is completely determined, it must be as it is. It cannot be otherwise than it is. No gap remains into which God can be fitted. Hence, Hawking's idea attacks both arguments for the existence of God: from the origin and from the contingency of the universe.

We must remember that his original characterization is correct. The theory is just a proposal. It is not the only theory that fits the observations. There is a hint of circularity in his choice here since, like Hoyle before him, he is clearly more comfortable with a universe without beginning or end. His reason is the same as Hoyle's: no beginning, no God.

An important feature of this theory that is easily overlooked is that time, for technical reasons, is treated as a space dimension. That is, real time is not used but is replaced by imaginary time (time multiplied by the square root of -1). Therefore, the lack of a beginning and end occurs in imaginary time. Conversion to real time reintroduces the singularities that imply a beginning and an end. Hawking then suggests "the so-called imaginary time is really the real time."[15] He supports this thought with the remark "it is meaningless to ask: Which is real, 'real' or 'imaginary' time? It is simply a matter of which is the more useful description."[16] The usefulness of a description surely is determined by the use one has in mind. If one wants to describe a universe containing no room for God, Hawking's theory may be useful. Hawking has made his choice but no scientific criteria demand we follow him.

---

[14] Ibid., pp. 140–41.

[15] Ibid., p. 139.

[16] Ibid., p. 139.

Hawking's views are presently not representative of the main stream of cosmological thinking. They do serve to show that there is always the potential for the scientific consensus to swing away from what may have become a comfortable accord with prevailing philosophical or theological ideas.

CRITIQUES AND COMMENTARY FROM PHILOSOPHY

Of course, philosophical ideas also impinge on the validity and utility of Adler's argument. J.L. Mackie, an atheist, has examined cosmological arguments generally in the fifth chapter of his book, *The Miracle of Theism* (the name indicates his surprise that theism is still believed by anyone).[17] His critique consists of denials. He denies the certainty of the assertions that: (1) "nothing comes from nothing," (2) a necessary being exists, (3) past time must have been finite, and (4) nothing occurs without a sufficient reason. As one might expect, these denials enable him to survey the remnants of variations of the cosmological argument like the proverbial bull might be imagined surveying the wreckage of the china shop.

Adler assumes an infinite past for the universe, so his form of the cosmological argument is impervious to Mackie's third denial. Denying that "nothing comes from nothing" threatens the idea that the "somethingness" of the universe requires a source in something other than itself. The first denial is thus a form of the fourth, which I will consider shortly. Also, since Adler's argument supports but does not assume the existence of a necessary being, only the denial of sufficient reason has a potential for damaging Adler's argument.

Mackie denies the principle of sufficient reason on two grounds. First, the principle of sufficient reason is empirically derived. We expect to find sufficient reason for any occurrence because we previously could do so for other occurrences. His thinking here is like Hume's idea that the sun need not rise tomorrow; we just expect it to because it always has before. What Mackie does not say, though it is implicit in the very nature of his counter-argument, is that the expectation of sufficient reason is very prob-

---

[17] *The Miracle of Theism* (Oxford: Clarendon, 1982).

ably correct. After all, if our experience prejudices us to expect everything to happen as it does for sufficient reasons, it must be true that things usually do occur for sufficient reason. Since Adler is constructing a plausible or probable argument rather than a deductive one, it might not be damaged by this denial.

However, it is just at the point where Adler most needs sufficient reason that Mackie is most determined to deny it. His second ground for denying the principle of sufficient reason is that what is true of parts of the universe need not be true of the universe as a whole. "Even if, within the world, everything seemed to have a sufficient reason . . . this would give us little ground for expecting the world as a whole, or its basic causal laws themselves, to have a sufficient reason of some different sort."[18] That is, Mackie is also saying the existence of the universe is of a different sort from the existence of things in the universe. Therefore, our experience of things in the universe provides no information about the universe in its entirety. Even if things generally have a sufficient reason for being, we have no right to use that information when we think about the whole universe. Mackie quickly goes on to deny that he is rejecting intelligibility of the world. He had, of course, asserted a restriction to that intelligibility, a point I will return to later.

While Mackie's concern is only with the sufficient reason of coming into existence of the universe his remarks also apply to the sufficient reason of the continuing in existence of the universe. Presuming to read the mind of the late J.L. Mackie, I think he would agree with Adler that the continuing in existence of the universe is radically different from the continuing in existence of a part of the universe. This radical difference actually strengthens Mackie's case for denying that the principle of sufficient reason is applicable to the continuing in existence of the whole universe. That is, Mackie's point is that the existence of the whole universe may be very different from that of any part of the universe. Adler's argument for a radically contingent universe affirms this point.

What can be said in response to Mackie? Adler denies any form of the principle of sufficient reason that would amount to assuming God does not exist. Since the simple statement of the principle (used by Mackie and others) "everything that exists is caused to exist" runs into the problem that "God's existence, if God exists,

---

[18] Ibid., p. 85.

is uncaused,"[19] Adler restates the principle: "Everything that exists or happens has a reason for its existing or happening either (a) in itself or (b) in something else."[20] In distinction from all other entities, the sufficient cause of God's existence resides in God alone.

If, for the sake of argument, we expand Mackie's denial to include Adler's form of the principle of sufficient reason, what impact does that have on Adler's conclusions? Since Adler is framing a plausibility argument, which is more plausible: Adler's affirmation or Mackie's denial?

I have problems with Mackie's mode of argument in this area. For example, he rejects the form of the cosmological argument that posits God as the *terminus* of a sequence of causes by raising the possibility that other (unspecified) things might be the *terminus*. Otherwise, he believes we must "simply accept this [that God is the *terminus*] as sheer mystery (which would be to abandon rational theology and take refuge in faith)."[21] But, by denying that the universe exists (or continues in existence) by sufficient reason, Mackie himself takes a large step in the direction of "sheer mystery." Denying that the principle of sufficient reason applies to the universe views the universe as a great, and apparently, permanently impenetrable mystery. Is "sheer mystery" acceptable in an atheistic position and not in a theistic one?

Perhaps I am being too hard on him. He clearly denies that *we know* the principle applies to the universe and I think it fair to read him as denying that the principle applies in actuality. For example, at the end of his consideration of the use of the principle in the cosmological argument, he says this sort of argument "fails completely as a demonstrative proof."[22] If he only meant to deny that we know the principle can be applied, it would be more appropriate to say that the argument is incomplete and, if it is to be used, must be supplemented with reasons showing how we can know the principle is relevant. Saying the argument fails "completely" implies considerable confidence in the counter-arguments.

I may, of course, be wrong. Perhaps Mackie only intended to deny that *we know* the principle applies to the universe. Then, the

---

[19] Adler, p. 104.
[20] Ibid., p. 103.
[21] Mackie. p. 92.
[22] Ibid., p. 87.

state of our knowledge becomes relevant. From the earlier discussion of Big Bang theories we can see that modern cosmologists have doubts about either form of Mackie's denial; some of them, at any rate, assume the origin of the universe was caused and that we can think about that cause. They even hold out hope that an improved physics will provide a naturalistic explanation of the singularity. Their efforts also imply that we even now have evidence (but certainly not proof) that can be interpreted to mean that the universe exists by sufficient cause. In turn, evidence that the universe had sufficient reason for coming into existence implies it is likely that the continuing in existence of the universe is by sufficient cause.

Mackie denies that his rejection of sufficient reason undermines the scientific enterprise, saying,

> The sort of intelligibility that is achieved by successful and causal inquiry and scientific explanation is not undermined by its inability to make things intelligible through and through. Any particular explanation starts with premises which state `brute facts,' and although the brutally factual starting-points of one explanation may themselves be further explained by another, the latter in turn will have to start with something that it does not explain, *and so on however far we go.*[23]

I accept this picture of the fabric of explanations, scientific or philosophical, but note that a primary assumption is that unexplained features of an explanation can be investigated at another level. Mackie is positing a level at which explanation must terminate with something still unexplained. What he seems to be saying is that the suggested failure of sufficient reason is not unusual. Indeed, he is trying to persuade us that it would fit a familiar pattern. The irony is that he is simultaneously denying the already familiar pattern in which things happen for sufficient reason.

Furthermore, Mackie does not appear to appreciate just how necessary motivation is in science. The history of science generally and the history of cosmology in particular can be read as one long lesson in how deeply-held beliefs, presuppositions, and prejudices have been a major force behind scientific discovery and invention. Think of Kepler's belief in God, The Supreme Mathematician, and

---

[23] Ibid., pp. 85–86.

how that belief sustained his thirty years of work toward the three laws. More recent examples of the same thing are Einstein's invention of the cosmological constant to satisfy his prejudice for a static universe and Hoyle's work on steady state theories because Big Bang theories were too Christian. Now, if one believes the universe came into existence for no reason, what motivation is there to investigate the origin of the universe? Mackie's denial does not undermine the entire scientific enterprise but it surely does undermine cosmogony.

We see that the costs of denying the principle of sufficient reason as it applies to the origin of the universe are significant. The overall consistency of Mackie's position has been jeopardized by it and motivation for scientific effort in cosmogony is undermined.

Granting the *possibility* that the universe came into existence for no reason or without cause, there is yet no reason to grant this idea higher status. While there is no calculus by which we can determine the plausibility level of an idea, all we know of the universe, of science, and even of Mackie's argumentation point to the conclusion that the idea is unlikely. The scientific mind rightly resists it. It seems fair to demand that the burden of proof lie with those who would deny the applicability of sufficient reason to the universe as a whole.

Since Adler concludes by affirming that the universe was created for sufficient reason, I should also briefly comment on an argument by the noted philosopher of science, Adolf Grünbaum.[24] Like Mackie, Grünbaum raises the question of how concepts of ordinary causality can be applied to creation out of nothing. He also denies that ordinary causation can apply to the origin of the universe because causes precede their effects in time. But before the universe existed, there was no time. Therefore, it is incoherent to speak of a cause of the origin of the universe since there was no time in which such a cause could have existed. With no cause of the origin of the universe, no argument can be made from the cause to a creator. Grünbaum apparently does not continue this line of thought to its full conclusion that scientific investigation of the origin of the universe is, therefore, an incoherent enterprise.

---

[24] "The Pseudo-Problem of Creation in Physical Cosmology," *Philosophy of Science* 56:3 (September 1989), pp. 373–394.

Now, causes may precede their effects incidentally but what is critical is that they must *co-exist* with their effects. A cause *never* produces an effect except on a body that exists in a place and time where the cause too exists. If I hold a stone in my outstretched hand, it will fall when I release it only if gravity is available to act on it from the time it is released. Surely the stone would behave in the same manner had a gravity field not existed in that region of space prior to its release but had sprung into existence exactly at the time of release. Grünbaum's argument has no force against *co-existent* causes.

The idea of co-existence of a cause and its effect is likely to seem strange because it is axiomatic that *a cause precedes its effects*. A little reflection should show that the axiom as stated goes beyond the known facts. A more reasonable statement in better accord with the facts is that *a cause never follows its effects*. In this latter form, the axiom does not conflict with the co-existence of a cause and its effects, while the former form obviously denies such a possibility. Thus, a better statement of the axiom takes away the starting point of Grünbaum's argument, leaving it unsupported.

A response to this change of the axiom might be that a cause co-existent with the beginning of the universe is still a cause that cannot "pre-exist" the universe. If time began with the beginning of the universe, then it is incoherent to speak of anything existing before the universe existed. Thus, it is incoherent to speak of God "pre-existing" the universe.

It may be incoherent to speak of God existing before the universe came into existence. But that may just be a trick of our limitations as creatures enmeshed in time. Even aside from questions of origins, the existence of God outside time has always been subject to this complaint of incoherence (a problem worth worrying about once we are sure of what time is). However, an idea may be incoherent or unintelligible and still true. For example, it is commonly recognized that a materialistic explanation of thought is self-defeating. If ideas are only neural epiphenomena, then the idea that ideas are only neural epiphenomena is itself only an epiphenomenon with no legitimate claim to being true. A truth claim for the idea is incoherent. Nonetheless, *it might be true*! "Incoherent" is not equivalent to "false."

CONCLUSIONS

Philosophically, we have found it can be doubted that the principle of sufficient reason applies to unique events such as those contemplated in cosmological arguments for the existence of God. Nevertheless, I have urged that it be not unreasonable to use it in such situations. If that is so, Adler's argument remains a plausible argument as he claimed.

Recent developments in cosmology appear to converge with and support Adler's argument. Trends in cosmology surely strengthen the plausibility one might claim for the argument. There is, of course, no way to *quantify* the impact of these developments on the plausibility of Adler's argument. A warranted, *qualitative* judgment is that the argument is no worse for the wear and may, indeed, now be judged somewhat more probable than it was originally.

III

Adler's Early Struggles with the God Question

8 The Demonstration of God's Existence (1943)

MORTIMER J. ADLER

I

I came upon the work of Jacques Maritain during the early years of my study of St. Thomas. I can express my debt of gratitude to him as a teacher in no better way than by saying that he taught me how to read St. Thomas *formalissime*.[1] The manner and spirit of his discipleship to St. Thomas shows that allegiance to an intellectual tradition need not blind one to the limitations of the past, nor relieve one from facing the exigencies of the present. Not merely by his insistence on the necessity for stripping "the great truths of antiquity of the errors which grow parasitically on them,"[2] but by his own rethinking of traditional positions does he show us how to disengage philosophical truths from the adventitious imagery of an historical culture, be it ancient or mediaeval, and how to exorcise irrelevant errors of fact.[3]

My study of the philosophy of St. Thomas began twenty years ago with the reading of the question on God's existence in the *Summa Theologica*. It was then that the vocation of the philosopher first became clear to me—not irresponsible poetizing, not system building, not the pretensions of a *Weltanschauung*, but the plain hard work of demonstration. Unless the philosopher solves problems by laying adequate analytical foundations for demonstration and, in the light thereof, by proving conclusions from self-evident premises, he does nothing.

Though the major part of his own work was theological,[4] St. Thomas has been for me the exemplar of philosophical method. Nevertheless, it seems to me that, in some instances, more work remains to be done on proofs which St. Thomas advanced. A case in point is provided by his arguments for God's existence. What once seemed clear has, in the light of fuller study, become problematic.

I am aware that I am not the first to have encountered difficulties concerning the probative force of the five ways of demonstrating God's

109

existence. Cajetan indicates some of the difficulties by his contention that these arguments do not conclude directly to the existence of the God of revelation, but require interpretation in the light of analysis to be found in questions of the *Summa* which follow the question on the existence of God.[5] Banez accepts this point of view, but only with certain very definite qualifications.[6] At the same time he criticizes Cajetan sharply for leaving the impression that St. Thomas wishes these arguments to be understood in the unamended sense of Aristotle, especially the first two which *appear* to be restricted to corporeal motions.[7] Yet Banez himself seems to raise a new difficulty when he remarks that the factual sempiternity of contingent beings is compatible with the third argument, as stated by St. Thomas.[8] Difficulties similar to these are reflected in the writings of more recent Thomists.[9] Because of their bearing on my own analysis, I wish to mention here specifically the views of Etienne Gilson and Jacques Maritain.

Gilson has shown that there is no proof for God's existence in Aristotle—neither in Book VIII of the *Physics,* nor in Book XII of the *Metaphysics.*[10] The unmoved mover is not the Uncreated Creator, any more than the demiurge fashioning primordial matter, according to the "likely story" of Plato's *Timaeus,* is the God in which Jews and Christians believe through His revelation of Himself. In this connection it should be noted that St. Thomas explicitly condemned "the error of the ancient physicists . . . who say that God is not the cause of the being of heaven, but only of its movement "(*Contra Gentiles,* II, 15). St. Thomas also knew that the proposition upon which Aristotle's proof depends (that motion is "eternal" in the sense of everlasting, or without beginning and end in time) is neither self-evident nor demonstrable.[11] There is, furthermore, ample evidence outside of *Summa Theologica,* I, 2, 3, and *Contra Gentiles,* I, 13, to show that St. Thomas's philosophy does not permit a strictly Aristotelian proof of God's existence.

Maritain supports this insight when he points out in his *Degrees of Knowledge* that

> . . . whatever the *way* in which it is employed, the consideration of intermediary causes is used in an entirely other fashion by St. Thomas than it is by Aristotle. . . . The Pure Act to whom these ways lead will be explicitly known as the creator, and the creation of things admits of no intermediary (*S.T.,* I, 45, 5). Thus, from the beginning, if St. Thomas shared Aristotle's image of the physical universe, his metaphysics is, on the other hand, from the first line, free of that image.[12]

This is a crucial point in support of the thesis I shall try to develop. If the proof of God's existence must be an argument for the existence of a creative cause—or, more generally, a *cause of being*—then it cannot proceed directly from the facts of motion or of becoming, nor can it proceed through the dependence of secondary causes upon a first cause; for if God is directly and without intermediaries the cause of the being of things, then His existence should be demonstrable directly from *their being*, which is His proper and unique effect. The problem about an infinite series of causes would seem to be irrelevant because, in truth, there is no series at all, not even a finite series having two members.

It may be said that the last two of the five Thomistic arguments do not appeal to the impossibility of an infinite series and that, moreover, these are proofs which have little or no lineage from Aristotle. This, of course, raises the question, often debated by Thomists, whether there are five *logically distinct* proofs. If there can be *only one* logically adequate demonstration of any proposition that is established with certitude—which seems to be St. Thomas's opinion on the matter[13]—then we must ask whether the five arguments stated by St. Thomas are five *ways* of stating the same argument, or whether one of these is the valid proof and the others not, or whether none of these *as written* is strictly a demonstration but only an indication of where a demonstration might lie. These are questions I shall not now answer in detail. The analysis to follow does, I think, determine the answer which must be given.[14]

Before I begin that analysis, I wish to declare as explicitly as possible my firm belief in God's existence and my equally firm conviction that God's existence can be proved by reason without recourse to faith. Though I am not a Catholic, I would say that I hold these things by faith. It is not contradictory to say that I affirm by faith that God's existence can be known to reason without recourse to faith; nor does it in any way indicate a lack of such faith for an individual to admit that he does not *yet* know by reason what his faith affirms *can* be so known.[15] St. Thomas's explanation of why the proposition "God exists" is both a rational conclusion and an article of faith applies perfectly to the fact that the proposition "God's existence can be demonstrated" is both a matter of faith and open to reason's ascertainment.[16]

The faith that God's existence can be proved is needed by those who do not yet know the demonstration and who, because believing in God's existence and benevolence toward man, might wonder whether God created man with a natural endowment for knowledge of divine things. It is also needed by those who, thinking they have demonstrated a truth, nevertheless remember the fallibility and pitfalls of any merely human reasoning, and so have recourse to the certitude of faith that what they have *tried* to prove *can be* proved, even if their most elaborate and diligent efforts have, from some human weakness, failed of perfection. But, above all, it seems to me, faith that a proof of God's existence is *attainable* is needed to sustain all those who desire to know whatever can be known of God by natural reason in this life; it is needed to sustain them in this most arduous of all intellectual efforts, to help them to persist in pursuit of a proof, despite all the obstacles, despite all the controversies of men and the failures of the past, despite all the *apparent insolubilia*.[17]

In view of this, I hope that I will not be accused of undue temerity because I here set forth the difficulties which it seems to me must be overcome in any *purely philosophical* proof of God's existence. I shall first try to show the critical impact of St. Thomas's own theory of causality upon the usual rendering of the arguments about God's existence. Such criticism, it will be seen, everywhere appeals to Thomistic principles, and never to anything extrinsic or foreign. Then I shall try to proceed constructively toward the statement of a proof which satisfies all the critical conditions imposed upon the undertaking by St. Thomas's own theory of causality. Since the best statement I can make is not free from difficulties, I shall conclude with a summary of what has been seen, and an intimation of what remains to be done.

II

For brevity's sake, let me present in outline form the several critical points which impose antecedent limitations upon any attempt to prove God's existence.

  A. For any given effect, there are the following causal possibilities.
     a. Either one efficient cause only or many are productive of the effect. (In connection with *a posteriori* reasoning, only efficient causes need be considered.)
     b. If many, then
        (1) Either the number is finite or infinite;
        (2) Either the many causes are ordered to one another by succession in time or they are simultaneously co-operative and, as conjoined in action, they must be co-existent.
     c. We know at once that an infinite number of co-operative causes is impossible, because an actual infinite, that is, an infinite multitude of co-existent things, is impossible.
     d. But we also must concede that an infinite number of successive causes is possible, for the possibility of such a series is the possibility of an infinite time, time without beginning or end, and this is a potential and not an actual infinite. (Vd. *S.T.*, I, p. 7, aa. 3, 4.)
     e. I shall henceforth use the word "series" only for a plurality of causes ordered successively to one another; and I shall use the word "set" for a plurality of co-operative causes.

B. The possibility of an infinite series of efficient causes, each a mover and a thing moved, or each a generator and a generated thing, must be conceded because the proposition that the world is "eternal" (i.e., of infinite duration) is neither self-evidently nor demonstrably false. (Vd. *S.T.*, I, q. 46, aa. 1, 2; II *Con. Gen.*, 31–38; esp. Ch. 38, wherein St. Thomas says: "It is impossible to have an infinite number of active causes which act together simultaneously, or an infinite number of simultaneous actions. Such are causes that are *per se* infinite, because their infinity is required for their effect. On the other hand, in causes which do not act simultaneously, this is not impossible, according to those who assert that generation has always been.")

    f. Hence no argument for the existence of God is valid which appeals to the impossibility of an infinite *series* of efficient causes (or of movers and things moved); even as no argument is valid which rests upon the premise that the world or motion is "eternal"; for the one falsely denies what is possible, and the other affirms to be true what is neither self-evident nor demonstrable.

    g. When it is said that "in efficient causes it is impossible to proceed to infinity *per se* because there cannot be an infinite number of causes that are *per se* required for a certain effect" (*Sum. Th.*, I, q. 46, a. 2, ad 7) it is suggested that a plurality of essential causes cannot be infinite because such causes must be simultaneous in action and co-existent in being. (Vd. the passage from *II Con. Gen.*, 38, cited above.) This requires further examination.

C. The distinction between a plurality of causes *per se* and an accidental plurality of causes must be understood as a distinction between a plurality of causes which differ from one another in *essence* and a plurality of causes which differ only numerically or *accidentally*.

    h. In the potentially infinite series of fathers and sons, one generator differs from another accidentally or numerically, not essentially.

    i. In the plurality of causes productive of an artistic effect, the physical thing (e. g., the stick which moves the stone), the living bodily member (e.g., the hand), and the psychic powers (e. g., reason and will) differ from one another essentially.

    j. But the distinction between an essential and an accidental plurality of causes is not identical with the distinction between a *set* of (co-operative) causes and a *series* of (successive) causes;

        (1) For in a set of co-operative causes, some of the members may differ only accidentally, as, for example, two sticks simultaneously used to move a stone;

(2) And in a series of successive causes, some of the members may differ essentially, as, for example, the man who at an earlier time trained the dog to carry a burden, that operation being performed at a later time.

f.   Hence it cannot be said that an infinity of causes is possible because they differ accidentally, for that possibility depends not on their being accidentally different, but upon their being serially ordered in succession nor can it be said that an infinity of essential causes is impossible, unless these causes are ordered to one another as members of a co-operative set. A particular series of causes may have a finite number of essentially different members, but this does not exclude the *possibility* of an infinite number. An infinite regression is always possible in *a series* of causes—whether these causes be essentially or accidentally different.

g.   It follows, therefore, that the impossibility of a plurality of causes "that are *per se* infinite" must be understood as the impossibility of an infinite set of causes—impossible because as cooperative "their infinity is required for their effect."

D. We have seen that essentially differentiated causes may be ordered in two ways: either successively or simultaneously. This fact determines a distinction between causes applicable only to a number of causes which are essentially different. That distinction is between higher and lower causes, each of which is a principal cause of *its own* proximate effect, and higher and lower causes, one of which is the principal and another the instrumental cause of *their common* proximate effect.

m. Wherever there is essential diversity, there is hierarchical gradation. The words "higher" and "lower" are to be understood in terms of such gradation.

n. In a *series* of essentially diverse causes (be it finite or infinite), a higher can be distinguished from a lower cause as a primary principal cause from a secondary principal cause. (Vd. Maritain, *Science and Wisdom*, New York: 1940, pp. 193ff.) Only if such a series is *known* to be finite, and not from the supposition that all such series must be finite, can it be said that there is a *first* principal cause. Here the word "first" has its proper ordinal significance, meaning that before which in the series there is no prior member.

o. In a *set* of essentially diverse causes (always necessarily finite), a higher cause can be distinguished from a lower cause as a principal from an instrumental cause. Unlike primary and secondary principal causes, each of which has *its own* proximate effect, a principal and an instrumental cause cooperate to produce *one and the same* proximate effect.

p. In a *set* of essentially diverse causes, there may be more than one principal cause, for any cause except the highest or the lowest in the set may be both instrumental in relation to a higher cause and principal in relation to a lower cause. But the highest principal cause cannot be called a "first cause" in the same ordinal sense in which "first" is said of the prime member of a series. Nevertheless, it remains true that just as we know there is a *first* principal cause if the series of essentially diverse causes be finite, so we know that there must be a *highest* principal cause in any set of causes related as principal and instrumental, because any *set* of causes must be finite.

E. Our analysis so far has eliminated two possibilities of demonstrating the existence of God as a cause required for effects known to exist; and we must, therefore, inquire whether a third possibility that has been indicated remains tenable.

q. The first possibility was that in *any series* of causes, *without regard* for the distinction between accidental and essential diversity among the members, there must be a first or uncaused efficient cause. This was eliminated in B. above.

r. The second possibility was that in a *series* of essentially diverse causes, there must be a first or uncaused efficient cause. This was eliminated in C. above.

s. The remaining possibility, indicated in D. above, is that in *a set* of essentially diverse causes, there must always exist a *highest* principal cause, and this is God, whose existence was to be proved. But, as I shall now attempt to show, this possibility is not tenable either.

t. Before that can be shown, one further point must be noted, namely, that all the distinctions among efficient causes which we have been considering are relevant *only* to efficient causes of becoming (whether the becoming is *simpliciter* as in substantial change or *secundum quid* as in the several accidental motions). In the *efficient* causation of being (i. e., of existence itself), there can be no plurality of causes: there is neither a series of such causes nor a set of such causes, and so there is no secondary principal cause of being and no instrumental cause of being. Hence to argue that God cannot be proved as a *first* cause or as a *principal* cause is only to argue that God cannot be proved as *causa fiendi*; it does not mean that God cannot be proved as *causa essendi*.[18]

F. That God cannot be proved as the highest principal cause of any
    known effect in the order of becoming does not involve the denial
    of God's efficient causality in the production of every effect which
    occurs in the course of worldly motions and generations. *After* we
    know that God exists, and something of His essence and power, we
    can learn of His operation in the *occurrence* of every *event* which
    happens in this world. But from the occurrence of such events,
    from worldly motions and generations, we cannot infer God's exis-
    tence as an indispensable efficient cause, co-operating as *causa
    fiendi* with other causes of becoming, and related to them as prin-
    cipal to instrumental cause in the set of causes productive of each
    particular effect. The reasons for this are as follows:

    u. From the point of view of our knowledge, there are two situa-
        tions in which an effect is produced by the co-operation of
        principal and instrumental causes

        (1) One is the situation in which all the causes are known to
            us as cognate objects of knowledge, as, for example, in the
            aetiology of an artistic product. In such cases, our study of
            the causal nexus may instruct us as to the order of the
            causes, which is principal and which instrumental, but
            since the causes are known or knowable to us apart from
            the effect, we need not infer the existence of any of these
            causes from the effect.

        (2) The other is the situation in which not all the causes are
            known to us as cognate objects. In this case, whatever
            cause is a transcendent object cannot he known to exist
            apart from its effect—its existence being know-able only by
            inference from effects. Clearly God is such a transcendent
            object, whose existence must be proved by *a posteriori* infer-
            ence from His effects.

    v. Now when an effect is not the *proper* (i.e., unique, exclusive)
        effect of a single cause, but the effect of cooperative action on
        the part of several causes related as principal and instrumen-
        tal, it is impossible to infer from the effect the existence of any
        cause which is not knowable apart from the effect.

        (1) According to St. Thomas, natural agents are genuinely effi-
            cacious as efficient causes of becoming. (Vd. III *Con. Gen.*,
            69.) If this were not so, "all knowledge of physical science
            would be denied to us" (*loc. cit.*).

        (2) But St. Thomas also holds that *the same effect* (in the order
            of becoming) is both from God and from the natural
            agent—"not as though part were effected by God and part
            by the natural agent; but the whole effect proceeds from

each, yet in different ways, just as the whole of one same effect is ascribed to the instrument, and again the whole is ascribed to the principal agent" (*ibid.*, 70)

(3) Hence since the whole effect can be ascribed to the natural agent, as is done in the science of physical things, we are not compelled to infer the existence of God in order to give an adequate causal explanation of the effect. But we can only know the existence of a transcendent object if a known effect cannot be causally explained without positing this object as its cause. Hence we cannot infer the existence of God from any effect (in the order of becoming) with respect to which God is only the principal cause, but not the unique or exclusive cause, as He is in the case of being which is His proper effect. We cannot know that the natural agent is related to God as instrumental to principal cause in the production of a natural effect (i.e., a generation or a motion) *until we know that God exists.*

(4) With one exception, nothing that has here been said is inconsistent with St. Thomas's whole theory of principal and instrumental causality. Vd. *S.T.*, I, q. 105, a. 5; III, q. 62, a. 1; I, q. 45, a. 5; *II Con. Gen.*, 21: *III*, 69, 70; *De Pot.*, 3, 7. The one exception is my insistence that there is no instrumental cause of being, which St. Thomas *appears* to contradict when he says that God does not preserve the being of every creature *immediately*, but rather through the operation of subordinate causes. Vd. *S.T.*, I, q. 104, a. 2. I shall return to this point presently.

w. If it be objected that natural things do not operate except in terms of their natures, which they themselves do not cause, and hence the fact of their causal operation implies the existence of that which causes their natures, two points must be made in reply.

(1) God as the cause of the *natures* of natural agents is not the principal cause of the effects of their action, for to cause the nature of a thing, to give it its form, or its form and matter, is to cause its *being*, not its becoming. (On this, St. Thomas speaks plainly in *S.T.*, I, q. 104, a. 1.) Hence though the facts of becoming may lead us to ask whence comes the being of the things which are both causes and effects in the order of becoming, this does not lead us to infer God's existence as a principal *causa fiendi.*

(2) That things *exist* (have being) as well as *become* (are subject to change) may require us to look for the cause of their

essences and existences, as well as for the cause of each becoming that occurs, but it remains to be seen whether the existence and causality of God affords the only explanation for the existence and natures of things. That is precisely the problem of proving God's existence, which remains to be solved.

G. The preceding analysis compels us to admit that God cannot be proved as *causa fiendi* of known effects. We are thus brought to the conclusion that the only way in which God can be proved is as *causa essendi*—as the cause of the being of things, not of their changes. Moreover, this way does not, like the other ways, turn out upon examination to be unavailable, due to the character of the causal nexus involved. This is confirmed by St. Thomas's insight into the character of *being* as an effect.

x. We are told that being is the *proper* effect of God. Vd. *Sum. Th.*, I, q. 8, a. 1; q. 19, a. 5, ad 3; q. 45, a. 5; q. 65, a. 3; q. 104, a. I; *II Con. Gen.*, 6, 15, 17–21.

y. Primarily, we understand from this that to cause being is to create, and that creation is neither movement nor change, and that in creation there is no succession. (I shall subsequently consider the *causa essendi* as preserving being.)

z. Furthermore, in creation there are no intermediary causes, no secondary principal and no instrumental causes. Hence, to say that being is the *proper* effect of God means that God is the *unique* and *exclusive* cause of being, as He is the sole creative cause.

aa. If these things be so, then it should be possible to prove God's existence as the cause of the being of whatever needs to have its being caused, for here we are dealing with an effect which can have only one cause. Hence we should not be involved in all the problems about finite and infinite series, primary and secondary, principal and instrumental causes, which arise wherever a plurality of causes is possible.

bb. But all these points about the causation of being are made by St. Thomas *after* he has offered arguments for God's existence, four of which do not seem to prove God as the *direct* cause of His *proper* effect. If, because of this, these arguments do not demonstrate God's existence, it may be possible, nevertheless, to formulate the one remaining argument in such a way that it is valid inference from *being* as an effect to its cause. It is certainly not sufficient to try to read into the arguments *as written* the force of the basic insight that God is the *sole* cause of being, His *proper* effect, for the notion of a *proper* effect, an effect due to a unique cause, does not occur in the reasoning, and is violated by every reference to God as a "first" cause, implying a plurality of causes. (God can be called a "first cause" only in the sense that being, as prior to becoming, is a *first effect.* Vd. *S.T.*, I, q. 19, a. 5, ad 3: "Since God wills effects to come from causes, all effects that presuppose some other effect do not depend solely on the will of God, but on something else besides, but the first effect depends on the divine will alone.") Garrigou-Lagrange recognizes the crucial significance of the notion of being as God's *proper* effect, but tries vainly to render the traditional arguments in the light of this notion; whereas it is obvious that, in doing so, he departs from the arguments *as written* and approaches the formulation of a single proof which is none of the five ways. (Vd. *op. cit.*, Appendix, pp. 379–390.) I leave to the reader to judge how nearly his *approach* and mine converge.

H. In attempting to prove God as the unique cause of the being of things, it is necessary to remember that such causality is compatible with two possibilities, neither of which can be proved or disproved: the possibility of an "eternal" world, and the possibility of a world which began to be.

    a. If it were supposed that the only sense in which God is the cause of being is equivalent to the usual meaning of "creation"—namely, causing the world to *begin* to be (vd. *S.T.*, I, q. 66, aa. 1, 4, on the creation of time)—then the irrefutable possibility that things never began to be would entail the consequence that an everlasting world does not have a cause of being. On the contrary, if things are contingent in being, it would seem that they must have a cause of being, whether or not the whole order of contingent things has or has not always existed.[19]

    b. Now if we assume the truth of the second possibility, which is assuming that the world was created, there is no way of proving God's existence, for we have assumed it, and the same proposition cannot be both assumed and proved. The fact of creation is inseparable from the fact of a Creator; hence to assume the one is to assume the other.

    c. Furthermore, the fact of creation (i.e., the fact of an absolute beginning of the world) cannot be proved, but must either be assumed by reason or known to faith. Hence the existence of a Creator (in the sense indicated) must either be assumed by reason or known to faith. It cannot be proved.

    d. Therefore, it is necessary to proceed in terms of the other possibility (i.e., a world without beginning), and show that such a world, at every instant and in every particular, needs a cause of its being, which is itself uncaused in being. This procedure has two merits.

(1) St. Thomas says that "the most effective way to prove God's existence is from the supposition of the eternity of the world, which being supposed, it seems less manifest that God exists" (*I Con. Gen.*, 13). I would go further and say that no other way is possible. And I must also point out that the supposition of the eternity of the world is not a premise in the demonstration itself, as it is in the Aristotelian argument on which St. Thomas is here commenting.

(2) Supposing the eternity of the world, the demonstration abstracts from all temporal series, and proceeds to infer God's existence as *causa essendi* directly from the present existence of a single contingent thing.

I. Finally, we must observe two ways in which an efficient cause of being can act: CREATIVELY, by placing something *extra nihil* and *extra causas*; PRESERVATIVELY, by sustaining in being whatever does not exist by its own essence. In either case, the effect produced by the cause of being is *the actual existence of a possible being,* or of a series of such beings if they are the generable and corruptible members of a species. (Vd. *S.T.*, I, q. 65, a. 9, ad 1 on annihilation vs. corruption.) This is important, because on the supposition of the world's eternity, we cannot prove God as a creative, but only as a preservative, cause of being. Therefore, we must overcome the difficulty raised by St. Thomas's statement that in the preservation of beings God operates through intermediate causes (vd. *S.T.*, I, q. 104, a. 2).

a. If this were so, then the being of things would not be the *proper* effect of God's action; and as we have seen the existence of a transcendent cause can be proved only from its *proper* effect, the effect which it alone directly causes.

b. But there are many passages in which St. Thomas seems to take a contrary position. In *S.T.*, I, q. 8, he says that God is in all things by His power, causing the being of things "not only when they first begin to be, but as long as they are preserved in being." And "it belongs to the great power of God that He acts immediately in all things" (*ibid.*, ad 3). In *S.T.*, I, q. 45, a. 5, he says that God alone can create and therefore acts creatively without intermediary causes of any sort; following which, in *S.T.*, I, q. 104, a. 1, ad 4, he writes: "The preservation of things by God is a continuation of that action whereby He gives existence, which action is without either motion or time." Hence it would seem that just as God gives existence by direct causal action (creatively) so, acting preservatively, He sustains existence in the same way. But this is contradicted by the statement that "a thing is kept in being by that which gives it being. But God gives being by means of certain intermediate causes. Therefore, He also keeps things in being by means of certain causes" (*S.T.*, I, q. 104, a. 2, *per contra*).

c. The contradiction could be easily resolved, were it merely *apparent* and due to verbal ambiguity. In q. 104, a. 1, St. Thomas indicates two distinct meanings of the word "preserves"—one, to sustain in existence as such, the other, to counteract causes tending toward a thing's corruption. In the first meaning, to preserve a thing is to operate as *causa essendi*, in the second, to preserve is to operate as *causa fiendi*. But in q. 104, a. 2, St. Thomas, referring back to both of these meanings, says: "In both ways, a created thing keeps another in being." Since the contradiction is not apparent, but real, we must resolve it by making a choice between conflicting texts. In view of the fact that the only *relevant* illustration given in q. 104, a. 2 is of the action whereby corruptibles are preserved from corruption, and in view of the greater weight of all the contrary texts, I choose to take the position that only God preserves in being, as only God creates, and that whatever action hinders corruption, like any action affecting generation, operates only as a *causa fiendi*. This is not to deny that, with respect to corruption as with respect to generation, the Divine power may cooperate with natural agents, or may appoint secondary principal agents, to work an effect; but since the effect is a change (whether produced or prevented) God does not thus act as *causa essendi*. In what follows, I shall always use the word "preserve" to signify the action of a *causa essendi*, and never to signify the action of a *causa fiendi*.

d. The position I have taken is confirmed by the distinction St. Thomas makes between the work of creation and the work of propagation. (Vd. *Sum. Th.*, I, q. 69, a. 2; q. 73, aa. 1, 2; q. 74, a. 2.) With respect to things generable and corruptible, God creates the species, not the individual; only self-subsistent things are created as individuals. Hence, since the preservation of things in being is a continuation of God's creative action, as the generation of new individuals is not, God preserves in being only what He creates: self-subsistent individuals, and the *series* of generable and corruptible things which constitutes the endurance of a species.

   e. We can conclude, therefore, that a *causa essendi*, whether it acts creatively or preservatively, acts directly in the production of its effect. Furthermore, whatever holds for the creative action of a *causa essendi* holds for its preservative action: thus, if it is true that no natural agent can create, it must be similarly true that no natural agent can preserve the being of either a self-subsistent individual or a species. The fact that St. Thomas uses the prejacent matter of a work of art as an example of *causa essendi*, in contradistinction to the artist's activity as *causa fiendi* (vd. *S.T.*, I, q. 104, a. 1) does not violate this point, because the wood is the material cause of the chair's *being*, as any substance is the material cause of its accidents' *being*, and we are here considering God as *efficient causa essendi*. Furthermore, accidents need only a material cause for their existence, though an efficient cause for their becoming, whereas substances need an efficient cause both for their being and their becoming.

J. All this being so, it should be possible to prove the existence of God, even on the supposition that nothing is created. That possibility lies in the conception of being as the *proper* effect of a unique cause, an effect incapable of being produced (whether creatively or preservatively) by either a *series* or a *set* of *causes. If* this conception is sound, then there will be no difficulty in showing that this unique cause is God, by whom everything needs to be preserved, since "not for a moment could it subsist, but would fall into nothingness, were it not kept in being by the operation of the Divine power" (*S.T.*, I, q. 104, a. 1) But in that "if" lies the problem of proving God's existence. Is this conception sound? Is it true, in short, that one contingent being cannot be the *efficient* cause of another's being?

III

Nothing so far said provides the proof of God's existence. Many propositions have been made about the Divine causality *in fieri*, but none of these can be affirmed as true by reason until the existence and character of God as a cause is proved *a posteriori* from our knowledge of the world. So far I have merely set forth the conditions which causal theory imposes upon *a posteriori* inference from cognate effects to a transcendent cause. Thus we have determined the several ways *in* which God *cannot* be proved, and we have come at last to the one possibility of a demonstration which satisfies all the prerequisite conditions.

That one possibility can be formulated in the following syllogism (hypothetical, as every *a posteriori* syllogism must be).

MAJOR: IF anything exists whose continuation in existence requires the operation of an efficient cause at this very moment, THEN a being exists whose existence is uncaused.

DEFINITIONS:

(1) By "contingent being" I understand that which requires the operation of an efficient cause for perseverance in being at any moment, and this may be either a self-subsistent entity or the series of generable and corruptible things constituting a species. Another name for contingent being is *"ens ab alio,"* and *ens ab alio is* equivalent in meaning to "caused being" which, in turn, is equivalent in meaning to "that whose essence is not its existence."

(2) By "necessary being" I understand, not an incorruptible being, but an uncaused being. Another name for necessary being is, therefore, *"ens a sé"* and this is equivalent in meaning to "that whose essence is its existence."

(3) By "corporeal substance" I understand not merely *ens per se,* but a corruptible individual, and therefore an entity which, participating in the contingent being of the species to which it belongs, is *ens ab alio.*

(4) By "God" I understand a necessary being or *ens a se.*

MINOR: Corporeal substances *do* exist.

CONCLUSION: THEREFORE, God *does* exist.

With regard to this, as with any other proffered demonstration, the conclusion remains problematic until the premises can be affirmed. The problematic character of the conclusion can, therefore, be understood in terms of whatever problems or difficulties attach to the premises. Let me outline the problems which must be solved before the conclusion "God exists" can be regarded as demonstrated.
  1. *With respect to the minor premise.*
     a. That a plurality of corporeal substances *does* exist is not self-evident to reason, nor is it evident to sensitive intellection. That a numerical diversity exists is evident, but this evident truth will not function as the minor premise; for supposing all these to

be accidents, the existence of *one* substance will suffice to explain their being. From *ens per aliud,* one can only infer *ens per se,* not *ens a se.*

b. Furthermore, while it is true that *ens per aliud* implies *ens per se,* so that if anything at all exists (which is a fact directly evident to our sensitive intellection), substance must exist, it does not follow that there exists a plurality of individual substances, which as the generable and corruptible members of a species show themselves to have contingent being. From the existence of accidents, all that can be proved is the existence of *one* substance and *only* one, which will then be both *per se* and *a se.* This is the fallacious reasoning of Spinoza; it results in the denial of a transcendent God, but it cannot be avoided if the ultimate fact appealed to is simply the evident existence of something.

c. The evident fact of motion or accidental change is the starting point from which, in my opinion, it can be proved that a plurality of corporeal substances exists. The proof is too difficult to state here, but I think it can be validly made against objections of the sort raised by followers of Spinoza, Hegel, or Whitehead. Unless it can, God's existence cannot be proved, because if we cannot prove the existence of corruptible substances, we certainly cannot prove the existence of incorruptible substances, and without knowledge that there is *ens per se et ab alio* we cannot infer *ens a se.* Thus we see how the fact of motion is relevant, not as the minor premise in the proof of God's existence, but as the minor premise in the proof of corruptible substances, which conclusion is the minor premise in the proof of God.

2. *With respect to the definition of God.*

a. The word "definition" is, of course, being used loosely, for God is indefinable *secundum se* as well as *quoad nos.* But in order to prove the existence of something, we must have at least a nominal definition of that thing—we must be able to express with some definiteness the conceptual medium through which the name signifies. Furthermore, we cannot learn what meaning to attach to the name "God" from an *a posteriori* demonstration of His existence. Unless prior to the demonstration itself the name "God" signifies for us a necessary being, one whose essence is its existence, we cannot say, after we have proved that a being exists *a se,* that this being is God. The name "God" may mean more than this: it may mean for us an infinite, perfect, immutable, eternal being. If it be asked how we are able to "conceive" God by an enumeration of such notes, before we have proved that God exists, and *supposedly* deduced other propositions about His nature, the answer is that we conceive God by negation and remotion from corporeal things. We know what such things are, we know that if God is, He must be as *unlike* these things as possible, and so by negating the characteristics of things, we construct—not abstract—a notion of God. Of the various negative notes which enter therein, it so happens that only one is useful in the proof of God's existence, for since the proof is from effect to cause, in the sphere of being, one of the terms in the major premise must be "uncaused being."

b. A difficulty arises here with the Kantian charge that if in order to prove God *a posteriori*, one must first conceive Him as a necessary being, a being whose essence is its existence, then from such knowledge of His essence, His existence is self-evident, and the ontological argument is covertly present, invalidating the demonstration. The objection can, I think, be overcome in two ways: first, by pointing out that a nominal definition does not give us knowledge of the Divine essence; second, by showing that the process by which we attach meaning to the name "God"—the process of *constructing a* notion negatively—merely enables us to *think* of a possibility, even though that possibility is the possibility of a necessary being. It is *a logical* possibility, by which we mean that the constructed notion is not self-contradictory, in which case it would be a logical impossibility. But although we know that a logical impossibility *cannot* exist, we do not know that a logical possibility *does* exist. Hence, prior to the proof that a necessary being *does* exist, the existence of a necessary being is, so far as our knowledge goes, merely a logical possibility. Should no proof be available, the notion of a necessary being would still remain a logical possibility, for while it is self-contradictory to say that a *real* being whose essence is its existence does not exist, it is not self-contradictory to say that we do not know whether there *is* a *real* being which corresponds to our *ideal* construction. It should be noted, furthermore, that the modality of our conclusion is assertoric, not apodictic: we cannot ever conclude an *a posteriori* argument with a "must" proposition. This fact completely refutes the Kantian charge, for if the ontological argument were involved, the contradictory of the conclusion would be impossible, and hence the conclusion would be a necessary proposition. But "a necessary being *does* exist" is not a necessary proposition, *as we know it.*

c. There is one other problem here, namely, whether the other negative notes in our understanding of God can be demonstrated once we have proved that a necessary being does exist. An "unmoved mover" would seem to be an immutable being, but is a necessary being immutable, infinite, unique? How do we know, for example, from our proof that a necessary being exists, that *only one* such being exists? And unless we know that, have we proved God's existence? I shall return to this problem presently in another connection.

3. *With respect to the major premise.*

a. The inescapable problem here is presented by the dilemma that the major premise must either be self-evident or demonstrable. But which? Let me consider each alternative briefly.

b. A proposition is self-evident if its truth is known immediately upon an understanding of its terms. To test the major premise for self-evidence, let me state it in such a way that its terms are emphasized: "the existence of a contingent being *(ens ab alio)—implies—*the existence of a necessary being *(ens a se)."* I have italicized the word "implies" to indicate that, even though I have avoided the words "if" and "then," my proposition remains hypothetical: it is certainly not a categorical predication. Now the terms to be examined are obviously "contingent being" and "necessary being."

(1) In order for the proposition to be self-evident, we would have to understand *contingent being* as (a) that which needs a cause for its existence and (b) that which cannot cause the existence of any other thing; and we would have to understand *necessary being* as (a) that which needs no cause for its existence and (b) that which can cause the existence of anything contingent. If both notes—(a) and (b)—are involved in our understanding of these two terms, then it is self-evident that the existence of a contingent being, which must be caused and cannot be caused by another contingent being, *implies* the existence of a necessary being which need not be caused and can cause the existence of a contingent being.

(2) But do our conceptions of contingent and necessary being involve the note I have marked as (b) in each case? (If not, the proposition is not self-evident.) The question can be asked another way: what in our understanding of *esse* and *causa essendi* requires us to see that *ens ab alio* cannot be *causa essendi*, that only *ens a se* can?

(3) The metaphysical problem here envisaged is so difficult that I dare say only that I do not know the answer, adding that if the answer is given by scholastic metaphysics, I am unacquainted with the texts in St. Thomas or others, which contain the problem's solution. Obviously it will not do in *natural* theology to appeal to knowledge by faith. We may know by faith that God is Creator, and thus be enabled to see that only the Creator can be *causa essendi;* but apart from faith, and on the intelligible supposition of no creation (i.e., no beginning of the world), the metaphysician may not be able so to penetrate the mystery of being that his understanding of *esse* and *causa essendi* renders the major premise self-evident.

c. The major premise cannot be demonstrated deductively by the direct method, for that would require antecedent terms more intelligible than *being* itself; moreover, since it is formally a hypothetical proposition, and irreducible to a categorical predication, it cannot be demonstrated by an ordinary syllogism through a middle term, which is the predicate of the minor term and the subject of the major term; furthermore, since it is not a proposition *asserting the existence* of anything, but rather the statement of an intelligible connection, it cannot be proved by *a posteriori* reasoning. Hence, the only mode of reasoning available is the *reductio ad absurdum*—a showing that the denial of the proposition leads to self-contradiction. (When the *only* method of arguing for a proposition is indirect, that proposition should be self-evident.)

(1) Let us suppose to be true what must be shown to be false, namely, that a contingent being can *efficiently* cause the existence of another contingent being. Then the existence of a given contingent being can be explained by reference to another contingent being as its *causa essendi*. But a cause of being must co-exist with its effect. The generator can perish without causing the generated to perish; the moving ball can come to rest while the ball it moved remains in motion; but "the being of a thing cannot continue after that action of the agent has ceased, which is the cause of the effect, not only in *becoming,* but also in *being*" (*S.T.*, I, q. 104, a. 1). Hence, if any contingent thing exists, all its causes *in esse*, proximate and remote, must co-exist, for if B is the cause of A's being, and C is the cause of B's being, and so on to N, all must co-exist with A, or A ceases to be. Now this set of causes cannot be infinite, for an actual

infinity of co-existent things is impossible. But if it is finite (letting "N" represent the last term in the ordered set), then either N's being is caused by A, in a circle of efficient causality, which would *seem* to be impossible, or N's being is uncaused, which is impossible by the definition of N as a contingent being. Hence we may be able to conclude that if only contingent beings exist, the existence of *all* of them cannot be explained causally. For at least one of them, the existence of *a* necessary being (as its *causa essendi*) seems to be required.

(2) This reasoning is defective for the following reasons. It does not show that one contingent being cannot cause the existence of another. It fails, therefore, to operate as does the indirect argument against those who deny the self-evidence of the principle of contradiction, for by that method Aristotle, in *Metaphysics,* IV, does not prove the principle, but rather defends its *self-evidence.* Our indirect reasoning here fails to defend the self-evidence of the major premise. Nevertheless, it seems to prove what that major premise asserts, namely, that if any contingent thing exists, a necessary being exists. It shows that in a finite set of co-existent things, there must be at least one whose existence is uncaused. It does not show, however, that there cannot be more than one, or that a necessary being causes the existence of a given contingent thing immediately rather than mediately. Furthermore, the reasoning depends on one proposition which holds in the order of *becoming,* but may not hold in the order of *being,* namely, that if A depends upon N for its existence, N cannot depend *on* A for its existence. Since the causation of being is without time or the motion of matter, the usual arguments against the possibility of A moving N and N moving A at the same time and in the same way, may not apply. I tentatively suggest that, in order to see the impossibility of this circle, in order to see this reciprocal causality as vicious, it may be necessary to understand *esse* and *causa essendi* well enough so that *we* can see the impossibility of existence being caused by a contingent being. But if we could do that, the major premise would be self-evident, and there would be no need for this mode of indirect reasoning.

d. *Supposing* for the moment that the major premise is either self-evident or demonstrable, it still remains to show that there can be *only one* necessary being, for upon the absolute uniqueness of the *causa essendi* proved to exist, depends our right to *say* that we have thereby proved God's existence. Nothing is more binding upon us than the requirement that we use the word "God" as the proper name of a unique being. But can we infer the uniqueness of an entity from the necessity (or uncaused status) of its existence? I think the answer is Yes on one condition, namely, that we *can* truly assert that if there is no composition of essence and existence in a thing, there can be no other composition in it—no composition of potency and act, of matter and form, of subject and accident; for then a necessary being would not only be absolutely simple and immutable, but also infinite in being (since all limitation of being derives from the composition of really distinct principles of being), and there cannot be more than one infinite being. This, I think, can be argued. But is the prerequisite condition of this chain of reasoning capable of being satisfied?

(1) Is it self-evident or demonstrable that the several compositions are so ordered that whatever lacks the first in order (essence and existence) lacks all the others, and that whatever has the last in order (subject and accident) has all the others? Upon the latter fact would depend our inference that whatever changes accidentally is generable and corruptible, and that whatever is generable and corruptible is contingent in being. Upon the former fact, would depend our inference that a necessary being is purely actual, absolutely simple, hence infinite, hence unique.

(2) If we do not *somehow* know that the identity of essence and existence excludes all other compositions, a necessary being may exist with potentialities for accidental change. Aristotle and St. Thomas saw no contradiction in the existence of incorruptible bodies with potentiality for accidental change. I say: either an incorruptible moving body is self-contradictory, or a changing necessary being is not. The contingent existence of spiritual substances which are not corruptible, but which are capable of change and are also composite of subject and accident, complicates the problem greatly.

(3) In short, the proof of God's existence depends in two ways upon *knowledge* concerning the order of the several compositions of really distinct principles of being: (a) we need such knowledge to prove from the facts of motion that a plurality of corruptible substances exist and, from their

corruptibility, that they are contingent in existence; (b) we need such knowledge to prove that there can be only one necessary being.

(4) I dare not say that such knowledge is lacking. I can only say that I am unacquainted with any texts in which this requisite knowledge is exhibited in a series of propositions shown to be self-evident or demonstrated. If there are no such texts, then there is work for metaphysicians to do on this problem, as there is also work for them on the problem of the self-evidence or demonstrability of the major premise which seems to be required for the proof of God's existence.

IV

In conclusion, I must add, as plainly as possible, what I now know from all this reasoning—*that no corporeal thing can cause the being of another corporeal thing.* I know this because I know that, among bodily things, every expression of efficiency and every communication of energy directly or reductively involves local motion and time; whereas the causation of being is an act totally apart from time and motion. Hence no corporeal substance can *efficiently* cause the being of anything. From this, and from the existence of corporeal substances, whose corruptibility implies their contingency, and whose contingency in being requires *a causa essendi* at every moment of their endurance, I know that there exists a cause of the existence of the whole material world, and also that this *causa essendi* must be a spiritual, i. e., an incorporeal, being. But though an incorporeal being cannot be corruptible by the decomposition of matter and form, it can be contingent in being by the composition of essence and existence. If that is so, it too will need a cause of its existence outside of itself, even though it has always existed. Furthermore, I know that if more than one incorporeal, contingent being exists, the number which do must be finite, for an actually infinite multitude is impossible.

This brings me to the heart of the problem which remains for me. It would *seem possible* for incorporeal beings, albeit contingent, to cause the existence of corporeal things, since spiritual action can take place without time or local motion. It would also *seem possible* for one incorporeal contingent being to cause the being of another. How can I learn that this is impossible, so that I may know by reason that a necessary being exists— the cause of the being of every contingent thing, corporeal and spiritual? The answer would seem to lie in the impossibility of a circle of causation in which, among a *finite* number of contingent beings, each causes the being of another. If such circularity in causation is impossible, then a necessary being is required, for every contingent being must be caused to be.[20] May I repeat once more that to see this last impossibility is tantamount to seeing that a contingent being cannot cause being, which makes self-evident the proposition that if anything contingent exists, a necessary being does. With the self-evidence of this proposition as a major premise, the conclusion "God exists" can be demonstrated with certitude.

One word more. Anyone who raises questions of the sort I have propounded, in the face of a long and venerable tradition in which it is presumed that these matters are settled, should acknowledge that his perplexities may be due to his own incompetence, and should beg indulgence for all the errors he has made, on the ground that he is earnestly seeking the truth. Because man is a social animal, the truth cannot be sought in private. The intellectual life is a social one. Each of us needs all the help he can get from his fellows in speculative work—that most difficult of all cooperative pursuits. Therefore, he should be encouraged to say publicly, after protracted reflection and mature judgment, what he knows and what he does not know, what he sees and what remains hidden, so that others can correct him where he has erred, and direct him where he is blind. If my discourse about God's existence rests upon my erroneous dismissal of traditionally accepted arguments, or upon my ignorance of solutions already available to remove the difficulties I have mentioned, then I hope it will be taken as a plea for instruction. I have reason to think that I am not alone in my difficulties. If they are due to errors and ignorance, then the scholastic metaphysician who is in possession of the knowledge has an obligation to expound it in a more effective manner—contrived with greater sympathy for those gentiles in the modern world who desire natural wisdom.

NOTES TO CHAPTER 8

[1] "Rien de plus tragique que ces glissements de l'intelligence, quand elle passe insensiblement d'un principe très éléve formellement vrai à une application ou matérialization menteuse; on trouve beaucoup de ces glissements chez les Grecs, c'est pourquoi les scolastiques disaient qu'il importe toujours d'entendre Aristote *formalissime*" (*Questions de Conscience,* Paris, 1933, p. 99).

[2] *Scholasticism and Politics,* New York, 1940, p. 189.

[3] "A sound philosophy can dispense with the particular system of scientific explanations of which it makes use in accordance with the state of science at a particular epoch, and if that system were one day proved false, the truth of that philosophy would not be affected. Only its language and the sensible illustrations with which it clothes its truths would require modification. . . From what has been

said we can understand why the purely scientific mistakes to be found in the older statements of Aristotelian and Thomistic philosophy, statements which inevitably bear the stamp of the scientific beliefs of their period, do nothing to discredit the truth of that philosophy" (*An Introduction to Philosophy;* New York, 1930, pp. 120–21). And he adds in a footnote on p. 122: "The 'crime' of the decadent Scholastics of the sixteenth and seventeenth centuries was that they believed, and made others believe, that the philosophy of Aristotle and St. Thomas was in this sense bound up with the mistakes of ancient science, of which it is in reality wholly independent." Cf. *Degrees of Knowledge,* 1938, pp. 58–63, 74–75. Vd. also *Scholasticism and Politics,* p. 207.

⁴ Vd. *Contra Gentiles,* I, 2. Maritain observes that "in the Middle Ages philosophy was usually treated as an instrument in the service of theology. Culturally, it was not in the state required by its nature. The coming of a philosophical or profane wisdom which had completed its own formulation, for itself and according to its finalities, responded therefore to an historical necessity. But unfortunately this was accomplished under the emblem of separatism and a sectarian rationalism; Descartes *separated* philosophy from all higher wisdom, from everything in man which comes from above man. I am certain that what the world and civilization have lacked for three centuries has been a philosophy which would have developed its autonomous exigencies in a Christian climate, a wisdom of reason not closed but open to the wisdom of grace" (from an essay contributed to *Living Philosophies,* edited by Clifton Fadiman, New York, 1939).

⁵ Cajetan, in *S.Tl.,* I, q. 2, a. 3, n. II: ". . . primae viae, ex parte motus, sat est quod inferatur, *ergo datur primum movens immobile,* non curando utrum illud sit anima caeli aut mundi: hoc enim quaeretur in sequenti quaestione. Secundae quoque viae, ex parte efficientis, sat est quod ducat ad primum efficiens, non curando an illud sit corpus vel incorporeum: hoc enim quaeretur in sequenti quaestione. Tertiae vero viae, ex parte necessarii, sat est quod ducat ad primum necessarium non ex alio, non curando an sit unum vel plura: hoc enim quaeretur in question xi . . ."

⁶ Banez, in I, q. 2, a. 3, ad 1. arg.: ". . . licet omnes illae rationes simul sumptae non probent immediate et explicite, *Deum esse,* et multo minus Deum esse illud ens perfectissimum, quo perfectius quid excogitari nequit (hoc enim reservatur ad probandum in sequentibus quaestionibus) nihilominus rationes illae efficacissime probent quod in rerum natura reperiuntur perfectiones quaedam, et proprietates, quae alteri quam Deo nequeunt competere, et ex consequenti virtualiter et implicite probant Deum esse."

⁷ Cajetan had said: "Et sic istae rationes habent plurimum disputationis: eo quod prima via, ut in I Contra Gent., cap. xiii, dicitur, non ducit ad motorem magis immobilem quam sit anima intellectiva; secunda autem, . . . non ducit nisi ad corpus caeleste et ejus motorem; . . ." (*loc. cit.*). To which Banez answers: ". . . si nomine motus solum intelligatur motus physicus, bene dicit Cajetanus quod per illam rationem solum devenitur ad primum motorem, immobilem quidem per se, per accidens tamen potest esse mobilis. Sed non debet sic sumi, sed ut comprehendat etiam motus spirituales et metaphysicos, qualis est quaevis operatio, et etiam quaevis applicatio potentiae spiritualis ad swum actum; . . ." (*loc. cit.,* ad 2 arg.).

⁸ Banez, *loc. cit.*, ad 4 contra tertian rationem: ". . . ad demonstrationem D. Tho. satis est, si res contingentes ex natura sua non possint semper esse, licet ab extrinseco et par accidens id habeatur: nam ex se sunt indifferentes ad esse et non esse: et ideo ut semper sint, oportet ponere causam necessariam, quae illas reducat in actum."

⁹ Vd. for example, Garrigou-Lagrange, *God, His Existence, and His Nature,* St. Louis, 1934: Volume I. (I shall subsequently comment on the significance of the appendix which is added at the end of this volume.) I should like to add here that my problems concerning the arguments as stated in *Summa Theologica,* I, 2, 8 and in *Contra Gentiles,* I, 13, do not arise from difficulties of the sort which Kant supposed to be insurmountable. Garrigou-Lagrange, it seems to me, has detected Kant's error (vd. *op. cit.,* p. 299ff.), but in his own formulation of the *a posteriori* argument he does not explicate the reasoning in such a way that some knowledge of *what* God is (including the note of necessity) is openly acknowledged to be prior to the knowledge *that* God is, without undermining the *a posteriori* character of the proof. Cf. Maritain, *Degrees of Knowledge,* p. 276.

¹⁰ Vd. *The Spirit of Mediaeval Philosophy,* New York, 1936: Ch. I–III, and esp. pp. 43–51; and also *God and Philosophy,* New Haven, 1941, Ch. I. Vd. *ibid.,* Ch. II, wherein M. Gilson reveals the difficulties which beset the usual rendering of the Thomistic arguments.

¹¹ In *Contra Gentiles,* I, 15, St. Thomas uses the word "eternal" both in the Aristotelian sense of "without beginning or end in time" and in his own sense of "absolutely timeless"; cf. *Summa Theologica,* I, 10, 3 and 4, which indicate the incompatibility of these two meanings of the word. The so-called "eternity" of the world or of motion is not merely contrary to religious faith (vd. *Summa Theologica.,* I, 46, 2); it is, according to St. Thomas, indemonstrable (vd. *ibid.,* I, 46, 1); and he cites an extraordinary passage from Aristotle's *Topics* (I, 2, 104ᵇ 10-17) which uses the question, whether the universe is eternal or not, as an example of a scientifically insoluble problem.

In view of all this, historical scholarship must try to explain why St. Thomas chose to expand at greatest length in *Contra Gentiles,* I, 13, the first of the five ways, which he derived from Aristotle's *Physics,* Bk. VIII. At the end of this unamended piece of Aristotelian reasoning, St. Thomas acknowledges that this argument "proceeds from the supposition of the eternity of the world, and among Catholics this is a false supposition." Does the word "proceeds" here mean "follows as from a premise"? I shall try to show subsequently why the true argument for God's existence must be *compatible with* the false supposition of the world's eternity, but it obviously cannot *follow from* that supposition as a premise.

It is a historical, not a philosophical, question whether St. Thomas thought better of Aristotle than Gilson does. The historian cannot ignore the fact that, in his commentary on *Physics,* VIII (Lect. 2, #5), St. Thomas says: "Plato and Aristotle arrived at knowledge of the source of all being (*principium totius esse*)." I trust the reader will be able to separate the philosophical from the merely scholarly questions that are involved.

¹² *Op. cit.,* p. 275, fn. 1, Maritain goes on to say that "in the *conservation* of things, where created causalities have their part, our image of the physical universe fits better than that of Aristotle with St. Thomas's metaphysical doctrine

(*S.T.*, I, 104, 2)." I shall presently try to show that if, according to the text cited, there are secondary and instrumental efficient (*not material*) causes of the preservation of the being of things, then no proof is possible for God's existence. I hold that a proof is possible because I regard what is said in *S.T.*, I, 104, 5 as inconsistent with St. Thomas's doctrine concerning *cause essendi*.

¹³ "In speculative things," says St. Thomas, "the medium of demonstration, which demonstrates the conclusion perfectly, is one only; whereas probable means of proof are many" (*S.T.*, I, 47, 1 ad 3). This logical rule applies to demonstrations *quia* as well as to demonstrations *propter quid*. It does not apply, of course, to reasoning which establishes a conclusion as *probable* (rather than *certain*), for the probability of a conclusion is increased by the number of independent lines of proof corroborating one another. Furthermore, the fact that the same conclusion may be capable of indirect proof (by *reductio ad impossibile*) as well as direct proof does not violate this rule, for the indirect proof is imperfect: it is dialectical rather than scientific, since it appeals to some proposition which the opponent himself affirms, without certifying this proposition in itself. There may also be material diversity which permits one and the same proof to be stated—for rhetorical purposes—in several different ways, but such differences are in language and imagery and in the rhetorical order; they are not differences in the terms whose concatenation establishes the connection between the subject and predicate of the conclusion.

¹⁴ Let me say here at once that the first and second of the five ways are obviously reducible to one another; and that the third way is independent of the first two *only* if it be interpreted, contrary to much of its language, to mean that the existence of possible (i.e., contingent) beings implies the existence of a necessary (i.e., purely actual) being. The actual steps of this argument, following Aristotle's reasoning in *Metaphysics*, XII, 6, do not establish the causal nexus whereby we must infer the existence of a necessary being as the efficient cause of contingent beings; furthermore, because it uses the word "necessary" to name the merely incorruptible as well as the purely actual, the argument is forced to fall back upon the impossibility of an infinite series of necessary beings, each one caused by another. As it stands, this third way adds little to the first two. The fifth way does not seem to me to be a demonstration of God's existence, but rather of God's providence, as will be seen by a consideration of its terms in the light of Q. 22 on the providence of God. The teleological fact that everything has an *immanent* final cause of motion does not imply the existence of a *transcendent* final cause. That wherever there is a nature, be it unintelligent or intelligent, there natural appetite tends toward an end, does not by itself prove the existence of an efficient cause of being or of natures. Unless it can be *independently* shown that the observed natures must be created, whatever characteristics *follow* from these natures will not demand the existence of a creator.

Of the five ways, the fourth seems to me the nearest approach to a valid argument for God's existence. This argument will be found better stated in *De Pot.*, 3, 5 than in *S.T.*, I, 2, 3. It is this argument which Maritain rephrases, with different imagery, in *Degrees of Knowledge,* pp. 274–76. But neither Maritain's statement nor the statement in *De Pot.*, 3, 5 faces the difficulties inherent in the unstated major premise on which the proof rests.

The analysis to follow will show why, in terms of Thomistic principles, the first two ways cannot be used to prove God's existence. Since the proof must be in terms of efficient, not final, causality, and from the causation of being, not of becoming, the outlines of a proof can be drawn from some elements in the third way combined with the basic insight expressed in the fourth way. The proof thus outlined must then be tested by examining the truth of the major and minor premises.

[15] The Vatican Council declared that God "can be known with certitude by the natural light of human reason, by means of created things," to which declaration of faith, they added the canon: If any one shall say that the one true God, our Creator and Lord, cannot be certainly known by the natural light of human reason through created things; let him be anathema." Vd. H. Denzinger and J. Umberg, *Enchiridion Symbolorum,* Nos. 1785 and 1806.

[16] Vd. *Contra Gentiles,* I, 4: We must show, says St. Thomas, that certain truths are fittingly proposed by God as an object of belief. "We must first show this with regard to that truth which is attainable by the inquiry of reason, lest it appear to some, that since it can be attained by reason, it was useless to make it an object of faith by supernatural knowledge. Now three disadvantages would result if this truth were left solely to the inquiry of reason. One is that few men would have knowledge of God, because very many are hindered from gathering the fruit of diligent inquiry, which is the discovery of truth." Here St. Thomas enumerates three obstacles to the discovery of truth which operate *ut in pluribus.* "The second disadvantage is that those who would arrive at the discovery of the aforesaid truth would not succeed in doing so for a long time. . . . The third disadvantage is that much falsehood is mingled with the investigations of human reason, on account of the weakness of our intellect in forming its judgments, and by reason of the admixture of phantasms. Consequently many would remain in doubt about even those things which are truly demonstrated, through ignoring the force of the demonstration, especially when they perceive that different things are taught by the various men who are called wise. Moreover among the many demonstrated truths, there is sometimes a mixture of falsehood that is not demonstrated, but assumed for some probable or sophistical reason which at times is mistaken for a demonstration. Therefore it was necessary that definite certainty and pure truth about divine things should be offered to man by the way of faith."

[17] In considering St. Thomas's *actual statement* of the arguments for God's existence, we must remember two things: first, that in the cultural circumstances of his time, he was the great polemicist for the genuine worth of purely philosophical wisdom; second, that he himself, nevertheless, wrote as a theologian, not as a philosopher. Vd. fn. 4 *supra.* The first fact may help to explain why he defended Aristotle as the symbol of Philosophy, why he took arguments from Aristotle which later criticism has questioned. The second fact is even more important, because it calls our attention to an insoluble rhetorical problem. The proof of God's existence is a work of *natural* theology, and in the proper order of natural learning, it can come only at the very end of metaphysics—it can be understood only after much prior analysis has prepared the way. But in an orderly exposition of *dogmatic* theology, according to the order of the articles of faith, the question about God's existence must come at the very beginning, where an ade-

quate statement of the proof cannot possibly be made. If, by accident, anyone were to read Part I of the *Summa Theologica* but skipping Question 2, and then were to return to Question 2 after having mastered the basic metaphysical points concerning being and becoming, causality, etc., such a person would see at once why the proof of God's existence could not be written—i.e., adequately expounded—in Q. 2, A. 3.

[18] Neither can Aristotle's "prime mover" be proved to exist from the *known facts* of motion, for the "prime mover" is a *causa fiendi*, and no transcendent *causa fiendi* can be inferred from the cognate facts of motion, or proved to exist by *a posteriori* reasoning. Vd. #6 and 7 *infra*. Hence it is impossible to demonstrate God's existence in two separate steps, the first of which proves the existence of a prime mover as *first* cause *in fieri;* and the second of which proves that the prime mover is really God as the *only* cause *in esse.* This has an obvious bearing on the efforts by Cajetan and Banez to interpret the first two of the five Thomistic arguments. Cf. fn. 5 and 7 *supra.*

[19] The word "creation" is ambiguously used, when it is sometimes used to mean *both* the causation of being *and* the definite origin of what is thus caused; and sometimes to mean *only* the causation of being without specifying whether what is thus caused to be ever *began* to be or *always* existed. When "creation" is used with both notes it is contradictory to speak of a "created eternal world," for if the created is what has a definite beginning, it cannot also be everlasting or without beginning. When "creation" is used with only one note (omitting the notion of a beginning), then the phrase "created eternal world" is not contradictory, because an everlasting world, without beginning or end, may nevertheless be contingent in its being *at every moment* and so at every moment require the action of an efficient cause of being.

For analytical clarity, it is absolutely necessary to use the word "creation" in one sense, and one sense only. Despite the fact that scholastic theology has always used the word ambiguously, playing back and forth from one meaning to the other as the occasion demands, I am compelled to resolve the ambiguity in order to avoid analytical confusion, and I shall do so by using the word with these two notes in its signification: (a) to create is to cause being; (b) to create is to cause to begin to be—understanding such "beginning," of course, as neither a change nor a motion of any kind. There seem to me several good reasons for making this choice. In the first place, the note of origin or beginning enters into the usual theological sense of the word "creation" when, in the light of faith, God is called "creator," for by faith it is known that God not only is the cause of the world's being, but is also the cause of its beginning to be. In the second place, to use the word "creation" with *only* the first note—(a) above—in its signification, is to say that God is creating the world at every instant, and this does some violence to discourse. And in the third place, to use the word "creation" with only the (a) note is to make the word synonymous with "cause of being," in which case, it would be impossible to distinguish between God's creative and God's preservative action, for in both God acts as an efficient cause of being. Hence, in order to use the word "preservation" with a meaning clearly distinct from "creation," I shall use both words to signify "cause of being" (this is their common note), but I shall use "creation" with the additional and distinctive note—(b) above—namely, to signify "cause of beginning to be." In terms of such verbal usage, there should be no difficulty about understanding what is meant by saying that God can be the cause of being of either an everlasting world or a world with beginning, but he cannot be the "creative" cause of an everlasting world, though he can be its "preservative" cause, if it is the sort of world which requires a cause of its being.

The analytical points that are involved remain exactly the same, however one uses words. There are four: (1) that an everlasting world may be either one which is caused in being or one which is uncaused in being; (2) that a world which is caused in being may be either an everlasting world or one with a definite beginning; (3) that a world which is uncaused in being cannot have a beginning, but must be everlasting; and (4) that a world which has a beginning cannot be uncaused in being. We can never know by reason whether the world did or did not have a beginning; but we can know by reason that the world requires a cause for its being whether it is everlasting or had a beginning. We must, therefore, *prove* God's existence without *assuming* that the world had a beginning, and in a way that is *compatible* with the contrary assumption.

[20] We are obligated to remember that, in the sphere of becoming, intellect and will seem to be engaged in perfectly reciprocal causality, for each moves the other in the production of a free choice. Furthermore, we must note that it may not follow from the fact that a thing cannot cause its own being, that it cannot cause the being of another, for, as we know, a generated thing generates others, even if it is not able to generate itself.

9 | A Reply to Adler on God's Existence

HERBERT THOMAS SCHWARTZ, T.O.P.

She knoweth the subtilties of speeches, and the solutions of arguments.

—*Wisdom*, VIII, 8

I have written this refutation of Mr. Adler's essay on "The Demonstration of God's Existence"[1] for three reasons.

First, to confirm those of the faithful who might well have been dismayed by the thought that the teaching of St. Thomas, who is eminent among the Doctors of the Church, was open to such radical criticism as Mr. Adler has directed to it, and this in a matter which is a necessary preamble to the very Faith itself.

Secondly, to correct Mr. Adler and any others who might be obstructed in their quest of truth (which truth is the Living Truth Who is Christ) by errors of natural reason concerning the teaching of the Church, in so far as that teaching is accessible to the natural light of reason.

Thirdly, I have been moved to write these pages out of a sense of filial gratitude and reverence for St. Thomas, as well as for the other holy Doctors of the Church, in the hope that what is written here might, in some small measure, dispel the erroneous, but widespread, notion that adherence to Catholic doctrine begets sterility of thought. Whatever there is of truth, I have received from that inexhaustible Spring: whatever there is of intellectual error, and pride of spirit, is my own.

For prudence, as it is subordinated to the Faith, determines the proper disposition to the truths which we have inherited from men notable as much for their sanctity as for their learning and intellectual powers. Just as we venerate not only the Blessed Trinity of Persons in One Divine Nature, but also Christ and His Blessed Mother, as well as their

---

[1] Pp. 188–218 in both *The Maritain Volume of The Thomist* (New York: Sheed and Ward, 1943), and *The Thomist* V (January, 1943).

saints, so our reverence for truth, as it comes from God Himself, is participated in by our reverence for the teachings of the Doctors of the Church, and even of those outside the Visible Church whom tradition has established to be of sound doctrine. Experience, reason, and the admonitions of the Holy Ghost manifest that such reverence, far from being opposed to intellectual vitality, is the indispensable requirement for a truly healthy intellectual condition. It appears otherwise only in contrast with a ruthless pursuit of what is called reason, or when we have failed in the difficult task of perpetuating and therefore renovating tradition.

My only misgiving is in the conviction that what I have written is entirely unworthy to be associated with the teaching of St. Thomas. May he forgive me my presumption, for it was expedient that this work should be done.

Mr. Adler's article, excluding a short introduction and conclusion, is divided into two parts. In the first he intends to prove that God's existence cannot be demonstrated as He is a first cause in the order of becoming *(causa fiendi)*. In the second he considers the possibility of demonstrating the existence of God as a cause of being *(causa essendi)*. In the latter, although he admits the possibility in this line of causality as opposed to the order of becoming, he ends on a note of doubt principally because of difficulties concerning the premises of that demonstration (p. 209, III).

The first part is divided into three parts. In the first he argues against the possibility of demonstration by any temporal succession of causes, which he calls "series," and this indeterminately, i.e., not specified as causes *per se* or causes *per accidens* (p. 197, #2). In the second he argues against the possibility of demonstration through a temporal succession ("series") of "essentially diverse causes," i.e., causes which are causes *per se* of a given effect (p. 198, #3). In the third part he argues against the possibility of demonstration through a simultaneous plurality, i.e., "set" as opposed to "series" of "essentially diverse causes."

For convenience of reference I have adopted the following system: Since the article is divided into three parts which are numbered I, II, III, the first reference will be to the part of the article, designated by the roman numeral; the second will indicate the arabic numerals which Mr. Adler has used for the main divisions of his outline, e.g., II, #2, indicates the second main division in the second part of the article. This is followed by the page reference, so that the complete reference will be: II, #2, pp. 197, 198.

Mr. Adler—FIRST ARGUMENT, II, #2, PP. 197, 198.

Any demonstration of God's existence through a "series," i.e., a temporal succession of causes, presupposes the non-eternity of the universe. But the latter cannot be known by natural reason. Therefore no demonstration of God's existence through such a "series" of causes is possible.

The major is proved as follows: Any demonstrations of God's existence requires a finite number of causes. But if the universe were eternal, the number of causes in temporal succession would be infinite. Therefore, etc. The minor is an admitted truth of the tradition.[2]

REFUTATION

St. Thomas never attempts to demonstrate the existence of God through a temporal succession of causes. To the contrary, he says: "But it is manifest that when something moves because it is moved, the mover is moved simultaneously with this moveable; as when the hand by its motion moves a stick, the hand and the stick are moved simultaneously."[3]

Mr. Adler—SECOND ARGUMENT, II, #3, PP. 198, 199.

The existence of God cannot be demonstrated through any "series" of causes which is not finite in number. But a "series" of "essentially diverse causes" is not necessarily finite in number. Therefore the existence of God cannot be demonstrated from such a "series" of causes.

The major is evident from the nature of demonstration, and besides it is an accepted truth of the tradition. The minor is shown from examples: two sticks are used to move a stone; the two sticks are not "essentially diverse," i.e., different in kind, yet they are simultaneous and therefore finite in number. The man trains the dog to carry a burden, which the dog carries at a later time; these two causes, the man and the dog, are essentially diverse, and yet they are in temporal succession, and therefore could be infinite in number. Therefore "essentially diverse causes" are not necessarily finite in number.

---

[2] *II Contra Gentiles*, cc. 31–38; In *XII Met.*, 1. 5, #2497, 2498; In *VIII Phys.*, 1. 13, #8, 1.2, #17; *Summa Theol.*, I, q. 46, a. 2, corpus.
[3] In *VII Phys.*, 1. 1. Cf. in *VII Phys.*, 11. 3 and 4, where it is demonstrated that mover and moved are simultaneous in every species of motion.

Refutation

1. St. Thomas does not demonstrate the existence of God through any temporal succession of causes.

2. A temporal succession ("series") of causes *per se* of an effect ("essentially diverse causes") is impossible. For, if causes *per se* of an effect could be, as the author asserts here, in a temporal relation, the existence of a first cause could be demonstrated through a temporal succession of causes, and the universe, contrary to Mr. Adler's repeated assertion, could be demonstrated to have had a beginning in time. For unless a "series" of "essentially diverse causes" (causes *per se*) has a first cause, none of the other causes will be a cause, and it is false to call them a *series* of causes, for none of them is a cause. "Thus, therefore, if the moving causes proceeded to infinity, there would be no first cause; but the first cause was the source of all (the causes): therefore it would follow that all the causes as a whole would be removed: for when the cause is taken away, those things of which it is the cause are removed."[4] There must, then, be a first cause of such a "series."

But if it is said that this first cause is outside the temporal order, but the number of such causes in the temporal order is infinite, thus again, there will be no first cause of the whole "series," and they will not be causes. For, since it is held that these causes are infinite, there will not be a cause among them which can itself be caused by a cause outside the temporal succession. For whichever one is acted upon by the extra-temporal cause must be a determinate cause, and therefore it will be separated from the ultimate effect by a finite number of steps. It will therefore be in fact the first cause in the temporal order, and the remaining "causes" after it will be causes in no way. Therefore it is necessary that a "series of essentially diverse causes" should have a *first* cause in the order of time. Now the absolutely first efficient cause *per se* in the temporal order could not be caused by anything else in the temporal order, since, in that case, it would not be absolutely first in that order. Either, then, it is itself uncaused, or it is caused by higher causes which are not in the temporal order, for it is absolutely first, it has no efficient cause, not only no efficient cause which is before it in time, but no efficient cause which is before it in any way.

But if it has no efficient cause in any way, it must have its being of itself, which is impossible; for the first cause *per se* in temporal order must be a body. Otherwise it would not be in time at all, except *per accidens*, as a soul is in time because it informs a body: but in this way it would not be a first cause *per se* in the order of time.

---

[4] In *II Met.*, 1. 3.

But it is impossible for one body to be the cause of itself: for this would require that it should be both mover and moved at the same time, and this in one respect, in respect of the thing caused. Therefore no efficient cause *per se* which is first in the order of time can be the cause of itself; consequently it must have its being from a cause which is outside the temporal order.

Now either all the things in the universe were produced in this way, i.e., the whole creature, and therefore the universe would have had a beginning in time, or they were not all produced in this way. If they were not, the other things in the universe would have no cause which was first in the temporal order. Therefore they could always have been. Let it be supposed, then, that they always were, for if they were not, again the whole universe had a beginning in time.

This body, then, which is a first cause in the order of time, could have been produced by the bodies which existed before it, since these always were. But the cause of both, i.e., the eternally existing bodies, and the body which was first in the order of time relative to the things produced by it, must be some intelligence, since both require a cause which is outside the material order. This was shown for a cause which would be first in the temporal order, and it is easily shown for eternally existing bodies, as follows: Such bodies or causes could not be caused by a first cause in the corporeal order, inasmuch as, by the hypothesis, there is no such first cause in the temporal order; otherwise they would not be eternal. Therefore they must have their first efficient cause outside the material order, and such a cause must be an intelligence, as is evident from the nature of intellect, i.e., that it is immaterial *per se*. But it would be vain to produce a body to be a first cause in the order of time when it could have been produced by bodies already existing. An intellect, however, does not act in vain. Therefore all bodies would have had a beginning in time, if one did.

From this it is seen that the whole universe could be demonstrated to have had a beginning in time, if there could be an efficient cause *per se* which is first in the order of time. But Mr. Adler holds that it is impossible to demonstrate this. Therefore, neither could there be a single cause *per se* which is first in the order of time.

3. In this argument Mr. Adler attempts to prove that the existence of God cannot be demonstrated through a "series," i.e., a temporal succession of "*essentially diverse causes*." But the first argument, according to his intention, eliminated the possibility of demonstrating the existence of God through *any* temporal succession of causes, i.e., "series." Therefore it is a violation of the method of demonstration to prove this again for a "series" of "essentially diverse causes." For this is like demonstrating first that triangle as triangle has angles equal to two right angles, and then

demonstrating it for isosceles; and such demonstration is defective since the end of demonstration is to know the cause; but the cause is in what is commensurately universal with the effect, e.g., triangle and angles equal to two right angles, not isosceles and equal to two right angles, "series" of causes and the impossibility of demonstrating God's existence, not "series" of "essentially diverse causes" and that impossibility.

If it is argued that this objection is valid only in the demonstrative order, whereas in the dialectical order there may be many arguments proving the same conclusion, and that Mr. Adler's arguments are dialectical; we admit the major, but deny the minor. For St. Thomas's arguments are intended to be demonstrations. This is manifest from the fact that the first three ways end with the assertion of the consequent necessity of positing God to be, as well as from the following: "Since nature operates for a determinate end from the direction of a superior agent, it is *necessary* that those things which are done by nature should be reduced to God as to a first cause."[5] Now the conclusion may not be stated to be necessary unless the argument is demonstrative. The demonstrative intention is, besides, apparent in the last book of the *Physics* and the *Metaphysics,* and in many other places. But it would be again a defect in method to overthrow demonstrative arguments by dialectical ones. Further, Mr. Adler states his demonstrative intention in this article: "The analysis to follow does, I think, determine the answer which must be given" (I, p. 193). And again: "Our analysis so far has eliminated two possibilities of demonstrating the existence of God as a cause required for effects known to exist" (II, #5, p. 200).

But it may be argued that St. Thomas's proofs are merely dialectical, inasmuch as he proves the same thing in five ways. Thus the present author says: "If there can be *only one* logically adequate demonstration of any proposition that is established with certitude—which seems to be St. Thomas's opinion on the matter—then we must ask whether the five arguments stated by St. Thomas are five *ways* of stating the same argument, or whether one of these is the valid proof and the others not, or whether none of these *as written* is strictly a demonstration but only an indication of where a demonstration might lie" (I, p. 193).

To this we answer that the five proofs of St. Thomas are not five proofs of the same conclusion formally, but only materially. For the first proof demonstrates the necessity of a first mover, the second demonstrates the necessity of a first efficient cause, the third demonstrates the necessity of a necessary being, the fourth demonstrates the necessity of a perfect being, the fifth demonstrates the necessity of a ruler of the universe. It

---

[5] *S.T.*, I, q. 2, a. 3, ad 2, italics mine.

happens that God is each of these, or, in the proofs, that we understand God by each of these terms which stand in the place of the definition. In this respect the demonstrations are imperfect, i.e., as not proceeding from the formal definition, and, for this same reason, more than one demonstration is possible, according to the number of things that stand in place of the definition and can be known from known effects. But this in no way affects the necessity of the conclusion *that* God exists, since it is known with necessity that *only* God could be a prime mover, first efficient cause, etc. Thus the imperfection in this mode of demonstration does not reduce it to dialectical proof.

And this explains the passage from St. Thomas which the present author adduces: "In speculative things the medium of demonstration which perfectly demonstrates the conclusion, is one only."[6] For the demonstration of God's existence is not perfect demonstration. But it in no way follows that a proof which is not a perfect demonstration is only dialectical, as we have explained. St. Thomas, it is true, opposes perfect demonstration to probable proof in the cited passage adduced by Mr. Adler. But he adds: "And similarly in operative things, when that which is for an end adequates, if I may use the expression, the end, there is only required one medium of demonstration. *But the creature is not so related to the end which is God*; whence it was necessary for creatures to be multiplied" *(loc. cit.,* italics mine). From this it is seen how the multiplicity of the creature founds the possibility of more than one demonstration of God's existence, and at the same time how each demonstration is imperfect without affecting the necessity of the conclusion.

4. "Essentially diverse causes," i.e., causes which are in a *per se* line of causality with respect to a given effect, contrary to the assumption of Mr. Adler's second argument, *must* be simultaneous, and for that reason, and this precisely as causes and causing. The cause *per se* of an effect is that which produces the effect in virtue of its proper nature, and not in virtue of something which it has received and which it may or may not have, its nature remaining the same."

The cause of the statue *per accidens* is indeed Polycletus, but *per se* the cause of the statue is making the statue *(faciens statuam)*: for Polycletus is the cause of the statue in so far as it happens to him *(accidit ei)* to he making the statue."[7] For it is making the statue which of itself produces the statue, not Polycletus as that in virtue of which the statue is made, but only as a subject. Likewise the stick which is moving is the cause *per accidens* of the motion of the stone when it is moved by the stick, because it

---

[6] *S.T.,* I, q. 47, a. 1, ad 3.
[7] *In II Phys.,* 1. 1, n.4.

is the motion of the stick which moves the stone. But this is only because the stick *happens* to be moved. For just as making the statue is the cause *per se* of the statue being made, so motion is the cause *per se* of a thing being moved.

But motion does not subsist in itself; therefore, as a subsisting agent, that is a cause *per se* which has the act by which it causes in virtue of its own nature, as e.g., the hand moves of itself as a living thing, not in virtue of being moved by something outside itself, and therefore the motion of the hand is a cause *per se* of the motion of the stick. But the virtue which the hand has of moving itself, granted it has this in virtue of its nature, is something which it received from a higher principle, i.e., the soul. Therefore the soul is a cause *per se* of the motion of the stick by the hand. Again the virtue of the soul to move the body is something it has by its proper nature; nevertheless it does not have this of itself as from an ultimate principle, for it does not have its being of itself.

Further, that is a cause of a thing's being which acts as an agent; and since what comes to be receives its act from the agent, it must be moved simultaneously with the agent, and this is necessary whether the mover causes the motion *per se* or *per accidens*, as the motion of the hand is the cause *per se* of the motion of the stick, and is moved simultaneously with the stick; or if the stick moves a stone, the stick is a cause *per accidens* of the motion of the stone, yet it too is moved simultaneously with the stone. For this reason, i.e., that action and passion are simultaneous, it is impossible that causes in temporal succession should be causes of one effect. For example, if water is first heated, it is used later to heat a bed, then again later the bed is used to heat a body. But the temporal succession is brought about by the duration of the effect which subsequently acts as a cause in another motion.

Now although it is not necessary for causes *per accidens* to be in temporal succession, inasmuch as all the causes of a single motion must be simultaneous, as we have explained, nevertheless this is necessary, that causes which are in temporal succession should be causes *per accidens*, which can be seen in the following way: By temporal succession, that which first receives the heat now heats. Evidently, therefore, it does not heat *per se*, that is, in virtue of itself, but in virtue of what it has received. But this is, by definition, what it is to be a cause *per accidens*. Therefore, it is impossible for causes *per se*, what Mr. Adler calls "essentially diverse causes," to be in temporal succession, upon which assumption the whole of his present argument is founded. For if it is impossible for causes *per se* to be in temporal succession, it is futile to attempt to prove that the existence of God could not be demonstrated from such a succession of causes. For such a succession of causes could not exist.

Hence it is entirely irrelevant to the demonstration of God's existence whether the universe be eternal or not. For, on the former hypothesis, the infinite succession of causes would be causes *per accidens*, as it has been explained; but *at any moment* the causes *per se* of any change would be necessarily finite, and this, not because they are simultaneous, as Mr. Adler asserts, but for the following reason: Whatever the causes may be of a single effect, whether *per se* or *per accidens*, e.g., the movement of a stone by several sticks, the first of which is moved by a hand, the causes *per accidens* must themselves be caused by a cause *per se*, and this is necessary from the nature of cause *per accidens*. For a cause *per accidens* causes the effect not in virtue of itself but in virtue of something which it has received. The motion of the hand, in turn, must be caused by another cause *per se*. But there must be a first cause in this order: otherwise the effect would have no cause, since the intermediary causes are only causes in so far as they are caused. Consequently, the number of causes must be finite, not because they are simultaneous, and not even because they are all causes *per se*, but because they are reducible to causes which are causes *per se* and therefore necessary to the effect by definition. But the number of accidental causes in a single motion cannot be infinite since they must receive their effect from a cause *per se*; but if the causes *per accidens* were infinite in number, there would be no first one to receive its act from the proximate *per se* cause, and consequently the so-called causes *per accidens* would not be causes at all.

The principle of simultaneity of causes, therefore, is the singleness of the motion or effect, which causes are ultimately reduced to causes *per se* of that effect, which must be finite in number as necessary to that effect and to the intermediary causes, since a first is essential to the causality of the intermediary causes. Corresponding to this, an infinite number of causes has its principle in this, that there must be a succession of motions or effects, since the infinite number of causes requires a temporal succession of causes (on the assumption that an actual infinite cannot exist which is only absolutely certain for the corporeal order). A succession of effects is necessary because the causes of a single motion must be simultaneous. But to be in temporal succession, the causes must be causes *per accidens*, as has been shown. Thus, as the principle of a finite number of causes is, ultimately, causality *per se*, the principle of an infinite number of causes, i.e., the principle of its possibility, is causality *per accidens*. "But in causes *which do not act simultaneously*, this (infinitude of causes) is not impossible, following those who posit perpetual generation. But this infinitude *befalls (accidit)* causes: for it is accidental to the father of Sortes that he is or is not himself the son of someone else. But it is not accidental to the stick, in so far as it moves the stone, that it is moved by the hand: for it moves in so far as it is moved."[8]

The true doctrine in this matter, as well as the indubitability of St. Thomas's teaching, is manifest in the following passage:

> It is impossible in efficient causes *per se* to proceed to an infinite: as if, for example, the causes which are *per se* required for some effect should be multiplied in infinitum; as if the stone should be moved by the stick, the stick by the hand, and so on in infinitum. But it is not reputed impossible to proceed in infinitum in agent causes *per accidens*; as if, for example, all the causes which would be multiplied in infinitum would only have the order of one cause, but their multiplication would be *per accidens*; as the artisan operates with many hammers *per accidens*, because one is broken after the other. Therefore it happens to this hammer that it acts after the action of another hammer. And similarly it happens to this man insofar as he generates, that he should have been generated by another man. For he generates insofar as he is man (*inquantum homo*) and not insofar as he is the son of another man. For all men generating have one grade in efficient causes; namely the grade of particular generator. Whence it is not impossible that man should be generated by man in infinitum. But it would be impossible if the generation of this man depended on this man, and on the elementary body, and on the sun, and so on in infinitum.[9]

5. The act of training the dog is not a cause *per se* of the subsequent carrying the burden; but the habit of being trained is a cause *per se* of this operation; as the generation of the father is not a cause *per se* of the generation of the son, but man is the cause of the generation of the son, since to be a man is *per se* required to generate a son, as having a habit is *per se* required to perform an operation proceeding from such a habit. Two things cause *per se*: being in act; and the cause of what acts being in act, in the respect in which it acts, when it acts. But what caused the com-

---

[8] *II Con. Gent.*, c. 38, ad 5, italics mine. In respect of the motion of the stone, i.e., of the effect, the motion of the stick is not accidental, but in respect of the nature of the stick, it is accidental, for the motion *befalls* the stick. Cf. the above. On the part of the effect, that is a cause *per se* without which the effect would not be produced, as the stone would not be moved unless the stick, as it was moved, moved it. But on the part of the cause, that is a cause *per se*, in virtue of whose nature the effect proceeds, and in this sense the stick is not a cause *per se*. Again, the cause *per as*, as it is a created cause, must be reduced from potency to act by a higher cause, either in the order of nature, or operation, and this is the *ratio* for demonstration through motion, and through efficient cause respectively, consequently the term, cause *per se*, must be understood analogically: for all the causes *per se*, except the first cause, cause in virtue of an act received.

[9] *S.T.*, I, q. 46, a. 2, ad 7.

ing to be of the thing which acts, causes *per accidens.* Unless the same thing is at once the cause of a thing's being in act and having come to be, e.g., the sun is the cause both of the generation of a man and his act of generating another. But the act of training the dog is *per se* the cause of the dog's being trained, since it is *per se* required for someone to be training the dog when it is being trained. And these are simultaneous.

Likewise in every motion, for motion is one with action and passion, and action and passion must be simultaneous. In the order of particular causes, it is true, *this* dog is able to carry the burden in virtue of having been trained previously, just as *this* man is able to generate in virtue of having been generated himself. But to be trained does not *per se* require to have come to be trained, just as to be a man does not *per se* require to have come to be a man. Thus it is evident that the cause *per se*, and the effect, must be simultaneous. Therefore it is impossible, as Mr. Adler supposes, for there to be a "series," i.e., a temporal succession of causes *per se* of one effect, "essentially diverse causes."

Hence Mr. Adler's example supporting the minor does not exemplify; for the cause as causing, i.e., the man training the dog, is *simultaneous* with its effect; i.e., the dog being trained.

Mr. Adler—THIRD ARGUMENT, II, #6, B, PP. 201, 202

The existence of God cannot be demonstrated by a set of causes which are the cause of an effect which is not proper to a single ultimate cause. But "a set of essentially diverse causes" (causes which are simultaneous and in a *per se* line of causality with respect to a given effect) is constituted of causes of an effect (becoming) which is not proper to a single ultimate cause. Therefore the existence of God cannot be demonstrated by "a set of essentially diverse causes."

The major is known from the nature of demonstration *a posteriori.* The minor is proved as follows: Becoming is the effect of physical causes (instrumental) and, hypothetically, of God (principal cause), each of which is a total cause of the effect according to St. Thomas.[10] Therefore there is not one ultimate cause, but two, at least in possibility, the ultimate instrumental cause, and the principal cause which would be God.

REFUTATION

As is evident, the only difficulty can be with the minor of this argument which, in Mr. Adler's statement, rests chiefly on the authority of St.

---

[10] *III Con. Gent.*, c. 70.

Thomas, who ascribes the totality of the cause both to the instrumental and to the principal cause. Arguing dialectically first, then, since the adduced proof is from authority, it should be said that if this were indeed St. Thomas's teaching, he would have had to be either stupid or maliciously dishonest, inasmuch as he would have failed either intellectually in respect of an elementary inference, that God's existence could not be demonstrated from physical effects, or, seeing this, he would have adduced sophistic reasoning to save a truth of the Faith. Now since neither of these conclusions is tenable, it follows that Mr. Adler's interpretation is not according to the authority of St. Thomas.

But indeed neither the fact nor the teaching of St. Thomas accords with Mr. Adler's interpretation. For the instrumental cause and the principal cause are not independent lines of causality, as St. Thomas manifests in many places, but the instrumental is subordinated to the principal cause, as the term instrument, is intended to show. The instrumental cause is a total cause in the sense that from it, proximately, the whole effect proceeds, as the movement of the pencil may be said to be the total cause of the writing which is produced by that movement. But the pencil, since it is only an instrument, must itself be moved:

> For in any agent there are two things to consider, namely, the thing itself which acts, and the virtue by which it acts: as fire heats through heat. But the virtue of an inferior agent depends on the virtue of the superior agent, in so far as the superior agent gives this virtue to the inferior agent through which it acts; or conserves it, or even applies it to action, as the artisan applies the instrument to its proper effect; to which he does not give the form through which the instrument acts, nor does he conserve it, but only gives it motion. It is necessary, therefore, that the action of an inferior agent should be not only from it through its proper virtue, but through the virtue of all the superior agents: for it acts in virtue of all of them. And just as the lowest agent is found to be active without any intermediary, so the virtue of the first agent is found to be without any intermediary with respect to producing the effect: for the virtue of the lowest agent does not have the virtue to produce this effect of itself, but from the virtue of the proximate superior; and thus the virtue of that (superior) has it from the virtue of (its) superior; and thus the virtue of the supreme agent is found to be productive of the effect of itself, as if immediate; as appears in the principles of demonstration, of which the first is immediate. Therefore, just as there is no difficulty in this, that one action should be produced (both) by some agent and its virtue, so there is no difficulty in this, that the same effect is produced by the inferior agent and by God: by both immediately, although by each in a different way.[11]

---

[11] *III Con. Gent.*, c. 70.

The author's difficulty here is twofold: in the first place he fails to understand the analogy of causality, through which causes are not ultimate until we arrive at what is first without qualification; secondly, through a rationalistic proclivity to ontologize every distinction, he fails to see how a thing can be formally many (according to the relations which things have to it) and in itself one, as there is no contradiction in this, that God is the first *causa movens* and *causa efficiens* in the order of becoming, as well as the first cause in the order of being *(causa essendi)* . In this, as in other places, he applies too readily the law of excluded middle.

Mr. Adler—FOURTH ARGUMENT, II, #9, PP. 206–09, AND III, PP. 209–216

This argument is divided into three parts. In the first Mr. Adler intends to show that there is a single remaining possible way to demonstrate God's existence (II, #9), having eliminated, in his view, the traditional ways; in the second he states what he thinks is the only possible demonstration (III, pp. 209, 210). In the third part he raises difficulties and doubts concerning this proposed demonstration (III, pp. 210–16). For the sake of clarity we shall follow each of these parts with its refutation.

Mr. Adler—Fourth Argument, first part, II, #9.

The existence of God can be demonstrated from a known effect which is the proper effect of God. But preservation in being is a known effect which is the proper effect of God. Therefore, etc.

The major is evident. The minor is established by the authority of St. Thomas.

REFUTATION

The whole difficulty, evidently, lies in the minor of the argument. The refutations, consequently, are all directed to this premise.

1. No demonstration should rest formally on a premise accepted from authority; and Mr. Adler neither demonstrates the necessity of the proposition that preservation in being is the proper effect of God, nor does he manifest or even assert that it is self-evident.

2. The authority of St. Thomas can have little weight with Mr. Adler inasmuch as he has dismissed all the ways by which that authority claims to have demonstrated the existence of God, as well as many of his conclusions in other matters, e.g., in politics, in law, in logic; so that the

dialectical weight of his authority must be negligible for the present author. In fact, in the very act of determining the basic teaching of St. Thomas, Mr. Adler accuses him of contradicting himself: "The contradiction could be easily resolved, were it *merely* apparent and due to verbal ambiguity" (II, #9, c, p. 207). Yet he goes on to say: "Since the contradiction is not apparent, but real, we must resolve it by making a choice between conflicting texts." Now this procedure is altogether unintelligible; for, if St. Thomas is so untrustworthy as he appears to be to Mr. Adler, how could a demonstration be founded on what is at best a probable determination of his more fundamental teaching?

3. There is no authority whatsoever in St. Thomas for the proposition that God is the *unique* cause of conservation of being. The one citation which Mr. Adler gives for this opinion *(S.T.,* I, q. *65,* a. 9, ad 1) is, unfortunately, incorrect; there are only four articles in question 65 of the first part.

Now the teaching of St. Thomas is manifest in the other passages cited by Mr. Adler. Thus, St. Thomas says that what is proper to God in relation to the creature is not to sustain in being but to be the cause of being absolutely, i.e., universally: "But that which is properly the effect of God creating, is that which is presupposed relative to all the other (causes), namely, being absolutely. Whence nothing else can operate dispositively and instrumentally to this effect; since creation is not from something presupposed which could be disposed through the action of the instrumental agent. Thus, therefore, it is impossible that it should convene to some creature to create; neither by its proper virtue, nor instrumentally or by ministering."[12]

In this it is seen that, in St. Thomas's doctrine, it is proper to God to cause being in its universality. And this may be seen again: "For being itself is the most common *(communissimus)* first effect and more intimate than all the other effects; and therefore it belongs to God alone according to the proper virtue of such an effect."[13] But lest it be thought that conservation could also be the proper effect of God, it should be said that conservation is the proper effect of God not as such, but as it is the continuation of creation: " It should be said that the conservation of things by God is not by any new action, but by the continuation of the action which gives being; which action indeed is without motion and without time."[14] But if it is argued that this is the only conservation of being in St. Thomas's teaching, we may adduce this passage from many to show that he taught that there are secondary causes of the preservation of being:

---

[12] *12 S.T.,* I, q. 45, a. 5, corpus.
[13] *De Pot.,* q. 3, a. 7, corpus.
[14] *S.T.,* I, q. 104, a. 1, ad 4.

And therefore, principally indeed, the first cause is conservative of the effect; but secondarily all the mediate causes; and in proportion more so as a cause is higher and more proximate to the first cause. Whence the conservation and preservation of things is attributed to the superior causes also concerning corporeal things.[15]

It is clear, therefore, that, in the teaching of St. Thomas, the conservation of things is proper to God only in respect of the conservation of immaterial things. But immaterial things, *qua* immaterial, are not contingent but necessary, i.e., considered naturally they cannot not be. Therefore, in order to know that they are sustained in being, we should have to know that they could not sustain themselves in being, i.e., the mere fact that such things exist does not imply that God exists; but when God is known to exist, it becomes manifest that even such beings depend on God for their existence. Consequently, although in fact the existence of such things is preserved by God, we do not know this from the knowledge that such things exist, but only when we understand that the existence of such beings is received, through the analogy of potency and act in the order of efficient cause, which is in fact St. Thomas's second way of demonstrating the existence of God. For, as the above citation[16] makes clear, there is no distinction on the part of God between the efficient cause of a thing in the order of production and in the order of conservation, and this not even by a distinction of reason *cum fundamento in re* with respect to the production of immaterial things, since these are necessarily created, not generated.

Mr. Adler, consequently, cannot intend by the "unique effect" the existence of immaterial things, for, as such, his proposed demonstration would be at best nothing more than an almost unintelligible version of St. Thomas's second way; whereas he has dismissed that way as untenable. Further this is clear from the minor of the final demonstration he proposes: "Minor: Corporeal substances do exist." From this it is evident that the unique effect of God is not, in his intention, the preservation of the being of incorporeal substances, but of corporeal substances. And it is precisely this effect, the preservation of corporeal substances, which is not the unique effect of God in St. Thomas's teaching.

The root of Mr. Adler's difficulty with St. Thomas in this question, and the reason why St. Thomas, in his view, appears to contradict in one place what he says in another, may now be manifested. For Mr. Adler, evidently, has again applied the law of excluded middle in an uncritical fashion. Indeed, if we start with this disjunction: either God is the unique cause of conservation, or the creature, as well as God, conserves the being of

---

[15] *S.T.*, I, q. 104, a, 2, corpus.
[16] *S.T.*, I, q. 104, a. 1, ad 4.

things, what Mr. Adler has concluded would follow. For at one time St. Thomas is explaining the dependence of all things for their being on God, i.e., as God is the principal and universal cause of the being of things inasmuch as His nature is to be and His alone; at another time he is explaining how lower causes co-operate in the conservation of corporeal things, when those causes are universal with respect to the effects, and therefore equivocal causes:

But sometimes the effect is not apt to receive the impression of the agent according to the same ratio which it has in the agent, as appears in all agents which do not produce something similar according to species; as the celestial bodies are the cause of the generation of inferior bodies dissimilar according to species: and such an agent can be the cause of the form according to the ratio of such a form, and not only according as it is acquired in this matter; *and therefore it is the cause not only of the becoming (fiendi), but of the being (essendi).*[17]

Relative to the absolute disjunction postulated, this would appear to contradict the statement that God is the universal cause of the conservation of being. But when the proper qualifications are made, i.e., that God is the unique cause of conservation as the universal and principal cause, but the creature is also a cause of conservation in so far as it too is universal in respect of a more particular effect, the contradiction is seen to be only apparent. But to resolve this contradiction the causes must be seen analogically, according as causes in their universality approach the universality of God's causality, and not univocally as Mr. Adler has regarded them.

From this we may see, too, why a demonstration of God's existence as the cause of being seemed feasible to Mr. Adler where the other demonstrations seemed to fail of their end. For it seemed as if only in the order of being was God a unique cause: this intention is evident from the following where he is preparing the way for "the one possible demonstration":

Furthermore, in creation there are no intermediary causes, no secondary principal and no instrumental causes. Hence, to say that being is the *proper* effect of God means that God is the *unique and exclusive* cause of being, as He is the sole creative cause. If these things be so, then it should be possible to prove God's existence as the cause of the being of whatever needs to have its being caused, for here we are dealing with an effect which can have only one cause. Hence we should not be involved in all the problems about finite and infinite series, primary and secondary, principal and instrumental causes, which arise whenever a plurality of causes is possible (II, #7, c, d).

---

[17] *S.T.*, I, q. 104, a. 1, corpus, italics mine.

But, both in the order of becoming and in the order of being, God is not a unique cause, in the sense that He is the only cause, cause being taken indeterminately as something common. Rather His uniqueness is as a principal cause, i.e., as a first cause; and this problem, i.e., the problem of analogy, is no more obviated in the order of being than it is in the order of becoming. The principal cause of Mr. Adler's error, then, is his insistence on a univocally distinct causality on the part of God, e.g., a sense in which God is a cause as man is risible, whereas in fact, because the creature participates in and imitates the Divine causality, no such distinction can be found: the causality of God is necessarily analogically common with the causality of the creature. But causality is proper to God as it is absolutely principal and most universal. Indeed, Mr. Adler's procedure presupposes this theological impossibility, that God should create a creature that should not imitate its Creator.

In the second part of this argument Mr. Adler presents what he considers the only possible demonstration of God's existence. It is evident from what has been said in the refutation of the first part of his argument why the existence of God cannot be demonstrated in the way he intends, namely, because God is not a unique cause in the order of being, as this demonstration presupposes. Further, inasmuch as he himself finds this demonstration dubious, it is difficult to conceive in what a refutation of it would consist. Proceeding formally, we shall assume a positive intention, i.e., that Mr. Adler's intention is that what he presents as a demonstration is *probably* a demonstration. But probability is opposed to impossibility. Therefore the refutation will consist in showing that it is *impossible* to demonstrate the existence of God in the way Mr. Adler proposes. From this it will follow that, contrary to the declaration of faith in the demonstrability of God's existence, it cannot be demonstrated in any of the ways indicated by Mr. Adler; and since these are exhaustive of all possible ways, in his view, the existence of God is altogether indemonstrable according to his position.

As we have said, this has been shown already; for the whole demonstration depends, as the author admits, on the proposition that God is the unique cause of the preservation of being in things, and this has been shown to be false, both according to St. Thomas's teaching and demonstratively. But for the sake of completeness we shall adduce the supposed demonstration, refuting it, as we said, by manifesting further its impossibility.

Mr. Adler—Fourth Argument, Second Part, III, pp. 209, 210.

Mr. Adler states this argument in two ways. The first way is as follows:

If anything exists whose continuation in existence requires the operation of an efficient cause at this very moment, then a being exists whose existence is uncaused. But corporeal substances do exist. Therefore, etc.

In its second form, which, in Mr. Adler's opinion, is equivalent to the first, the argument reads:

The existence of a contingent being implies the existence of a necessary being. But a contingent being exists. Therefore, etc.

The minor of both forms is evident from experience, and is universally admitted. The major is supported by the previous proof (Part One of the Fourth Argument) wherein Mr. Adler attempted to establish that God was the unique cause of preservation in being of other things.

REFUTATION

1. The major presupposes the truth of the proposition that God is the unique cause of the preservation of things. But this has been demonstrated to be false (refutation of the First Part of Mr. Adler's Fourth Argument). Therefore the major is false, and the demonstration is impossible.

2. Again, against the major: no proposition of the form, A implies B, or if A then B, when A and B are in the real order, can be self-evident formally. This follows from the nature of a self-evident proposition; for a proposition is self-evident when there is no middle term necessary or possible to manifest the material identity of subject and predicate. But in a proposition of logical form, such as the major of the above proof, the illation being logical, a self-evident proposition would require the subject and predicate to be in the logical order; as it is self-evident that the differentia is predicable of the species which it differentiates. But when A and B are in the real order, as in the present case, the proposition cannot be self-evident formally, inasmuch as it would have to be shown, and understood, that the real being fell under the logical formality required by the logical nature of the proposition; and this would require a middle term; as risible implies rational because risible is a property of rational, and the property necessarily implies the subject of which it is the property; and likewise for the differentia or any predicable necessarily predicated of a subject.

If the major in Mr. Adler's supposed demonstration, then, is true and materially self-evident, as he must think possible (for otherwise it would be meaningless to suggest it as a demonstration), it is not in virtue of the logical relation, but because of the real material identity of the terms, i.e., that the very notion of contingent existence contains the idea of dependence in being on an existent which is absolutely necessary. But this is patently false in respect to the human idea of contingency as such; otherwise God would enter into the definition of every created thing, which is not only contrary to the authority of St. Thomas, and known to be false from experience, but is contrary to reason. For this would imply that that which is furthest removed from the sensible order is known first by abstraction from sense; or again, that that which is most intelligible in itself is most intelligible to us.

But in fact, just as the existence of God is self-evident in that Knowledge of God which is God's and is God, but not in our knowledge of what we mean by the term, God (before we know that He exists), so, in God's knowledge of contingent things, contingent things depend for their being on the necessary Being which is God; but this cannot be known in our knowledge of contingent being as such.

The major of Mr. Adler's intended demonstration, therefore, cannot be self-evident; for self-evidence is understood according to the objective relation between the terms of a proposition as they are known according to their proper formality, and the immediate relation between "contingent" and "dependence on a necessary being" is not verified for these terms as they are adequately and formally known to us. Nevertheless, in fact there is a necessary connection between these terms, inasmuch as God necessarily exists and everything else necessarily depends on Him for its existence. But this necessity is in fact, and is known as a conclusion, not as a principle of demonstration, i.e., when God is known to exist, it is known that everything else depends on Him for existence.

3. Again, against the major, if contingent being implied a necessary being who is God, far from having to demonstrate the existence of God, that would be self-evident; but it would be necessary to demonstrate the existence of everything else, i.e., contingent beings.

Mr. Adler—Fourth Argument, Third Part, III, #3, pp. 212–16

In the third and last part of the Fourth Argument Mr. Adler raises doubts concerning the demonstration he has proposed and which he considers the only possible one. This section is divided into two parts, in the first of which he raises doubts concerning the major premise of the demonstration; in the second, assuming that the major is either self-evident or demonstrable, he questions whether the necessary being demonstrated to exist is God. He attacks the self-evidence of his major in two ways: first by showing the difficulties attending the manifestation of the immediate relation between the terms; second by showing the difficulties which arise when one attempts to prove its self-evidence by proving that it can *only* be argued through *reductio ad absurdum,* taking this as a property of a self-evident proposition. In the second part he raises doubts concerning the nature of the being whose existence is hypothetically assumed to be demonstrated, namely, that if it is God, it must be known to be one only, and to have no composition of potency and act, no composition of matter and form, no composition of subject and accident.

REFUTATION

Inasmuch as Mr. Adler's proposed demonstration has been shown to be impossible, it will not be necessary to defend it against the doubts which its author raises against it. However, for the purpose of clarifying the question generally, it may prove useful to manifest a few of the more important errors in this section. To facilitate following this part of the argument, we shall order the doubts Mr. Adler raises concerning his demonstration in outline form:

I. Is the major of the demonstration self-evident?

    a. Do the terms manifest their immediate relation?

    b. Does the method of proving the self-evidence by proving that it can only be argued through *reductio ad absurdum,* defend its self-evidence?

II. Assuming the major to be self-evident or demonstrable, does the demonstration demonstrate the existence of God, or only the existence of a necessary being, whose essence is its existence?

We may now answer the difficulties raised by Mr. Adler in order.

    I.a. Mr. Adler sees that, for his major to be self-evident, the term, contingent, would have to mean: *needing a cause for its existence,* and *unable to cause the existence of another.* Likewise, the term, necessary being, would have to mean: *having no cause for its existence,* and *causing the existence of contingent being* (III, #3, b, pp. 212, 213). He is entirely right in raising this difficulty, for reasons which have been adduced in the refutation of the previous part of this argument; for the proposition is not self-evident. But he fails to conclude, properly, that this proposition *cannot* be self-evident, since the formal meaning of these terms cannot include these notes.

    I.b. Here Mr. Adler attempts to demonstrate the self-evidence of his major in order to raise difficulties with that proof. But it seems apparent that the self-evidence of a proposition cannot be demonstrated, and Mr. Adler in no way explains how this can be done. He seems to employ the major: A proposition which can he proved *only* through *reductio*, is self-evident. That is true enough as a judgment; but how is one to know that it cannot be proved directly, except by an infinite number of attempted direct proofs, all of which are shown to be invalid? But this is manifestly impossible.

Mr. Adler's method of establishing this step is clearly fallacious. It is needless to repeat the arguments by which he attempts to establish that it cannot be proved directly. If the occasion should arise, any number of objections could be raised to his procedure here; but the matter is not important enough to warrant close analysis. Let it suffice to state that, when he attempts to prove the major by *reductio,* he does not prove it at all. What he does prove is the principle presupposed by his demonstration, which he attempted to establish in the second part of the fourth argument. For the major of the demonstration reads: The existence of a contingent being implies the existence of a necessary being. Therefore the contradictory of this, from which a *reductio* should properly proceed, should read: the existence of a contingent being does not imply the existence of a necessary being. Instead of this, Mr. Adler begins: A contingent being can efficiently cause the existence of another being, which is the contradictory of: The cause of existence in a contingent being is the proper effect of God, i.e., the contradictory of the principle presupposed in the demonstration proper. From here on, consequently, the doubts which Mr. Adler raises are unintelligible.

II. Here Mr. Adler attempts to show that, even assuming the validity of his demonstration, the existence of *God* is not necessarily demonstrated. But this difficulty proceeds from a misconception of what a demonstration is intended to demonstrate. In Mr. Adler's view, ostensibly, a demonstration of God's existence must demonstrate all of God's attributes. By the same reasoning, Euclid, in demonstrating the existence of an equilateral triangle, failed because he did not demonstrate at the same time all the properties of the triangle. Mr. Adler complains that he knows no place where it is demonstrated that this necessary being has no composition of potency and act, of matter and form, of subject and accident. This is founded indeed, if the demonstrations of God's existence are rejected as he rejects them. But when they are understood and pre-supposed, the requisite demonstration of the other negative attributes can be derived from them as principles.

Thus St. Thomas demonstrates that there is no composition of potency and act in the Being demonstrated to exist, i.e., in the Being which he, and, as he says, all men, understand to be God,[18] that there is no composition of matter and form,[19] that there is no composition of subject and accident.[20]

*   *   *   *   *

In conclusion we may say, then, that, far from attacking the demonstrations of St. Thomas, Mr. Adler has only shown his inability to understand them thus far. His difficulties are in fact his own and not those of the Angelic Doctor. For the "possibilities" he has considered, both in the order of becoming and in the order of being, are in fact impossible ways, and not at all supposed by St. Thomas or his commentators.

In fact, if not in Mr. Adler's mind, the demonstration of God is impossible as he conceives it, and, I am afraid, that is the effect his words would have on an undisciplined reader. For he appears convinced that he has exhausted all possible ways of demonstration, and he ends with grave doubts concerning the one way which seemed possible to him. But what he has shown, really, is that the existence of God cannot be demonstrated from any connection of causes in the univocal order, i.e., as things temporally or simultaneously related in the order of becoming, employing here a logically univocal notion of *causa efficiens fiendi* (his first three arguments), or in the order of being, employing here a logically univocal notion of *causa efficiens essendi* (his fourth argument). His search has been for a causal relation which is univocally distinct as it is verified in God, and not analogically common; and this is impossible *qua* univocally distinct, i.e., as found in God but not found in any way in the creature.

In this he manifests a failure to grasp the concept of order, not as it is in St. Thomas merely, but as it is in the universe. For that order is realized in an assimilation of the creature to God. Therefore it is precisely as cause, taken indifferently, or efficient cause, taken in this way, that God is not unique. His uniqueness is as a first and most universal cause. But He is unique, and utterly diverse from the creature in His Incommunicable Nature which is known only to Himself, to the blessed, and in the darkness of Faith to those who believe what He has revealed of Himself as He is, the Blessed Trinity of Three Persons in One Divine Nature.

In the last part of his essay Mr. Adler asks, as one of "those gentiles in the modern world who desire natural wisdom," for instruction, "if my dis-

---

[18] *S.T.*, I, q. 2, a. 3.

[19] *Ibid.*, q. 3, a. 2

[20] *Ibid.*, a. 6.

course rests upon any erroneous dismissal of traditionally accepted arguments." I have tried sincerely, and not without a measure of painstaking effort, to understand his difficulties and to clarify the essential points of the doctrine in relation to them, having in view not only the defense of traditional teaching but also the obligation to manifest these preambles to the Faith for those who might be denied that most precious of all gifts through a misunderstanding of truths accessible to the natural light of reason. Neither do I ignore the great service Mr. Adler has done the Church by rousing her servants, the theologians, to a greater awareness of their shortcomings in relation to the perennial truths which it is their vocation to defend, and to look for means they had hitherto neglected to bring the power of Christ's doctrine to bear on the difficulties of our times.

For these reasons, it does not seem unfitting to suggest that it is not enough to "desire natural wisdom" after Christ. For history has shown abundantly that "He that hath, to him shall be given, and he shall abound: but he that hath not, from him shall be taken away that also which he hath." It would be misleading therefore, in the name of Christ, to impart instruction in natural wisdom, except as it leads to the Faith. But, for that, the principal means is not study. For we are exhorted to "seek first the kingdom of heaven, and everything else shall be given to you." The firm conviction in the existence of God, which Mr. Adler protests at the beginning of his essay, is surely sufficient foundation to pray to that God for the light to know His true Faith. By that Faith we know that such a prayer must be answered, albeit in God's own good time. And, by the teaching of Christ and His saints, we know that a certain interior quiet is necessary to hear the answer, such quiet as is not secured by the intense pursuit of natural wisdom. Therefore, by any instruction requiring undue activity of reason, we should only lead one seeking the truth more and more astray, confirming him in the erroneous conviction that the path of reason alone is pleasing to God. In this we do him a grave injustice, and more harm to ourselves.

This counsel, indeed, is not irrelevant to the plea for instruction in natural wisdom. For the Faith proves itself by its works: the quest of truth is a human act, and subject, therefore, to the movement of the passions, the more so because the good at stake is a greater good. Without that detachment and tranquility in relation to created truth, therefore, which the Faith alone assures when it is properly cultivated, it is most unlikely that men will be able to free themselves of that subjectivity which foredooms philosophical inquiry to failure; particularly inasmuch as the truths of philosophy bear most directly on the human appetite.

If, then, a man would have natural wisdom, he must bear with the generosity of God, who will only give more than natural wisdom, and with His Justice, for, if He is rejected, He will not give even what is natural.

In conclusion, by way of pointing out a confusion which, I think, is a source of much of Mr. Adler's difficulty, I would suggest that he consider the following passages from St. Thomas's commentary on the *De Trinitate* of Boethius:

> Nevertheless it should be known that, since that material something whence the genus is taken, contains in itself both form and matter, the logician considers the genus only on the part of that which is formal in it, whence his definitions are called formal, but the natural philosopher considers the genus on the part of both (the form and the matter). And therefore it sometimes happens that some things communicate in a genus according to the logician, which do not communicate according to the natural philosopher. For it sometimes happens, with respect to the similitude of first act, that that which a thing attains when it is in *such* matter, another thing attains without matter, still another attains it when it is in matter altogether diverse. E.g., it is evident that stone in matter which is (matter) according to the potency to existence, tends *(pertingit)* to this, that it should subsist, to which same thing the sun tends according to the matter which is potency to place, but not to existence, and (likewise) the angel lacking all matter. Whence the logician, finding in all these that from which the genus was taken, posits all these to be in one genus of substance. But the natural philosopher and the metaphysician, who consider the principles of things, finding that they do not all convene in matter, say that they differ in genus, according to that which is said in the tenth book of the *Metaphysics,* that the corruptible and the incorruptible differ in genus, and that those things convene in genus of which the matter is one and which are generated one from the other.[21]

> And although, logically considered, they (immaterial substances) convene with these sensible things in the remote genus which is substance, nevertheless, naturally speaking, they do not convene in the same genus, just as neither do the heavenly bodies with the inferior (bodies). For the corporeal and the incorporeal are not of the same genus, as is said in the tenth book of the *Metaphysics.* For the logician considers intentions absolutely, according to which nothing prevents material things convening to immaterial things, and incorruptible to corruptible. But the natural philosopher and the first philosopher consider essences according as they have being in things, and therefore where they find a diverse mode of potency and act, and through this a diverse mode of being, they say that the things are diverse in genus.[22]

[21] *In Boeth. De Trinitate,* q. 4, a. 2, corpus.
[22] *Ibid.,* q. 4, a. 3, corpus.

10 A New Approach to God's Existence

MORTIMER J. ADLER

PREFATORY NOTE

In the Maritain volume of *The Thomist* (Vol. V, January, 1943), I published an article concerning the demonstration of God's existence. The circumstances required a condensation and brevity which prevented the exposition of the argument from being analytically adequate and which did not permit extensive examination of the relevant texts in Aristotle and St. Thomas.

Since the publication of the article, I have been engaged in fairly lengthy correspondence with a number of persons seriously interested in the questions raised. For the most part, my correspondents have agreed that a precise and adequate statement of the proof for God's existence is an intellectual task yet to be accomplished. They are of various opinions concerning the significance or validity of the "five ways" proposed by St. Thomas. They locate the critical issues at different points. Some have defended St. Thomas against what they took to be my attack, and some, quite apart from St. Thomas, have attacked the proof I proposed. But with few exceptions all seem to concur in the view that the problem is far from solved.

In the course of this correspondence, I have learned how to state my own position more effectively, how to amplify my analysis, how to argue for or explain points which, at first, I thought were obvious. I can summarize the total effect of all this discussion, so far as I am concerned, by saying: first, that I am more certain now than before that there can be no proof of God's existence from *motion* as the known effect; and second, that I now see better than before how to expound and argue a valid proof for God's existence from *being* as the known effect. The primary problems for me are now, and have always been, whether these two things are true, and *not* what effect their truth has upon the problem of interpreting St. Thomas's writings. There is no point in even raising the scholarly question, until the philosophical questions have been resolved.

As I review the original article in the light of subsequent discussion and thought, I find that it was quite sound negatively, but both incomplete and in error positively. The original article did give, in outline at least, a correct indication of the arguments against proofs from motion. But the analysis of motion and

163

of the causes of motion was too brief and insufficiently explicit. That is one of the defects I hope to remedy in the present article. On the positive side, the original article confessed its inadequacy. It outlined a possible proof of God as *causa essendi*, but it failed to establish this proof by a verification of the premises. I now see what errors prevented me from completing the task I had undertaken. The basic error was a radically incomplete statement of the premises. Once I was able to state explicitly all the premises on which the conclusion 'God exists' depends for its *a posteriori* demonstration, I was able to verify these premises either as self-evident or demonstrable; and where the premises are demonstrable I think I can offer demonstrations. I have outlined this revised and perfected proof of God's existence and circulated it among a few of my correspondents. They have raised some further objections and difficulties, but I think I can defend the proof against all of these.

I should add one more thing. Since the publication of the Maritain volume, there have been a number of reviews which commented on my article. I have in mind one by Dr. Otto Bird in *The Commonweal* (March 12th, 1943), one by Dr. James V. Mullaney in *The New Scholasticism* (XVII, 2, April, 1943), and one by Dr. Herbert Schwartz in *The Thomist* (VI, 1, April, 1943). Of these, only the last is an extensive critique of my article. Unlike the other reviews, and unlike the criticisms offered by my correspondents, the Schwartz critique aims to show that my original paper is wrong in every particular. I have studied it carefully and I think that I can show that it almost fails as criticism, even though in many particulars it is right and argues for points or principles with which I thoroughly agree, and which I had in mind in writing the article under consideration.

With all these things in mind, I have undertaken the drafting of a second article on the demonstration of God's existence. In the course of this paper, I shall try to do the following things.

1. I shall expand the analysis of motion and of the causes of motion on which the negative argument of my original paper (its Part II, points #1–6) rested. This will provide a more adequate showing that there can be no proof of God as *causa fiendi*.

2. I shall present a more precise and explicit formulation of the proof of God as *causa essendi*, correcting the errors in my original formulation and verifying all the premises involved in the demonstration.

3. In the course of doing both of the foregoing things, I shall have in mind all the points raised by my correspondents. I hope that the difficulties they have raised will be resolved by the present essay. In addition, I shall deal explicitly and at some length with the Schwartz critique, showing point by point why and wherein it fails to establish its adverse judgments. I do this, not because the Schwartz critique by itself deserves so much attention, but because I am aware that in contemporary scholastic circles Schwartz reflects many persons both in turn and tenor of mind and also in the specific misunderstandings and errors so plainly exhibited by his thinking.

4. Finally, I shall defend the proof against the difficulties or objections raised by those of my correspondents who have seen provisional and incomplete outlines of it.

This present memorandum is only a rough draft of the article to be written. I do not wish to publish the second article until I have done what I can to get a careful and critical reading of the analyses and arguments presented in this memorandum. It is with that in mind that I have had these pages mimeographed, so that they could be circulated among persons competent to make the critical judgments and to give me the help I need in the fulfillment of this undertaking. I shall not attempt to write a final draft of the article, and certainly not to publish it, until I am reasonably sure that I have received and considered whatever can be said about this memorandum, whether that be a point of adverse criticism or a point of positive elaboration. I ask my readers to remember that this is a *rough* draft, and not a finished piece of writing; that it is submitted to them in order to solicit their help in what seems to me the most important, as well as the most difficult, task a modern philosopher faces. I shall appreciate, therefore, any suggestions they may have for greater refinement or precision of statement, or indications of where analysis needs to be amplified, or comments on errors of facts or fallacies in reasoning. In every case, I hope that my correspondents will do more than merely state their critical point, whether adverse or amplifying. I hope they will give reasons as fully as they know how; and though they may be inclined to cite the authority of Aristotle or St. Thomas, I hope they will not rest with such citations, but will also try to argue the case independently.

I shall be grateful for any comments which the recipients of this memorandum may feel impelled to send me—whether they deal with this essay as a whole, or merely discuss this or that part of it. I shall also be grateful to them if they will pass this memorandum on to other persons who may be interested in the problem and who may contribute to this cooperative venture. If they know of anyone to whom a copy of this memorandum should be sent and advise me of that, I will try to provide copies as long as the supply lasts.

It is with pleasure that I take this opportunity to make explicit acknowledgment of my gratitude to the following persons, for their patience and understanding, for their time and effort, in carrying on the discussion of the problem in conversation or by correspondence: A.C. Pegis, Fr. Gerard Smith, William O'Meara, Fr. Ernest Kilzer, William Bryar, Brother Theodore, Jacques Maritain, James L. Hagerty, Fr. Robert Slavin, Herman Bernick, Fr. R.J. Belleperche, Paul Weiss, Scott Buchanan, William Gorman, Fr. Richard Mignault, Leo Camp, Fr. Roger Maltais, Fr. George Thompson, Jacob Klein.

MORTIMER J. ADLER
University of Chicago June 1st, 1943

I. *Introduction*

1. The motion of the original paper was as follows:
    a. To show that there is no valid argument for God's existence which
        proceeds from a *particular motion* as an effect to God as the first mover
        of every natural motion, or as the first efficient cause of every natural
        motion, or as the highest principal cause of every natural motion. Two
        things should be noted here:
        (1) The arguments under consideration must start from some par-
             ticular natural motion which is an actual effect immediately
             known. The first step in any *a posteriori* argument is the existence
             of the effect. And the arguments must proceed from this known
             effect to God as a cause, through steps in which every cause men-
             tioned is a cause of *motion*, and not a cause of *existence*, as for
             example, the existence of mobile and moving substances. The
             traditional arguments being criticized at no point shift from
             causes of motion to causes of existence (i.e., from *causa fiendi* to
             causa essendi). If they did, they would all become rhetorical vari-
             ants of the one possible proof, which is of God as *causa essendi*.
        (2) The criticism of these arguments does not fail to take account of
             the fact that if God is a cause of natural motions, He is not a cause
             in the same sense as natural agents are. If God is the cause, or one
             of the causes, of any particular natural motion, He is the cause, or
             one of the causes, of every particular natural motion. This cannot
             be said of any natural agent which is limited in its causality, its effi-
             ciency extending only to the production of certain effects. Using
             the traditional language, which is bad on many counts, I would say
             that the words "*causa fiendi*" said of God and of any natural agent
             are said analogically, not univocally or equivocally. There are
             many ways in which the word "cause" is said analogically—of an
             efficient and a material cause, for example, or in the phrases
             "*causa fiendi*" and "*causa essendi*"; and even of two efficient causes,
             both of which are *causa fiendi*, such as God and a natural agent, if
             their modes of causation (without and with motion) are radically
             diverse. An unmoving efficient cause of motion does not cause *in
             the same sense* as a moving efficient cause of motion. Furthermore,
             it should be observed that this point about the analogical signifi-
             cance of the word "cause" is quite independent of the traditional
             distinction between univocal, equivocal and analogical causes, for
             that depends not upon a comparison of two causes as such, but
             upon a consideration of the nature of the cause and the nature of
             the effect: when the cause and the effect are the *same* in specific
             or generic nature, the cause is said to be a "univocal" cause; when
             the cause and the effect are *only analogically the same*, the cause is
             said to be an "analogical" cause; when the cause and the effect are
             simply diverse, the cause is said to be an "equivocal" cause.

Whether there are any equivocal causes, as it is sometimes supposed, makes no difference, because for the purposes of this discussion it is only necessary to admit that if God is a cause of motion, He is not a univocal cause, by comparison with the effect produced.

b. To show that a valid argument for God's existence as *causa essendi* is possible, to outline this argument, and to consider the difficulties which must be overcome before the proof becomes tenable against all objections. Here two things should be observed:

(1) As already observed, the notion of 'cause' and of 'causation' is not the same when one deals with causes of motion and causes of existence. Furthermore, either there is only one *causa essendi* or there are many. If there are many, of which God is one and natural agents are all the rest, then "*causa essendi*" is said analogically of God and natural agents, just as "*causa fiendi*" is said analogically of God and natural agents.

(2) Even if there should be some sense or senses in which natural agents can be regarded as '*causa essendi*,' the question remains whether God as *causa essendi* operates through natural agents as intermediary causes of existence. In this connection, I used the words "proper effect" to mean an effect produced by a single cause, causing directly or without intermediaries. I am now aware of rhetorical difficulties about such a use of words, since these words have many other meanings. But the difficulties are only rhetorical. The philosophical question remains: whether, if existence is efficiently caused by God, the causation is direct and immediate. If it is, the fact that the existence of a substance is the unmediated *material* cause of the existence of its accidents, would not be incompatible. I shall, as I proceed, try to clarify the vocabulary which I employed, to make sure that there can be no misunderstanding of what is meant by the statement that "being is the *proper effect* of God." It should be noted that it is never said that "motion is the *proper effect* of God"—though obviously if God is the cause of motion, He is the cause of every motion, just as He is the cause of every participated existence. In other words, it is not the "universality" of God's causal power, extending to every effect, whether in the order of being or becoming, which is involved in speaking of being, rather than motion, as God's proper effect.

2. It is necessary to explain how the authority of St. Thomas was used in the first paper, and how the authority of Aristotle will be used in this one.

a. In no case did I or will I base any conclusion, which I myself assert, on the authority of anybody. No human authority can support an argument and make it demonstrative. In quoting either St. Thomas or Aristotle *with approval* at any point, I always intend that the matter quoted be regarded as a proposition or propositions that I would affirm independently of their authority, either as self-evident or demonstrable. The fact that I sometimes quote them with approval, and sometimes reject what they say, has no bearing, since their authority is never logically a factor in the argument. It follows, therefore, that no one can answer my arguments by quoting the authority of St. Thomas or Aristotle to the contrary, unless they will go further and attest the propositions quoted.

b. The only reasons for mentioning St. Thomas and Aristotle are rhetorical, and here primarily to connect my own work with the tradition. This, it seems to me, is justified in that the fundamental philosophical principles on which my own arguments rest *happen* to be philosophical principles traditionally accepted and expounded. This permits some abbreviation of exposition on my part; I do not need to prove every proposition that I advance, in so far as the audience for whom I am writing know or can learn the proofs for these propositions from traditional sources. But where I appear to reject a traditional position, the defender of the tradition on this point is obligated to do more than cite the authorities. He must actually argue for the position he wishes to defend.

c. In the original paper, moreover, I cited a series of passages from St. Thomas which bear on the proposition "being is the proper effect of God." I did this not because that proposition is proved by St. Thomas. I cited these texts merely to indicate to the reader how St. Thomas helped me to discover the one possible proof of God's existence. Hence whether or not the text of S.T., I, 104, 2 does or does not contradict, apparently or really, other passages in the *Summa* has no logical relevance at all. The interpretation of texts has a bearing only on what one thinks about St. Thomas, not upon the truth. Against those who do nothing but argue from the authority of St. Thomas, the citation of contrary texts is dialectical procedure which obliges them to defend, not the truth, but the authority of St. Thomas as used in their own weak arguments.

d. My citation of passages from Aristotle's *Physics* and *Metaphysics* in this article is not argument from authority. The citation here has another rhetorical purpose, namely, to show discrepancies between Aristotle's and St. Thomas's account of causes and causation. Also the citation is for the sake of brevity. The proofs for the propositions cited are to be found in Aristotle. The proofs, not Aristotle's authority, are my basis for holding these propositions. Where I depart from or reject anything that Aristotle said, as I shall do, I will argue independently for the position I have taken.

3. I shall proceed here in the following order, the Roman numerals indicating the subsequent parts of this discussion:

> In II: I shall set forth some observations about motion and its causes and about *a posteriori* proof, that will be more extensive analytically than the too brief discussion of these matters in the original paper.

In III: I shall restate the negative arguments of my original paper (against all proofs from motion), and comment on Schwartz's misunderstandings, confusions, and irrelevancies.

In IV: I shall develop the positive argument for God's existence as *causa essendi*, and here I will comment on Schwartz's failures, which are similar in kind, though greater in degree.

II. *Analysis of the Causes of Natural Motions*

1. In *Physics*, II, 3 and *Metaphysics*, V, 2, Aristotle sets forth his analysis of the causes of a motion. This analysis has two main parts: (a) a distinction of the causes in type, according to the relation each bears to the effect, the motion caused; and (b) a consideration of the modes of causation.
   a. The fourfold distinction of causes in type need not be discussed here. We are primarily concerned with the efficient cause, for this is the only cause that must be extrinsic to, rather than immanent in, the motion caused. Apart from the voluntary motions of men, in which an end for the motion lies beyond the term of the motion itself, the term of a natural motion is, in different aspects, both the formal and the final cause of the motion. The material and the formal (or final) cause of a motion are *in* the thing moved, according to the definition of motion as the act of that which is in potency in the respect in which it is potency—the formal cause being the act, the material cause the potency, mentioned. But the efficient cause is itself a motion, not simply the immanent principle of a motion, its constitutive act or potency; and, therefore, it must be the motion of a subject distinct from the subject whose motion is efficiently caused. Aristotle's examples here verify this: the man who gave advice, or the builder who makes, or the father who procreates, are mentioned as efficient causes; and generally the efficient cause is described as "what makes of what is made and what causes change of what is changed" (*Physics*, II, 3, 194b30-31). Efficient causation thus always involves the correlation of agent and patient, mover and moved. I shall return to this point and discuss it in the light of what is said about motions in *Physics*, III, 3.
   b. The distinction among modes of causation involves two points: what Aristotle calls "incidental" vs. "proper" causes, and what Aristotle calls "potential" vs. "actual" causes. I shall show presently that these distinctions apply only to one of the four causes, i.e., the efficient cause; or, at least, primarily to this one. In any case, we need consider these distinctions only in the sphere of efficient causation.
   c. In addition to the foregoing, Aristotle gives certain rules for accurate speech about causes. If the cause is named generically or specifically,

the effect must be similarly named; if the cause is named individually, the effect must be similarly named. Thus, the artist is generic cause of any work of art as generic effect; the sculptor, a specific artist, is cause of the specific effect, a statue; and this individual sculptor is the individual cause of this individual effect, this statue. Generic and specific causes or effects do not exist, any more than genera and species of substance do. Only individuals exist, apart from the order of understanding. Though a cause can be *understood* specifically or generically, it must be the cause of *this particular* motion, as effect, and so as operative in any way, it must be an individual or particular cause. What Aristotle means by "generic causes" must, therefore, not be confused with what a later tradition meant by a "universal cause"—a cause for many different particular effects. If one act by one existent agent could cause the particular effects (the motions) A, B, C, D, etc., that act would be a "universal cause" in this sense, and it would be an individual, rather than a generic, cause in Aristotle's sense. A universal cause, in short, is *one* cause for *many* particular effects.

d. All of the foregoing must be qualified by the distinction between incidental and proper causes, and between potential and actual causes, to which we must now pay attention.

2. INCIDENTAL VS. PROPER EFFICIENT CAUSES

a. The translators of Aristotle sometimes use the word "accidental" instead of "incidental" and sometimes what is called "proper" in English is also translated "*per se*" or "essential." These linguistic variations must not be permitted to obscure the analytic point involved. There is only one distinction here, however it is named. Let us first examine the distinction, and then see how it should be named—in one way for purposes of clarity.

b. The distinction rests upon the distinction between essential and accidental unities. The word "man" or the phrase "rational animal" names an essential unity; the word "aryan" or "musician" and the phrase "white man" or "musical man" names an accidental unity. Furthermore, the "white musical" names an accidental unity, the coincidence of accidents in a single subject. The proper name "Polyclitus" names an accidental unity insofar as it signifies an individual in whom a specific nature (man) is conjoined with individual accidents (white, musical, sculptor, etc.)

c. Now let the effect be the coming to be of a statue. It is not Polyclitus *qua man* or *qua living creature* or *qua white* or *qua musical*, but *qua sculptor*, that must be *named* as the proper cause. Any of the other modes of speech signifies something that is accidental to the effect, by coincidence with that which is proper to the effect.... If, however, the effect were the coming to be of a man, it would not be Polyclitus *qua* sculptor, but Polyclitus *qua* this individual man, which should be properly named as the cause.

d. In short, taken as a rule of naming, the distinction between "proper" and "incidental" comes to this: to name an efficient cause *properly*, we must indicate that in virtue of which the effect is produced; if we indicate only that which has some accidental connection with that in virtue of which the effect is produced, we name an efficient cause *incidentally* or *accidentally*. Or, as Aristotle points out, we can speak of the accidental and the proper causes in combination: "we may say not 'Polyclitus' nor 'the sculptor' but 'Polyclitus the sculptor' "(*Physics*, II, 3, 195b12).

e. This distinction is very much like Aristotle's distinction between the proper and the incidental or accidental sensible. Thus, *white* is a proper sensible, but *white man*, or *the white man, Corsicus*, is only an incidental object of the proper senses. Why is this so? Because it is not the eye as eye which sees a white *man*, or *Corsicus*, who happens to be white. So far as the proper functioning of vision is concerned, that the white happens to be a man or a horse is accidental. Substances, in short, are only accidental objects of the proper senses; only visible, audible, tangible, etc. qualities, which are accidents, are non-accidental objects. Hence we see that the distinction between substance and accident does not control the distinction between the accidental and the proper object of a sense; nor does it control the distinction between an accidental and a proper cause of an effect.

f. Before we can go further in understanding the significance of this distinction, it is necessary to consider the other distinction—between actual and potential causes.

3. ACTUAL AND POTENTIAL CAUSES

a. Aristotle's point here simply is that the actual cause of a house being built is a builder actually building; the potential cause is the man's power of building, which makes him a builder (having the art, capable of building) even when he is not actually building. But the potential cause cannot be the cause of an actual effect, but only of a potential effect. 'Powers are relative to potential effects; actually operating causes to motions actually being effected" (*Physics*, II, 3, 195b27). Cf. *Metaphysics*, V, 2, where it is said: "some are called causes as being able to act, others as acting, e.g., the cause of the house being built is a builder, or a builder who is building." Here it seems to be suggested that the potential cause can be stated in relation to an actual effect.

b. This last point is connected with an important fact about the simultaneity of cause and effect. Actual cause and actual effect must be simultaneous, either wholly, as in the case of the building of the house (wherein the house is being built or in process of actually building only while the builder is actually building it) or partly, as in the case of local motion (wherein one billiard ball which actually moves another and that other may both be actually in motion for some time but not for the whole time of their respective motions).

c. To cover the facts indicated, let us distinguish between the correlative and the residual effect: the correlative effect being that motion which is simultaneous with the actual motion of the cause; the residual effect being that part of the same continuous motion which occurs after the motion of the cause has ceased. Every actual cause must have a correlative actual effect, whether or not it also has a residual actual effect.

d. Now, strictly speaking, only the actual cause of a motion is its efficient cause, for if an efficient cause is that by which an actual motion is produced, a potential cause is not efficient. This is proved by the fact that the potential cause can exist without the effect occurring, just as the residual actual effect can exist without the actual cause of the motion existing simultaneously. This, however, does not mean that the potential cause is not a cause; it is simply not an efficient cause of a given effect. How is it related to the effect? Since the power (i.e., the art) of building is prior to the act of building, and since the act of building on the part of the builder is an act of this power, the power of building, which is a potential cause of the house being actually built, is also a material cause of the act of building which is the efficient cause of the house being built. Now a cause of a cause is remotely, not proximately, the cause of the latter's actual effect. It is necessary to consider proximate and remote causes in order to understand what is involved in Aristotle's distinction between incidental and proper causes, potential and actual causes.

4. PROXIMATE AND REMOTE CAUSES

a. We see two things at once: an incidental cause cannot be regarded as either the actual or potential cause of an effect, and a potential cause cannot be, in a strict sense, the proper cause of an effect.

(1) Let us now narrow the meaning of "proper" down to this: that cause is proper which cannot exist or occur without the effect also existing or occurring. It has contact with the effect in a sense to be more precisely defined in a moment. This contact may be direct or mediated, but if mediated, the main point remains true, namely, that a proper cause is one which is correlative to the effect. It is, therefore, always an actual cause. If the effect is a motion, the proper cause must be an actual motion correlated with the effect as agent with patient.

(2) The meaning of "incidental" cause then becomes that which can exist or occur without the effect occurring. Thus, this man can

exist, can be white, can be a builder (have the power or art), without this house being in the process of building. In this sense, and in this sense only, such causes are incidental to the effect. But this does not mean that all incidental causes are dispensable. On the contrary, some are and some are not. But a cause which is dispensable in the sense that the effect could occur entirely apart from it is not a cause at all. In this sense, the fact that Polyclitus is white is an accidental cause of his building the house, but the fact that he is a man is not; for if he were not a man, who would not have an intellect, and if he did not have an intellect, he could not acquire an art, the act of which is the building of this house, which is the actual and proper cause of this house being built.

(3) We see, therefore, that Aristotle's discussion of proper and incidental causes is quite inadequate for the account of the total causal nexus upon which any effect depends. It provides us only with a distinction between what does and does not belong to the total causal nexus; but it does not provide us with the important distinctions we need for the ordering of a plurality of causes all of which are required for the effect, though not in the same way.

b. In dealing with a plurality of causes, we must distinguish first between those causes which *require the effect*, and those causes which *the effect requires*.

(1) By "causes requiring the effect" I mean causes which are correlative with the effect in the sense of a simultaneous actuality of agent and patient, mover and moved, cause and effect. In this sense, the motion of one thing is not called a cause except in so far as it actually produces an actual effect. The motion may preexist the effect, but as such it is not a cause; the effected motion may post-exist the cause, but as such it is not an actual effect, but a residue, or residual effect. Only in the strict correlation of simultaneous action and passion, do we have actual cause and effect. I shall call such actual causes which require their effects "*proximate causes*." The definition of a proximate cause is that which cannot occur without the effect also occurring. I shall postpone for the moment further analysis of a plurality of proximate causes for a given effect.

NOTE: I shall use the phrase "*cause per se*" for any proximate cause, meaning thereby that it is cause *through itself* and that it is directly correlative with its effect.

(2) By "causes required by the effect" I mean to include, in addition to "causes requiring the effect" for these also are required by the effect, causes which *do not require* the effect but are *only required* by it. What Aristotle called a "potential" cause is such a cause, for it does not require the effect, yet it is required by it; some of the things Aristotle called "incidental" causes are also required by the effect, though they do not require it.

(a) That which neither requires nor is required by the effect is not a cause, except in an accidental sense of the word. Instead of calling such causes "accidental causes," I shall simply not refer to them at all, for they are not causes in any sense.

(b) The meaning of "cause" which dictates this determination is the meaning common to every proper sense of the word, namely, *that without which*, a *sine qua non* condition. We see at once two degrees of "that without which"—(1) that without which no effect occurs and with which it does; (2) that without which no effect occurs, but with which it does not. This is the familiar distinction between conditions which are both necessary and sufficient (1) and conditions which are merely necessary and not sufficient (2). What I have called "proximate" causes or causes "*per se*" are both necessary and sufficient conditions for an effect. What are merely necessary but not sufficient conditions for an effect I shall now call "remote" causes or causes "*per aliud.*"

NOTE: In using "*per aliud*" rather than "*per accidens*" as the opposite of "*per se*," I avoid the confusion attendant on the two meanings of "accidental cause—in one of which a condition is named that is neither necessary nor sufficient. Furthermore, the phrase "*per aliud*" signifies that a cause is remote, i.e., is separated from its effect by intermediaries, some but not all of which must be proximate to the effect. Hence a cause *per aliud* is not correlative with an effect, as agent to patient, even when it is an efficient cause. Every efficient cause must, of course, be a cause *per se* of some effect, but for a given effect there can be efficient causes which are not *per se* but *per aliud.*

(3) This distinction between "cause requiring the effect" and "cause required by the effect" is indispensable to the understanding of real contingency in the processes of nature. If every cause upon which an effect depended were also a cause which necessitated that effect's occurrence, no effect could be regarded as contingent in any way. The contingency of an effect is due to the fact that *not all* of its causes require it, i.e., that some of its causes being given, the effect need not occur unless other and independent causes supervene, and unless these be the sort of causes which require the effect to occur. In short, we see the contingency of an effect when we refer it only to the causes it requires, but which do not require it. (Cf. Aristotle's explanation of contingency in terms of the operation of "accidental causes"—the sort of causes I have here called "*per aliud.*" Vd. *Physics*, II, 4-6.) And when subsequently we come to an understanding *of residual effects*, we will see that there are effects not required by any cause, though these effects may be, in turn, causes requiring other

effects. The causal operation of residual effects is another source of real contingency in natural processes.

c. The proximate extrinsic causes of a given effect must all be efficient causes, but not all the remote extrinsic causes of a given effect need be efficient causes.

(1) Whatever is strictly correlative to a patiency must be an agency, and every agency correlative with a patiency is an efficient cause. Hence if there is a set of proximate or *per se* causes, all must be efficient causes of the motion which is the correlative effect of each.

(2) But a remote extrinsic cause, one which is located in the nature or activity of some thing *other than* the thing moved, may be a material or a formal as well as an efficient cause.

   (a) Let us suppose for the moment that it is both true and significant to say that the essence of a thing is a formal cause of its proper accidents or powers. Then, if a thing's operations are acts of its powers, the essence of the agent is a remote cause of the effect of these operations. The essence of a man is a cause *per aliud* of the building of this house (the effect), for which the proximate cause, cause *per se*, is the act of building which the man performs. But as a remote cause, the essence of this man is not an efficient, but a formal cause. I do not say that the essence of a man is the formal cause of the housebuilding *without qualification*. Without qualification, the formal cause of the house-building is the form of a house. This is the immanent formal cause; and as such it cannot be called either remote or proximate. I said rather that *as a remote cause*, which means always an extrinsic cause, the essence of a man is a formal cause of whatever belongs to the man in virtue of his essence.

   (b) Let us also suppose that the powers of a man are the material cause of his habits, among which are the arts. Now if a particular operation, such as building a house, is an artistic act, the power which is actualized by the artistic habit is, as a remote cause of the act, a material cause. Again I do not say it is the material cause of the house-building *without qualification*, for the immanent material cause here is the stone, etc.

   (c) But the remote causes of a particular effect can never be exclusively either formal or material causes. Some of them must be efficient causes. The power does not reduce itself to act in the formation of a habit; nor does the habit reduce itself to act in the occurrence of an artistic operation. The cause of the becoming of the habit must be an efficient cause, and so must be the cause of the operation of the habituated power. But here there is an important distinction. Whatever causes the operation of the habituated power requires the effect of this operation; hence it is not a remote cause. But whatever causes the acts which habituate the power are necessary but not sufficient conditions of subsequent acts of the habituated power, and so these are remote causes of the artistic operation. Thus, for example, a teacher teaching is an efficient and proximate cause of a man's learning an art, for teaching does not occur unless learning occurs. But a man can have an art he does not use, or uses subsequently. If he does use it subsequently, then his artistic acts (building a house) are the proximate efficient cause of the effect (house-building), whereas the teacher's acts are a remote efficient cause. They are not cause *per se* of the house-building as an effect, but cause *per aliud* of the house-building. If the man could not have built a house without possessing artistic skill, and if he needed the acts of teaching to learn the skill, then certainly the acts of teaching are a necessary but not a sufficient condition, and are therefore entitled to be called "causes"—efficient, albeit remote or *per aliud.*

(d) Furthermore, a potential man cannot build a house. But a potential man is one who is generable but not generated. Hence the efficient cause of the man's coming to be, the act of generation on the part of his parents, is a remote efficient cause of the house being built. Note here that the father *qua father* is not an efficient cause of this man's coming to be, for *qua father not generating* is like *qua house-builder not building.* The father *qua man* is a remote formal cause in the sense, again, that the essence of a thing is the formal cause of its powers: the power of generating a man is possessed only by that which is a man. Hence the father as man is not the efficient cause of his son, but the father as generating is the efficient cause of that which is coming to be or being generated.

(e) Thus we see that among the plurality of remote causes, there may be many efficient causes not in the same line; for the man generating is not an efficient cause of learning the art, and the man teaching is not an efficient cause of the learner's coming to be. Yet one of these is prior to the other obviously, for the teacher cannot teach a potential man.

(f) Furthermore, there are degrees of remotion in the same line of causality. Thus, if A teaches B, and B teaches C, and C teaches D, both A and B are remote efficient causes of D's learning; neither is a cause *per se*, since C can know through learning without teaching D; only teaching by C is a cause *per se* of learning by D. But if C could not have known (his knowledge being the formal cause of his teaching) without being taught by B, and similarly with respect to B in relation to A, then A's teaching and B's teaching are remote efficient causes of D's learning, and A's teaching is more remote than B's. The same analysis applies to A generating B, B generating C, C generating D, etc.; for the generated need not generate, but generable cannot generate unless generated, so far as the operation of natural causes is concerned.

d. The remote efficient cause of a given effect K must, of course, also be the proximate efficient cause of another effect M. Nothing in short can be an efficient cause *per aliud* without also being an efficient cause *per se*, though it is never both with respect to the same effect. On the other hand, a proximate efficient cause need not be also a remote efficient cause, because it can happen that the motion K is not itself the efficient cause of any other motion. Thus, a man may be caused to learn something he never subsequently considers or uses. The efficient cause of his learning, the act of his teacher, may therefore not be a remote cause of any effect, but only the proximate cause of this man's learning this knowledge. (This may not be true in the sphere of local motions where so long as a thing is in motion it is an efficient cause of something else being in motion.)

e. One situation in which there is a plurality of efficient causes has not yet been discussed, namely, that in which several efficient causes are all causes *per se* of the same effect. This is the case in which A moves B while B moves C while C moves D. Here let the effect be the motion E. In this case, no material or formal causes intervene between the motions A, B, and C and the motion D, or the motion E, the effect. In this case, the motion of A requires the effect B, and so B requires the effect C, and so on until D requires the effect E; hence A, B, C require the effect E as much as the motion D does. Hence they are all causes *per se* of the effect E; all are strictly correlative with it, in the manner of agent and patient.

(1) Yet there is mediation here, of a sort which must be differentiated from the mediation in the case of a series of causes *per aliud*.

(2) In one sense, all these causes are proximate to the effect E, and in another sense, A, B, and C are not proximate, whereas D is. I shall use the words "immediate" and "mediated" to distinguish, in a set of causes that are equally proximate in one sense to a given effect, those which are not from the one which is proximate in the sense of immediate. Thus, D is the immediate proximate cause of E, whereas A, B, and C are mediated proximate causes of E.

(3) In a series of causes all of which are *per aliud* with respect to a given effect, let us say K, none of the causes are immediate. All are mediated by whatever cause or causes are the causes *per se* of K.

(4) I shall subsequently discuss immediate and mediated proximate causes in relation to the distinction between principal and instrumental causes. A principal and an instrumental cause of a given

effect must be related as mediated and immediate proximate causes or causes *per se*, but the converse is not true: causes related as mediated and immediate causes *per se* need not be related as principal and instrumental. Furthermore, when it is said that the effect proceeds immediately from the principal as well as from the instrumental cause, what is meant is that both such causes are proximate to the effect, in that both are its causes *per se*, requiring it. This does not violate the distinction between the causes as principal and instrumental, i.e., as mediated and immediate.

f. So far this analysis amplifies what was presented in the original article in Part II, Point #1. That was obviously too brief for adequacy. Yet the essential point made there is here reaffirmed. If a given effect has a plurality of causes, these must either be simultaneous or successive. That was what was said. We now see that that means:

(1) That any effect (which is a motion) *must* have one or more simultaneous causes, for every effect must have some proximate efficient causes or causes *per se*.

(2) That, in addition to its cause or causes *per se*, any effect *may* have one or more remote causes, including efficient causes.

(3) That remote efficient causes or causes *per aliud* need not be simultaneous with the given effect, or with each other, but may be ordered in a temporal succession, as well as in an order of causal dependence.

(4) That proximate efficient causes or causes *per se* must be simultaneous with their effect, and such causes may or may not be in an order of causal dependence, as we shall see.

g. Now the problem involves the question whether, when an effect requires a plurality of causes, that plurality must be finite or can be infinite. The solution of this question turns on the character of the causes and the way in which they are ordered to one another. It is necessary, therefore, to examine more closely the matter of the simultaneity of a number of causes, for, regardless of any other relevant principle, it is true that an *actual multitude* of distinct items is impossible. Hence if a number of efficient causes or motions are numerically distinct, and also simultaneous, they form an *actual multitude*, and such a multitude must be finite. This principle applies to a number of causes, regardless of their character as causes. Hence two questions arise: (1) must a number of causes *per se* for a given effect be finite because they are causes *per se*, quite apart from the fact that the causes *per se* for a given effect must be simultaneous? and (2) what are the limitations upon the principle of simultaneity itself? The second question has this in mind: must the first member in a set of simultaneous causes *per se* for a given effect be itself an uncaused motion, or a nonmoving efficient cause of motion? Thus, if for the effect E, there are the simultaneous proximate causes, A, B, C, D (a finite set, for whatever reason), in which A is the first member in the sense that no other cause simultaneous with it moves it, the question is whether A must be "an uncaused cause," or "an unmoved mover."

NOTE: In order to answer this last question, it is necessary now to turn to the nature of motion itself, and to analyze the relation of agent and patient. In this way we shall discover the limitation on the principle of simultaneity. Then we shall be able to return to the main problem and show that no motion, as an effect, requires an unmoved mover or a first cause in any sense of "first" which implies no other prior cause.

5. THE ANALYSIS OF MOTION

a. In the first place, it is necessary to distinguish a motion from what Aristotle calls a "complete actuality."

(1) When fully explicated, the definition of a motion indicates the point of distinction. Motion cannot be classed, says Aristotle, either as a potentiality or as an actuality. "A thing that is merely capable of having a certain size is not undergoing change, nor is a thing which is actually of a certain size. Motion is a sort of actuality but incomplete, the reason for this being that the potential whose actuality it is is incomplete" (*Physics*, III, 2, 201b29–31). "Take for instance the buildable as buildable. The actuality of the buildable as buildable is the process of building. For the actuality of the buildable must either be this or the house. But when the house is completely actual, the buildable is no longer buildable. On the other hand, it is the buildable which is being built. The *process*, then, of being built must be the kind of actuality required. The process of building is a motion" (*Physics*, III, I, 201b9–15).

(2) The foregoing is formulated in the definition of motion, but it is necessary to be explicit on the point that the actuality and the potentiality referred to in that definition are both incomplete. For if both were complete, the definition would be self-contradictory. A motion is the act of that which is in potentiality and in a respect in which it is still in potentiality. If the potentiality were completely actualized, there would be no motion. If there were no partial actualization of the potentiality, there would be no motion. A motion therefore consists of all the degrees of actualization of a potentiality short of complete actualization, and therefore it involves something less than complete potentiality at every stage. The process of a motion consists in the progressive actualization tending toward completeness of actualization, which when reached terminates the motion, and which is complete actuality. The opposite of motion is rest; but rest is not necessarily complete actuality. It can be either complete actuality or complete potentiality. That which is merely capable of being built

is at rest. That which is completely built, the house, is at rest. Motion occurs between rest in a state of complete potentiality and rest in a state of complete actuality. Vd. *Physics*, V, 2.

(3) This is confirmed by Aristotle's other description of motion as involving a subject, that which moves, and that *from which* and that *to which* the motion takes place. Whether the motion be described as from contrary to contrary, or from privation to form, or from form to privation, a potency and an actuality are involved as the terms of the motion. Let X represent that which is capable of being in motion. Let A represent the potentiality on which this capacity for motion is founded. Let B represent the complete actualization of A. Then when X is neither completely in state A nor completely in state B, it is in motion toward B. And so a motion is the incomplete actuality of that which is in potentiality in a certain respect. The words "in a certain respect" mean that X's potentiality must be determinate, i.e., a potentiality for the complete actuality which is B. Until that complete actuality is achieved, X is still in potentiality in that respect, but while the motion is going on, that potentiality is partially actualized at every moment of the motion.

(4) This point about motion consisting in an incomplete actuality of the movable in a respect in which it is potential is reiterated in *Physics*, VIII, 5, 257b8: "The potential is in process to actuality, and motion is an incomplete actuality of the movable." And here it is said that, in contrast, the mover moves in virtue of its complete actuality. "That which produces the form is always something that possesses it" (*ibid.*, 257b9-10). Cf. *Metaphysics*, XI, 9. I shall return to this point presently. Here I wish to add another citation of importance: *Metaphysics*, IX, 6. Here again Aristotle distinguishes the sort of actuality which is a motion, and complete actuality. The discussion of potencies and actualities in *Metaphysics*, IX, has a bearing on the distinction t between immanent and transitive activity, the actualization of impassible and passible potencies. This must be connected with the discussion in the *De Anima*, II, 1. These important distinctions do not, however, affect the main course of our argument.

b. In the second place, we must observe that the *efficient* cause of a motion is itself a motion. Every motion can be looked at from two points of view, from the point of view of the mover and from the point of view of the moved. If anything moves another without itself participating in the motion, it does not operate as an efficient cause. An efficient cause of motion is a thing in motion, and in so far as it is in motion. To act on another is to be in motion. Unless one thing acts on another which is capable of being acted on, it is not the efficient cause of motion in that other.

(1) If the mover were completely potential in the same respect in which the movable is completely potential, it could not efficiently

cause motion in the movable. To cause motion in the movable, a thing must be actual in the respect in which the movable is potential. It need not be completely actual in this respect, but it must have some degree of actuality. For A to heat B, A must be hotter than B. This does not mean that A must be completely actual with respect to its potentiality for hotness; for it can be in the process of heating at the same time that it heats another, which is colder than itself.

(2) To be actual in a certain respect is not the same as to act on another. Thus, the teacher is one who is actual in respect to a certain piece of knowledge, but that actuality is not the same as the activity of teaching. The activity of teaching cannot be separated from the activity of learning on the part of another. The one motion is, therefore, in a sense the actualization of the teacher's capacity for teaching and the learner's capacity for learning. "Teaching is not the same as learning, or agency as patiency, in the full sense, though they belong to the same subject, the motion, for the 'actualization of X in Y' and the 'actualization of Y through the action of X' differ *in definition*" (*Physics*, III, 3, 202b18–22). To act and to be acted on, says Aristotle, are the same only in the sense in which the road from Thebes to Athens and the road from Athens to Thebes are the same.

(3) In ordinary transitive motions—the acts of passible potentialities, which are motions from contrary to contrary—action and reaction are equal and opposite. Thus, if A heats B, B at the same time cools A. "To act on the movable as such is to move it. This it does *by contact*, so that at the same time it is also acted upon" *Physics*, III, 2, 202a4–6). The same holds for local motions and increase-decrease, as well as for alterations, but not for such things as teaching, for the acquisition of knowledge is an impassible change. It is not a motion from contrary to contrary.

(4) In short, for one thing to move another, it too must have a potentiality that can be actualized, and that actualization must be in process at the same time that the actualization of the potentiality in the moved is in process. Though the two potentialities are not the same, there is a sense in which their actualization is the same. "There is a single actuality of both alike. . . . It is not absurd that the actualization of one thing should be in another. ...There is nothing to prevent two things having one and the same actualization, provided the actualizations are not described in the same way" (*Physics*, III, 3, 202a18, 202b6, 202b8–9).

(a) This common actualization is the point of contact between mover and moved. Because of this fact, efficient causation can be described as a communication of energy or actuality, or more accurately as a communication between two things with respect to a single actuality, that is at once the actuality of each, though not in an identical respect, and hence differing in definition or description.

(b) The point here being made is like the point made in the *De Anima*, that the sense in act and the sensible in act are one, and yet the act of the sensible (which is 'being sensed') and the act of the sense (which is 'sensing') are not the same in definition, because the one act is in respect to diverse potentialities of that which can be sensed and of that which can sense. So the process, which can be called either "teaching" or "learning" is one act or motion, differently described as an act of the teacher's capacity for teaching and as an act of the learner's capacity for learning. So, also, the motion which is change of temperature, and which can be described either as "cooling" or as "heating," is one motion differently described according to the distinction between agent and patient, i.e., according to whether the colder thing is called the agent or the hotter thing.

(c) The actuality which is common to mover and moved is always the incomplete actuality which is a motion, and never the complete actuality which each thing has when it is at rest, for two things at rest are not related as agent and patient. Only two things communicating in the same motion are related as agent and patient, or as mover and moved. If nothing could be actual except as acting or as acted upon, nothing could be at rest in any respect. But things which are movable can be at rest in a given respect. Hence not everything which is actual in a given respect is an agent in that respect; not everything which is potential in a given respect is a patient in that respect. Agency and patiency occur only when two things are involved in one motion, which, looked at from the point of view of each of them, is a process of actualization of its prior potentiality by the prior actuality of another.

c. In the third place, with respect to any given motion, rest is prior. On the part of the thing which is to be the patient when the motion occurs, rest consists in potentiality in a given respect. On the part of the thing which is to be the agent when the motion occurs, rest consists in actuality in the respect in which the patient-to-be is potential. "The mover or agent will always be the vehicle (or possessor) of a form which, when it acts, will be the source or cause of the change, i.e., the full-formed man begets man from what is potentially a man" (*Physics*, III, 2, 202a9–12).

(1) It is necessary to distinguish this actuality from the action by which that which is the agent-to-be actually operates as an agent.

(2) The form possessed by the agent-to-be is not the efficient cause of the motion, though it is indispensable to the motion. To say that nothing *acts* except as it is *in act* does not mean that to be *in*

act is identical with *acting-on-another*. Thus, nothing except an actual man can generate a man, but actually being a man is not the same as actually generating a man.

(3) Our prior analysis takes care of the point under discussion. The form or actuality of the agent-to-be is a formal cause, a remote cause, a cause *per aliud* not *per se*, of the effect which will be produced when the agent-to-be actually operates, i.e., is now in fact an agent.

(4) It is only the efficient cause of the effect, the act of generating, which must be simultaneous with the effect, the process of being generated.

(5) Nevertheless, it is also true that the form which is in the agent-to-be prior to the motion will be in the patient-to-be after the motion. The knowledge which the teacher possessed prior to teaching will be possessed by the learner after learning; the heat which the hot thing possessed prior to heating will be in the cold thing after it is heated.

   (a) Here, then, is another sense in which there is a communication of energy or actuality in causation. If the action is transitive, and the motion is from contrary to contrary, the communication will involve a gain and a loss; if the motion involves impassibility and the action is immanent as well as transitive, the energy or actuality will be communicated without loss.

   (b) But this communication of energy or actuality cannot take place without efficient causation, in which two things participate in the same motion as agent and patient. We can ignore the fact that each may be an agent and a patient in distinct respects.

(6) The importance of this point is its bearing on the notion of a *residual effect*. Whatever actuality the patient possesses after the action of the agent ceases is a residual effect of the agent. This actuality may either be incomplete or complete. The patient may continue to be in process of motion or may be at rest after the action of the agent ceases. In short, the residual effect may be either a continuing motion or a completed actuality. *A residual effect is related to an actual cause in the same way that a potential cause is related to an actual effect.*

   (a) A potential cause may pre-exist an actual effect. A residual effect may post-exist an actual cause.

   (b) Only an actual cause and an actual effect are simultaneous. But just as a potential cause is a cause, so a residual effect is an effect.

   (c) Nothing but an actual cause of an actual effect is cause *per se*, inseparable from its effect in the sense that both cause and effect are involved in a single motion, as correlative agent and patient. But from the point of view of an effect, causes can be either *per se* or *per aliud*, proximate or remote, actual or potential, and the effect depends upon all its causes, though not in the same way. Similarly, from the point of view of a cause, effects can be either actual or residual, proximate or remote, and the cause is the cause of both sorts of effects, though not in the same way.

d. This brings us to the problem of simultaneity. The question is, whether one thing can move another only at the same time that it, in turn, is moved by another? There are two possibilities here.

  (1) Let A be in motion, and let B be in motion as the efficient cause of the motion of A. Now let us suppose that B must be in motion as long as A is in motion, that the time of B's motion must be coincident with the time of A's motion. Let us call such coincidence "total simultaneity." Now let us suppose that what holds true for A and B holds true for B and C, for C and D, and so on. If each movable is in motion only under efficient causation by another movable in motion during a coincident time, such total simultaneity will require that the number of movers and moved, agents and patients, be finite. This follows from the fact that an actually coexistent multitude of distinct things cannot be infinite. Hence if total simultaneity is required, and an actually infinite multitude is impossible, there must be a finite set of movers, one of which is a *first* mover in the sense that it is not itself moved by another. Let us call this mover "an unmoved mover." For our present purposes, it makes no difference whether the "unmoved mover" moves whatever it moves "by moving itself" or "without itself moving in any way."

  (2) But suppose, on the contrary, that there need only be a point of contact between mover and moved; by which I mean that there must be *some* simultaneity between the motion of A and the motion of B, but not *total simultaneity*. In this case, the motion of B may begin before the motion of A begins, and the motion of A may continue after the motion of B ends; but some part of the motion of B must be coincident with the motion of A. This *partial coincidence* is required for contact, or participation in the same motion as agent and patient, as actual cause and actual effect. But the motion of B which precedes the motion of A may be a *potential cause* of A's motion, and the motion of A which continues after the motion of B ceases may be a *residual effect* of B's motion.

    (a) As Aristotle points out, "though the moved must be in motion, it need not move anything else." It is only that which moves something else which must be in motion simultaneously with that other. Yet where Aristotle points out that that which moves another must be in motion while it moves, he adds that it is perfectly clear from the case of local motion that the mover and the moved must be in contact "only up to a certain point" (*Physics*, VIII, 5, 256b18). Thus, a moving ball can be in motion without moving another ball, and though, when it does move another ball, there must be some simultaneity between the motion of the one and of the other, the second ball can continue in motion after the motion of the first has ceased, and as continuing in motion, it may move for some time without moving a third ball, and then at a later time, while still in motion, it may make contact with a third ball, and move it. Similarly, the fire heats the water, and after the fire has ceased heating the water, the water while continuing to boil can heat an egg., and after the water has ceased to heat the egg, the egg can heat a hand, and so on.. In these series, there must be some contact between each mover and each moved, for whatever period of time they are correlative as actual cause and actual effect, or agent and patient; but the motion of each member need not be *totally simultaneous* or *coincident* with the motion of the member which moves it or which it moves. Hence the simultaneity, the point of contact, between A and B may not occur at the same time as the point of contact between B and C. If they do not occur at the same time, if the motions of A and B are not totally simultaneous, and the motions of B and C are not totally simultaneous, then the motions of A and C will not be totally simultaneous; and, more than that, they need not be simultaneous at all. Only if A is totally simultaneous with B, and B is totally simultaneous with C, must A and C be totally simultaneous with each other.

(b) Hence we see that the occurrence of potential causes (i.e., the motion of B, which *can* cause the motion of A but which is not *actually* doing so) and the occurrence of residual effects (i.e., the motion of A which was an actual effect of the motion of B, but which continues after the motion of B has ceased) are facts of experience that make a *first* mover, an unmoved mover, unnecessary, Aristotle's argument for an unmoved mover depends upon a fact which is not a fact of experience and which cannot be proved, namely, the eternity of motion itself. The argument cannot be made from the experienced facts of motion, apart from the hypothesis of motion's eternity.

(c) Let me show this simply. If any motion can be caused by a motion that is not totally simultaneous with it, and if that motion can in turn be similarly caused, then the last of these motions can have ceased before the first begins, in which case they are not in any way co-existent or coincident. Then it is quite possible for there to be an infinite series of movers, for since all the members of this series need not be co-existent, the infinite multitude is only a potential infinite, and there is nothing impossible about a potential infinite of things in succession, given an infinite time, which cannot be denied. Furthermore, each member of this series is the *per se* cause of its actual effect, though the occurrence of a residual effect which may be a potential cause before it becomes an actual cause, prevents a given member, C, from being the *per se* cause of the remote effect, A.

(3) But it will be objected that there cannot be an infinite set of *per se* causes of a given effect, which is their actual effect, since this requires total simultaneity on the part of all the movers with each other and with the motion that is the effect under consideration. And it will be said that this is the argument for an unmoved mover. In order to meet this objection, and show why it fails to establish the need for an unmoved mover, I must return now to the general analysis of causes and causation, by examining the relation to each other of the causes which are causes *per se* of a given effect.

6. COMPLETION OF THE ANALYSIS OF CAUSES

a. In the first place, let me show that it is not the so-called principle of sufficient reason which demands a finite number of causes for a given effect.

(1) An effect depends upon all its causes, for whatever is truly a cause is that without which the effect would not occur. Every cause is a necessary condition, though every cause is not both necessary and sufficient. Hence, if there can be an infinite, temporal, series of causes, only some of which are *proximate* and *per se* causes of a given effect, all the others being *remote* and *per aliud*, the principle of sufficient reason operates only to the extent that it is required that each member of the series which is an effect have sufficient and necessary (proximate and *per se*) causes as well as merely necessary (remote and *per aliud* causes. But in an infinite series, each member which is an effect can be caused. An infinite series only requires an infinite time, which is not impossible. Hence the principle of sufficient reason does not require that a plurality of causes be finite. To suppose otherwise is to suppose that in an infinite series of causes and effects, there will be some effect without its necessary and sufficient causes. To suppose this is to affirm and deny the infinity of the series, which is self-contradictory. In an infinite series, there is an infinite number of members prior to any given member.

(2) It follows, on the same grounds, that if there could be an infinite multitude of co-actual causes for a given actual effect, the principle of sufficient reason would not be violated by the infinity of the set of *per se* causes for a given effect. In such an infinite set—

which is, of course, impossible—each mover would be both a mover and moved, and all movers and moved would be totally simultaneous. It is the total simultaneity of such a set of movers and moved that makes it impossible, and nothing else. In short, it is the fact that an actual number must be a determinate number which prevents an actual number from being an infinite number. If, contrary to the truth, an infinite number could be an actual number, a given effect could have an infinite number of proximate and *per se* causes.

(3) But it will be said that if a given effect has more than one *per se* cause, the plurality of its proximate *per se* causes must be a finite plurality, precisely because, by the very nature of such causes, they must all be totally simultaneous with their actual effect, and hence totally simultaneous with each other. It is, therefore, necessary to examine such a finite set of *per se* causes for a given effect. One point should be noted here.

(a) I shall use the word "series"—as I did in the original article—to designate any plurality of causes temporally disposed with respect to a given effect, such that only some of *all* its causes are proximate, and all the rest are remote. In so far as we consider only efficient causes, or things in motion, all the efficient causes will, then, not be totally simultaneous. Each efficient cause will have an actual effect, and will be the *per se* or proximate cause of that effect, but all the efficient causes in the series will not be *per se* or proximate causes of the ultimate effect, or the effect under consideration. Thus, let A be the effect in question, and AA be its proximate, efficient, *per se*, cause; let BB, CC, DD, etc. be remote efficient causes in the series. Then though BB is a *per se* cause of some effect, let us say B, it is not a *per se* cause of A.

(b) I shall use the word "set" to designate any plurality of causes which are totally simultaneous with each other and with a given effect under consideration. In this case, each of the efficient causes is a *per se* cause of the same ultimate effect, though each is not proximate to it in the same way, for some one cause will be immediately proximate, let us say B, and another cause will be only mediately proximate, for if C moves B *as* B moves A, then B is the immediate and C is the mediated proximate or *per se* cause of A, the one effect.

b. It is admitted at once that a set of causes must be finite, because by definition the members of a set are totally simultaneous with each other and with their common effect. We need only consider the first member of such a set, for the question is whether that first member must be an unmoved mover.

(1) By "first member" of a set of causes, I mean that cause which is not moved by another *qua patient* while it moves another *qua agent*. The important word here is "*while*." Thus, let A be the effected

motion, B its immediate *per se* cause, and C its mediated *per se*
cause, in such wise, that C is moving B throughout the whole
period in which B is moving A, so that B could not move A unless
C were moving it. Now let there be no other cause which moves
C *while* C is moving B, as is required by the fact that this set of
causes must be finite. This is what is meant by calling C the "first
member" of the set. If a set contains two causes or more, one of
these will always be the immediate proximate cause, directly in
contact with A, the effected motion during the entire period
when it is an actual effect; and one, but not more than one, will
always be the ultimate *per se* cause, mediated in its contact with A
during the whole period when A is an actual effect, but not similarly mediating between A and any other motion. The "first
member" is this mediated and unmediating *per se* cause of the
actual effect A.

(2)   Now just as this set of causes can have a residual effect as well as
an actual effect, so the first member of the set can be an actual
cause at a time when it is only a residual effect of some other *per
se* cause. Thus, let the continuous motion C be divided into two
parts, the part C1-C2 and the part C2-C3. Let the part C1-C2 be the
actual effect of the motion D, which is then its *per se* efficient
cause. Let the part C2-C3 be the residual effect of D—i.e., the continuation of the motion after D has ceased to be in motion. Now
in order for C to be an actual cause of the motion A, the ultimate
effect under consideration, it is only necessary that part of the
motion C be simultaneous with either all or part of the motion A.
Hence if C2-C3 is simultaneous with the motion B, its immediate
actual effect, and if the motion B is simultaneous with the motion
A, its immediate actual effect, then C2-C3 is a *per se* cause, though
mediated by B, of the motion A. Furthermore, the motion C2-C3
meets all the requirements of a "first member" of this set of *per se*
causes, because no other motion simultaneous with it is its actual
cause, for it is the residual, not the actual, effect of the motion. D,
which is simultaneous with C1-C2. But a motion which is a residual effect is a caused motion, even though it has an actual cause
only for part of its total period. Furthermore, such a motion, even
though a residual effect, can be the cause of another motion with
which it may be wholly simultaneous. Hence, it follows that the
first member in a finite set of *per se* causes need not be an
uncaused cause or an unmoved mover.

(3)   In short, unless we know *on other grounds* that the first member
in a finite set of *per se* causes for a given effect is an unmoved
mover, an uncaused cause, we cannot infer that such a cause or
mover exists from the character of *per se* causes or from the
finiteness of a set of such causes. For though every such set
must have a first member, that first member can be at once a *per
se* cause of the effect in question, and the residual effect of a

prior *per se* cause of a prior part of itself. The fact that the parts
Cl-C2 and C2-C3 form a single continuous motion is, of course,
of the greatest importance. That part of the motion which is a
residual effect does not need any actual cause other than the
actual cause of that prior part of itself which is an actual effect.
But though it is, *qua* effect, only residual, the posterior part of
the motion is, *qua motion*, actual, and *qua actual* it can be the *per
se* cause of an actual effect. Furthermore, since D, which is the
actual cause of the prior part, Cl-C2, is not simultaneous with
C2-C3, and since it is this part, which as the residual effect of D,
is the actual cause of the motion B, and through B, of A, it follows that D is not a *per se* or actual cause of A. The motion D can
occur without the motion A occurring. A is not required by D.
D is, therefore, not a sufficient condition for A. Yet D is a
remote cause of A, and a *per aliud* cause, through its residual
effect which is an actual and *per se* cause of A.

(4) The fact that the effect A has a finite set of *per se* causes does not
imply, therefore, that it has a finite plurality of causes, for it has
remote and *per aliud* causes as well as proximate and *per se* causes,
and the number of remote causes can always be infinite. Hence,
no known natural motion, as an effect under consideration, need
have a finite plurality of causes in which there is a first member;
and even though it may have a finite set of *per se* causes, the first
member of this set can be an effect, albeit residual; and hence in
the whole plurality of its causes, a given effect need not have any
"first cause" in the sense of an uncaused cause or an unmoved
mover, a cause which is not *somehow* the effect of another cause.

c. There are further distinctions to be made concerning the patterns to
be found in the plurality of causes for a given effect, but none of these
affect or alter the conclusion reached. It will be useful to show this,
however, both for its own sake and for its bearing on traditional points
of analysis.

(1) First, let us consider a series of causes for a given actual effect.
What remarks can be made about the members of this series?

(a) First, that some of the members, at least one, will be a proximate, *per se*, and efficient cause of the effect; and that all the
rest will be either the immanent formal and material causes
of that effect, or they will be remote causes.

1. As remote, they will be either efficient, formal, or final in
their mode of causality.

2, As remote, they will be causes *per aliud*.

(b) Next, considering the remote efficient causes in relation to
the proximate efficient cause of this effect, we can distinguish two possibilities:

1. Either the remote efficient causes will be the same in
kind or diverse in kind from each other and from the
proximate efficient cause of the given effect.

2. Thus, in the infinite series of fathers and sons, each efficient cause—*a generative act*—is the same essentially as every other. Each father *qua man* is not an efficient cause; it is only his generative act which is an efficient cause of an actual generation. The same picture is presented by an infinite series of men teaching and learning, each teaching another, and each learning from another. Now it is not the fact that each of the efficient causes in this series is the same in kind that makes all but one remote and *per aliud* causes of a given effect. Nor are any of these remote causes "accidental" in the sense that they are not necessary conditions, indispensable to the occurrence of the given effect. The only thing "accidental" about the series is the fact that the efficient causes under consideration are only accidentally, numerically, or individually, diverse. They are not essentially diverse. (In this connection, let it be said that St. Thomas's example of an infinite series of hammers is totally irrelevant, and should not be treated as if it were like the example of an infinite series of fathers, or more precisely, of generative acts. Vd. *S.T.*, I, 46, 2, and 7. The action of one hammer is not even a remote cause of the action of another. The several hammers, finite or infinite in number, are causally independent of one another, and do not form a causal series; but the series of generative acts are not causally independent of one another, for unless the prior generative act takes place, the posterior generative act will not take place, even though one generative act is not the proximate or *per se* cause of the other.)

3. The other possibility is that of a series of efficient causes in which the members are not only numerically but essentially distinct. This is the only way in which it differs from the series of fathers and sons, or more precisely, of generative acts. The example I gave in my original article (p. 198) is an accurate representation of this situation: one efficient cause being the training of the dog to carry a bundle, the other efficient cause being the operation of the dog in carrying the bundle. Now here, only the second of these causes is the *per se* or proximate cause of the effect under consideration, namely, the carrying of the bundle. The training of the dog is a proximate and *per se* effect of the dog's being trained, a residual effect of which is the dog's trained disposition to perform an operation which otherwise it could not perform. But neither the dog's trainer, nor his act of training, nor the dog's trained disposition, is the proximate efficient cause or cause *per se* of the effect in question, the carrying of the

bundle. That cause is an operation according to the trained disposition, and that operation must have its own *per se* efficient cause. Yet the training of the dog is certainly a remote, *per aliud*, efficient cause of the effect in question, and as such it is essentially distinct from the proximate, *per se*, efficient cause of the effect in question. Here then is a series of efficient causes which are essentially, as well as numerically, distinct. Now this fact that they are essentially distinct does not make them causes *per se* of the given effect, any more than the fact that in the series of father and sons, the several causes are accidentally distinct makes them causes per aliud of the given effect. In short, there are two quite separate distinctions here, and there is no reason to confuse them. One is a distinction between remote and proximate efficient causes, *per aliud* and *per se* efficient causes of a given effect; the other is a distinction between series in which all the efficient causes are essentially alike, and series in which some of the efficient causes are essentially diverse from others.

(c) The reason for making these distinctions in the original article was that the examples which St. Thomas uses in connection with his discussion of causes *per se* and causes *per aliud* are far from clear; and his discussion of this matter is neither adequate nor precise. It was, therefore, necessary to show that the fact that the members of a causal series were all essentially alike was not at all relevant to the possibility of an infinite series of causes. A series of causes can be infinite whether its members are essentially alike or essentially diverse. If the members of the series are essentially diverse, there may be some sense in which they are essentially subordinated to one another, but such essential subordination in a series of causes does not require the series to be finite and to have a first member. Moreover, there is no point in St. Thomas's remark that a series of generative acts reduce to a single cause, unless it be that such causes, which are only accidentally different, are all *one* in essence. But even if a number of causes be diverse in essence, the number need not be finite *unless* all the causes considered are proximate or *per se* causes of a given effect. Here St. Thomas confuses two things: (1) the essential sameness or diversity of two causes and (2) the character of two causes as *per se* or *per aliud* with respect to a given effect. Two causes can be essentially the same, and both be *per se* or *per aliud* causes of a given effect; or they can be essentially diverse and both be *per se* or *per aliud* causes of a given effect; or if one is a *per se* and the other a *per aliud* cause of a given effect, both can be essentially the same or essentially different. Hence, the relation of one cause to another, according to their essential sameness or difference, must be kept quite distinct from the relation each bears to the same effect—as either *per se* or *per aliud*. And obviously the problem is not whether a number of causes for the same effect are essentially the same or essentially different, but whether the causes being considered are all *per se* causes of the effect or whether some are *per se* causes and some *per aliud*.

(2) This leads us then, secondly, to the consideration of a set of *per se* causes for a given effect. What remarks can be made about the members of such a set?

    (a) Though they are all proximate to the actual effect in the sense of being co-actual with it, they are not all immediate causes of the effected motion. There can, however, be two or more immediate causes; as, for example, two or more levers being used by two or more men to pry a stone loose. The motions of the several levers are *per se* and immediate causes of the motion of the stone; and the motions of the men wielding the levers are *per se* and mediated causes of the motion of the stone. Now in this case we have a number of *per se* causes which are only accidentally distinct—the motions of the several levers. Furthermore, these causes are independent of each other in the sense that the motion of one is not the effect of the motion of another. Hence, two *per se* causes in a given set need not be subordinated to one another as effect to cause or patient to agent.

    (b) The fact that one *per se* cause is subordinated to another does not require the two motions to be essentially distinct. Thus, a man can use one stick to move another stick to move a stone; in which case all the motions must be simultaneous and *per se* causes of the motion of the stone, but though the motion of the max's arm is essentially distinct from the motion of each stick, the motion of one stick and the motion of the other which it causes, are not essentially distinct.

    (c) Furthermore, in a finite set of *per se* causes of local motion, it is quite possible for all the members to be essentially alike, just as the generative acts in an infinite series of fathers and sons are all essentially alike.

    (d) Only in some cases is it true that the *per se* causes will be essentially subordinated to one another. Let me be sure this is clear. Two *per se* causes of a given effect may not be subordinated to one another, as two levers moving one stone. Two *per se* causes of a given effect may be subordinated to one another, but not essentially, because either could have been the cause and the other effect, as in the case of the motion of two sticks, one moving the other to move a stone, all the motions being simultaneous, of course. Or, in the third alter-native, the subordination may be essential and irreversible, due to the essential difference in the motions, as for exam-ple, the human arm, under voluntary motion, moving the stick as the stick moves the stone, the ultimate effect.

(e) Now in this third case, there is one further distinction of the greatest importance. It turns on whether the effect *requires* essentially distinct *per se* causes. Thus, for example, the motion of the stone does not require essentially distinct *per se* causes; for either the man's arm can move the stone with-out moving the stick to do it, or the stick can move the stone without being simultaneously moved by a man's arm, but by another stick which is in motion, let say, as a residual effect of some other body in motion, the wind, etc. If one calls the man's moving arm and the moving stick "principal" and "instrumental" *per se* causes of the motion of the stone, one should qualify this by saying that either cause is dispensable, by which I mean that the motion of the stone, as the effect in question, does not require a principal *per se* cause or an instrumental *per se* cause, though it does require one or more *per se* causes. Causes are related as "principal" and "instrumental" only when both are *per se* for a given effect, and as such are also essentially distinct in type, and are essentially subordinated. But though such a relation of causes can occur, it may not be required by a given effect. Hence, in such cases, knowledge of the effect will not permit us to infer the existence of an unknown principal cause, which is needed by the known instrumental cause for the production of the effect.

(f) Let us consider the other possibility, i.e., where the effect by its very nature requires the cooperation of a principal and an instrumental cause, both *per se* causes of the effect. Such a case is a physical work of art. Here if we know the charac-ter of the effect to be a work of art and to be physical (i.e., trans-formed matter), we also know that its efficient *per se* causes must include the act of the artist's mind and the act of his bodily members—whether or not his hands, for exam-ple, also use inanimate instruments—and we know that the motion of his bodily members is a cause which by itself could not produce the work of art, even as the motion of his mind is a cause which could not transform matter. Here, then, is an unqualified case of principal and instrumental causality, in which the very nature of the effect, as known by us, requires us to posit at least two causes, both *per se*, both co-active, and simultaneous in their activity with the becoming of the effect, but each unable to produce the effect without the other, for the principal cause is ineffective without the instrument, and the instrument is ineffective except as moved by the principal cause.

d. These further distinctions are of some importance in our inquiry concerning the proof of God's existence, but they do not alter the fundamental point so far established, namely, that for any given effect there need not be a first cause or unmoved mover. However, the members of a finite set of *per se* causes are themselves related to each other, the first member of this set can always be a motion that is a residual effect of a prior cause, and so the fact that the set of *per se* causes must be finite does not permit us to say that its first member, however it be related to the others, is an unmoved mover or an uncaused cause.

7. The Conditions of A Posteriori Inference

a. In the light of the foregoing consideration of causality and motion, we can set forth the formal conditions by which reason is able to infer the existence of a cause from knowledge of effects.

b. In the first place, it should be obvious that this is a process of proof, not discovery. In a process of proof, one must know the conclusion to be proved, as a possible proposition. Thus, I don't discover the proposition "God exists" from the premises. I prove it by the premises, and before I prove this proposition, the proposition can be known by me as a question, or as a problem, i.e., a proposition to be proved.

(1) The existence of anything is either directly known or demonstrable. Furthermore, it may be directly knowable, though not directly known, as for example, the existence of a certain historical figure may be directly knowable (in the sense that it was known to his contemporaries) but not directly known or knowable to us. To us, the existence of this historical person is only indirectly knowable by means of historical demonstration, which is typically *a posteriori* in method.

(2) But the existence of God is not directly knowable to any man *qua* man, in the natural order of knowing. It can only be known by demonstration, and by demonstration *a posteriori* from effects. Since God is a transcendent, not a cognate or sensible object, there will be no causal nexus in which God will be seen to be the immediate cause actually producing the known effect. Not only must God's existence be inferred, but so must His causality.

(3) In proving the existence of such a cause, we must have some definition of it, at least a nominal definition, which is all we can have in this case.

(4) If we try to infer God's existence from the effect which is a natural motion—a natural motion of any sort—the nominal definition we must use is "unmoved mover" or "uncaused cause of motion" or "first cause." All these nominal definitions are strictly

synonymous.

c. Now the only conditions under which the existence of an unknown type of cause can be inferred from motion as an effect, are as follows:

(1) If a known motion, any particular motion, were such that it could have only one cause, which would then have to be its *per se* cause, and also an uncaused cause.

(2) If a known motion were such that the series of causes productive of it, including both proximate and remote causes, had to be finite, in which case the first member of the series would have to be a remote and *per aliud* cause of the given effect.

(3) If a known motion were such that the plurality of its *per se* causes were not only finite but also contained a first member that could have no cause, in which case that first member would be a first but mediated *per se* cause of the given effect.

(4) If a known motion were such that from its nature we knew it required a set of causes *per se*, related as principal and instrumental, among which must be included as the highest and indispensable principal cause an "unmoved mover."

d. These four conditions exhaust all the possible ways in which we can infer from the known facts about motions as effects, the existence of a cause that is not a natural agent, i.e., itself not a natural motion, for we know all natural agents to be moved movers or caused causes. I am, of course, excluding one condition, namely, that involving the hypothesis that the world of natural things in motion has everlastingly consisted of things in motion. Since this hypothesis is neither self-evident nor demonstrable, it cannot be used as a premise in an argument.

e. I am now prepared to show that God's existence cannot be proved as a cause of motion. I shall do this in the next section, and therein show that this more elaborate analysis confirms what was said in the original article, in Part II thereof, the first six points of which were devoted to this negative showing.

III. *Summary of the Negative Arguments*

1. According to the four conditions stated in Part II, above, at #7, God cannot be demonstrated as a cause of motion, if we employ the nominal definition "first cause" or "unmoved mover" or "uncaused cause."

   a. No known motion has a *single* efficient cause. By a single efficient cause, I mean a unique cause, which by itself provides all the necessary and sufficient conditions for that motion's occurring. Such a cause would, of course, be *per se*, and as proximate to its effect, it would also be immediate. Hence, God cannot be inferred as the unique cause of any known natural motion. If there were such a unique cause, it could be God because a unique cause is necessarily an uncaused cause. (If God exists, and performs miracles, some physical motions may be thus caused.)

      (1) This argument is confirmed by the fact that every natural motion within our experience is known by us to be caused by another natural motion within our experience. Even if this other natural motion were not itself the unique cause of the effect in question, its occurrence would prevent us from supposing God to be the unique cause of the effect in question.

      (2) But, in the second place, no natural motion is known by us as a unique cause, for since every natural motion is known by us to be caused by another natural motion, in part at least, we know that any given effect will have at least two natural motions among its causes—either both *per se*, one immediate and the other mediated, or one *per se* and one *per aliud*, i.e., one proximate and one remote.

   b. No natural motion is known to have a finite *series* of efficient causes, and there is nothing about a series of causes in temporal succession which requires that there be a first member of the series. Hence, God cannot be inferred as the temporally remote first or uncaused efficient cause in a series of causes for a given effect.

      (1) This argument is confirmed by another consideration. Suppose (what we do not know) that a given effect has a finite series of causes, some of which must be proximate and *per se* to it, and others remote and *per aliud* in varying degrees. Now the first member of such a series could not be a cause *per se* of the given natural motion which is the effect in question. But if the first member of such a series were an efficient cause of motion, it would have to be the cause *per se* of its own proximate effect, a natural motion prior in time to the natural motion which is the effect in question. Then if this first member were called God, because it corresponded to the nominal definition used, God would be the *per se* cause of one natural motion, and the *per aliud* cause of another natural motion. This is repugnant in itself.

      (2) Furthermore, if God were the *per se* cause of the first natural motion in a finite *series* of motions, God would have to be either

the immediate cause of that motion or the mediated cause of that motion. If the mediated cause of that motion, God would have to be the immediate cause of some other natural motion, for otherwise the set of *per se* causes would be infinite as such. Hence, God would have to be the immediate *per se* cause of some natural motions, but not of all. But no known natural motion is without a natural motion as its immediate *per se* cause.

(3) Despite these repugnant consequences, we might be forced to posit an unknown type of causality for an original natural motion, if there were some first natural motion in a temporal series of motions. Since, however, there is no ground whatsoever for asserting a finite temporal series of natural motions, with an original member, we can avoid the difficulties indicated. But, then, also we cannot infer God as a first cause in this way.

c. Although we know that the number of *per se* causes for a given effect must be finite, and that if these causes are subordinated to one another causally, there must be some first member in the set of such causes, all proximate and simultaneous with a given actual effect, we have no grounds for asserting that the first member of such a set must be an unmoved mover or an uncaused cause. The first member of such a set can always be a residual effect of a temporally prior cause which is the actual *per se* cause of a prior part of one continuous motion, of which this first member is a posterior part. Hence, God cannot be inferred from the fact that the *per se* causes of any motion must be finite, for none of these needs to be totally uncaused. A residual effect is not totally uncaused.

(1) Furthermore, we have the same difficulty here that we had before. If God were the first member in a set of *per se* causes, and if this set contained a natural motion as another *per se* cause, God would have to be the immediate *per se* cause of one natural motion, and the mediated *per se* cause of the natural motion which is the effect in question.

(2) But this is repugnant in the light of all our knowledge of natural motions. No one particular natural motion can be distinguished from all the rest as the immediate effect of God's *per se* efficient causality. Since God cannot be the mediated *per se* cause of all natural motions, for then there would be an infinite number of *per se* causes for any effect, the only other alternative is that God is the immediate *per se* cause of every natural motion. But if this is the case, then every natural motion must have two immediate *per se* causes, one of which is not subordinated to the other as a mediating cause, namely, a natural motion and God's efficient causality. For let the effect in question be the motion A. Then if God is the immediate *per se* efficient cause of every natural motion, God is the immediate cause of A. But let B be another natural motion which is also the immediate *per se* cause of A— mediated by no other natural motion. Then God is also the

immediate cause of B, as well as of A, and not of A through B, any more than of B through A. This may be true in fact, as Catholic dogma holds it to be true, but it cannot be known by reason from any analysis of natural motions and their causes. The type of efficient causation of a natural motion which is Divine is in itself unknown. The immediate cause of a known effect—any known natural motion—must itself be known, for it is simultaneous with the effect, participating in the one motion. If it is not known, it cannot be inferred from the character of the effect in so far as the effect is a motion.

(3) But, above all, it is clear that if the truth is that God is the immediate *per se* cause of every natural motion, and if, in addition to God as cause, each motion has another immediate *per se* cause which is a natural motion, then God certainly cannot be inferred as a first cause *per se* which is not an immediate cause of every natural motion.

(4) The foregoing reasoning is additional to the main point, which is that the finitude of a set of *per se* causes does not mean that its first member is in *no* way an effect of prior causes. Hence, God cannot be inferred as a first and mediated *per se* cause, because the nominal definition requires that we find a totally uncaused cause, a cause which is in no way the effect of prior causes.

d. Finally, there is no known natural motion which by its very nature as an effect requires anything other than natural motions as its *per se* causes. Hence, God cannot be inferred as the requisite principal cause, in the manner in which the mental activity of the artist can be inferred as the requisite principal cause for a work of art as an effect. In so far as what is here becoming is known to us as a physical work of art, we know that its *per se* causes must include (1) artistic activity as principal and (2) bodily activity, with or without auxiliary instruments, as instrumental. But in so far as what is here becoming is any natural motion, nothing about the nature of the effect, so far as it is known to us *as a motion*, requires anything but natural motions as its *per se* causes, whether or not these be related as principal and instrumental. Now since no natural motion is without a cause, and since by the nominal definition of God as uncaused we know that Divine activity is not a natural motion, we cannot infer God's causality from any known natural motion, as we can infer the artist's mental activity from the nature of a work of art. I mean by this, of course, that we cannot infer God as an efficient cause of whatever natural motion is taken as an effect.

(1) Again I do not mean to imply that it is in fact false that God is somehow the principal cause of every natural motion, using other natural motions as instruments in a manner only analogous to the way in which one natural motion is related to another as principal to instrumental cause. This may be true, but it cannot be known by reason from our knowledge of natural motions as effects.

(2) Furthermore, there is a difficulty here of the same sort we have previously met: either God is the principal cause of some natural motions or of all. If of some, then other natural motions can be his instrumental causes; but if of all, then no natural motion can be an instrumental cause, in which case it is confusing to speak of God as a principal cause. For even though the relation between God and natural agents is only analogous to the relation between natural agents as principal and instrumental causes of a given effect, that relationship implies that the principal cause is not the principal cause of the instrumental cause, but of the effect for which there is both a principal and an instrumental cause. Furthermore, if natural agents were truly instrumental causes in relation to God as principal cause, then miracles would be impossible, which dispense with natural agents in the production of natural effects.

(3) These considerations are offered merely to indicate difficulties involved in understanding what may be true, namely, that God is somehow a principal cause of some or all natural motions. But these are difficulties in the understanding of what can only be known by faith. By reason it cannot be inferred that God is in any way the efficient *per se* cause of a natural motion.

2. The foregoing seems to me to be an adequate negative showing that there can be no valid *a posteriori* demonstration of God's existence which (1) uses a natural motion as the known effect from which the reasoning starts, and (2) uses "unmoved mover" or "first efficient cause of motion" as the nominal definition of God, whose existence is to be proved.

    a. As I insisted in my original article, this does not mean that God's existence cannot be proved. It still remains possible for there to be a valid *a posteriori* demonstration in which (1) the known or demonstrated effect is contingent being, the existence of a contingent thing, rather than the occurence of a motion, and in which (2) the nominal definition of God is "necessary being" or "uncaused cause of being."

    b. Furthermore, what I have so far shown negatively does not deny dogmatic truths about Divine causality in relation to natural motions. It merely insists that these are dogmatic truths, which we can make some effort to understand. They are not truths we can know by reason from our knowledge of natural motions and their efficient causation.

    c. Before I go on to the positive task of formulating a valid proof of God as the unique and immediate efficient cause of the being of all contingent existences, I shall briefly show, first, that the more elaborate analysis here presented is on all essential points the same as the analysis in the original paper; and second, I shall briefly comment on Schwartz.

3. I shall here refer to the arguments presented in Part II of the original paper, by using the numbers in that outline.

    a. #1 presented the fundamental alternatives: if a given effect has a plurality of causes, these are either finite or infinite in number, and they are either simultaneous or ordered in temporal succession.

(1) This is subject to one correction which my more elaborate analysis has now made. Simultaneity or temporal succession are exhaustive, but they are not exclusive when applied to a plurality of causes. A plurality of causes need not be *all* simultaneous or *all* successive; such a plurality can include some causes which are simultaneous with each other and with the effect, and some which are temporally ordered and temporally prior to the effect.

(2) It remains true, however, that the number of simultaneous or *per se* causes must be finite, whereas the number of temporally successive or *per aliud* causes need not be finite. Hence, it follows that if a plurality of causes includes both simultaneous and successive causes, the plurality as a whole need not be finite.

(3) Though this was originally said without reference to the distinction between *per se* and *per aliud* causes, all further distinctions, such as this, merely verify the point which has been made.

b. #2 extended the analysis by showing that a cause *per se* for a given effect is an active cause, and hence one which is immediately or proximately productive of the effect, and it went on to say that if there be a plurality of *per se* causes for a given effect, that plurality must be finite, because "there cannot be an infinite number of simultaneous actions" (Aquinas, *C.G.*, II, 38).

(1) And St. Thomas goes on to say: "On the other hand, in causes which do not act simultaneously, this is not impossible, according to those who assert that generation has always been."

(a) Now, in the first place, it should be observed that St. Thomas concedes the irrefutability of the assertion that "generation"—or motion—"has always been." If it could be refuted, then it could be proved that the world of physical change had an absolute beginning—that there was some first natural motion. But this cannot be proved, Vd. *S.T.*, I, 46, 1, 2.

(b) In the second place, it should be observed that a cause which does not act simultaneously with the occurrence of its effect cannot be a *per se* or proximate cause; but must be a *per aliud* or remote cause. St. Thomas does not say that actions or motions which are not simultaneous with their effect are *not* causes. They are causes, and as such they are indispensable (i.e., necessary) to their effect, though they are not sufficient, or by themselves productive of the given effect.

(2) There can be no doubt that what St. Thomas means by a *per se* cause is what Aristotle means by a "proper, actual" cause—i.e., a cause which is simultaneous with its actual effect. Hence, it follows that if a given motion has two causes *per se*, they must be simultaneous with each other.

c. #3 tried to point out that the distinction between a *per se* cause and a *per aliud* cause, which is a distinction based on the relation of each cause to a given effect, is not the same as the distinction between an accidental and essential subordination of causes, for this distinction depends upon a comparison of the several causes for a given effect *with one* another, and not of each with the effect.

(1) The reason for the point made in #3 was the unclarity and ambiguity of the examples which St. Thomas used in *S.T.*, I, 46, 2, ad 7. For example, a series of fathers and sons presents the following elements for analysis:

(a) For a given effect, namely, the generation of A, all of the other men in the series, B,C,D, etc. are only *per aliud* causes, because a man as a man is not the efficient cause, but only the generative act as such. Hence, let us substitute a series of generative acts, by B, by C, by D, etc. Now of these generative acts, one, B's generative act, is a proximate and *per se* cause of the generation of A; all the others are remote and *per aliud* efficient causes, with respect to the generation of A, though each is a *per se* and proximate cause of some other effect; thus, the generative act of C, though *per aliud* with respect to A's generation, is *per se* with respect to B's.

(b) Now if one examines this series of temporally successive causes, one finds that they are all essentially alike; hence it should be said—even if St. Thomas doesn't say it—that though these actions are causally subordinated in the sense that a prior cause is necessary, nevertheless the causes as such, and in relation to one another, are not essentially subordinated to one another.

(c) The same thing can be true in a set of *per se* causes for a given effect. Two causes can both be *per se*, both be simultaneous in action with each other and with their common effect, and yet two things can be true of them:

(1) They can either be dependent, or independent of each other: dependent as one stick moving another to move a stone; independent as two sticks, neither of which moves another, together moving a stone.

(2) They can either be essentially or accidentally subordinated to one another if one is dependent on the other: accidentally, as one moving stick to another in motion; or essentially, as the moving stick to the moving hand which moves it.

(d) As I pointed out before, St. Thomas's other example is of minor relevance to the whole discussion. The substitution of one hammer for another, in temporal succession, is a case of a series of causes in which the members are independent of one another. The action of the first hammer and the action of the second hammer are independent. They are also only accidentally different.

(e) But if St. Thomas's two examples of successive causes be considered, and if my two examples. of simultaneous causes be added, we get the following four cases:

      (1) A series of causes in which a posterior is dependent on a prior, and which are, compared with one another, only accidentally different.

      (2) A series of causes in which a posterior is not dependent on a prior, and which are, compared with one another, only accidentally different.

      (3) A set of simultaneous causes in which one is dependent on the other and which are, compared with one another, only accidentally different.

      (4) A set of simultaneous causes in which one is not dependent on the other, and which are, compared with one another, essentially different.

(f) But this is not exhaustive of all possibilities. The fifth possibility is that of a series of temporally successive causes in which a posterior is dependent on a prior, and which are, compared with one another, essentially different. To illustrate this, I gave as a case: the man who trained a dog to carry a burden, that operation being performed at a later time.

      (1) Now obviously, the training of the dog—not the man as man—is the efficient cause of the dog's trained disposition, and it is a *per se* cause thereof. But with respect to the effect in question, the carrying of the burden, the proximate *per se* cause is the dog's operation, according to its disposition; and with respect to this effect, the man's act of training and even the dog's disposition as such are remote and *per aliud* causes.

      (2) Nevertheless, the operation depends upon the disposition, and the disposition is a residual effect of the training. Here is a series of de-pendent causes, and when we compare two efficient causes in this series, the man's act of training and the dog's act of carrying, we see that they are essentially, not accidentally, different.

(2) These distinctions being made, and not being without significance, it was then shown that they do not alter the primary point, namely, that a series of causes, whether dependent or independent, whether accidentally or essentially different, can be infinite; whereas a set of simultaneous causes, whether dependent or independent, whether accidentally or essentially different, must be finite.

      (a) Furthermore, it was of the greatest importance to see that the point about finiteness or infinity is in no way affected by these distinctions, but only by the simultaneity or non-simultaneity of the causes in relation to each other and to a given effect.

      (b) The fact that I brought more distinctions into the discussion than St. Thomas did explicitly is certainly not destructive of clarity; and, moreover, it was necessitated by the fact that traditional discussion is ambiguous and confused.

d. #4 aimed to introduce the traditional distinction between principal and instrumental causes, which applies only in the case of a set of *per se* causes for a given effect. It should be noted at once that this distinction is not a distinction based upon the relation of two causes to their common effect, but upon their relation to one another.

(1) Now here the distinction between essentially vs. accidentally subordinated *per se* causes becomes relevant, for only when two *per se* causes are essentially different can they be related as principal and instrumental.

(2) A principal cause is always a higher, an instrumental a lower, cause, for the same effect, and this gradation of higher and lower is inseparable from the hierarchical order in which essentially different causes can be placed.

(3) Furthermore, it was pointed out that unlike two principal causes, in a series of causes, which are essentially different, a principal and an instrumental cause in a set of causes, have "*one and the same proximate effect.*" This should have been obvious enough, but let me expand it briefly.

(a) Let A be the effected motion. Let AA and aa be its proximate *per se* causes, essentially different, hierarchically ordered. Then AA is here principal and aa instrumental cause of *one* effect, viz. A—on the condition, of course, that the motion of aa is dependent on the motion of AA. Furthermore, as I have shown, if there are only these two *per se* causes of A, then aa the moved mover moving A, will be both immediate and proximate, whereas AA, which moves aa as it moves A, will be proximate but mediated. The principal cause of a given effect is always a mediated proximate cause; the ultimate instrumental cause an immediate proximate cause.

(b) Now let the motion AA be the residual effect of the motion B; and let BB and bb be related to the motion B, as AA and aa are related to the motion A. Then BB will be a principal cause of the motion B, and a *per aliud* cause of the motion A. Hence, though both AA and BB are principal causes, they are not principal causes of the same effect; and furthermore, AA is dependent on BB, not as on a sufficient, but as on a necessary, condition. Hence, even if AA is causally dependent on BB, and even if AA and BB are essentially different, and BB is higher than AA hierarchically, AA and BB are not related as instrumental and principal causes, for such a relation only occurs between *per se* causes of one and the same effect.

(4) Now it was said that in any finite set of *per se* causes which are related as principal and instrumental, there must be some first or highest principal cause as well as some lowest or ultimate instrumental cause. This was obvious. But this analysis was incomplete.

(a) Our present account, being more elaborate, shows us that in a finite set of simultaneous *per se* causes, there must always be what I have called a "first member."

(b) Since the members of a set of *per se* causes need not be essentially different and subordinated in that way, it need not be true that the "first member" of the set is a principal cause in the strict meaning of "principal." In a loose meaning of "principal," the "first member" of the set can, of course, be called the highest or first principal cause, and all the other dependent causes are its instruments. But on a strict meaning of "principal" more than causal dependence is involved, namely, hierarchical subordination. This is important, because as we have seen, when two causes are related to a given effect as principal and instrumental, on the strict meaning, the effect requires their cooperation and their cooperation as *essentially different in type.*

(5) Hence, the more general conclusion here should have been that in a set of *per se* causes, in which some depend on others, there must be a "first member" because the set is finite; and this more general conclusion could then have been qualified by the statement that if, in addition, the causes are essentially different, and ordered to one another and to their effect because of this fact, the "first member" will also be the "highest principal cause" in the set.

e. #5 attempted to summarize what was shown so far. It merely said:

(1) First, the general truth: that no series of causes *qua* a series of temporally successive motions need be finite, hence need have a first member.

(2) Second, a qualification of this truth, added for greater precision, namely that the distinction between essentially and accidentally subordinated members in a *series* of causes, does not alter the truth.

(3) Third, that in any set of simultaneous causes, all of which are *per se* causes of one and the same effect, there must always be a *first member*—whether that first member is or is not, in a strict sense, also the highest principal cause. This follows from the finitude of the set.

(a) It was then pointed out that the one remaining question, therefore, was whether this "first member" in any set of *per se* causes was God, according to the nominal definition of "unmoved mover" or "uncaused efficient cause."

(b) And the caution was added: that so far the discussion was considering only motions as effects, and hence considering all efficient causes as causes of motion *as such.*

f. #6 attempted to show that it could not be argued that the "first member" in any set of *per se* causes for a given motion was God. Though the argument given was sound, it was only one of two arguments, and the more restricted in its scope. Let me state the more general argument first, and then repeat briefly, and more clearly, the restricted argument given in the first paper.

(1) The more general argument is the one already stated, namely, that any first member in a set of *per se* causes can be itself the residual effect of a *prior per se* cause. Hence, it follows that the first member in a set of *per se* causes need not be an *absolutely uncaused motion*, or a cause which is absolutely—that is, in no sense—the effect of a *prior* cause. This being so, the character of the first member of any set of *per se* causes does not satisfy the nominal definition of God. And it is seen that though any given natural motion as an effect can have only a finite plurality of *per se* causes of itself, it need not have a finite plurality of causes, for any effect can have *per aliud* as well as *per se* causes, and these can always be infinite.

(2) The restricted argument turns on the consideration of causes which are, in a strict sense, related as principal and instrumental causes of the same effect. Now there are two possibilities here:

(a) *Either*: the principal as well as the instrumental cause may be a cognate object, i.e., a natural motion within the sphere of experience. *Or*: it may be supposed that the set of causes includes, as its highest principal member, a transcendent cause. Only in the latter case, is it necessary to *infer* the existence of the "highest principal cause."

(b) But we have already shown that if the highest principal cause is a natural motion, it need not be an uncaused cause or an unmoved mover. Hence, we need consider only the second possibility.

(c) In the original paper, my argument against this second possibility was not adequately stated. But the truth was, nevertheless, implicit in what was there said. The truth is that we must be able to see that two causes are strictly related as principal and instrument by reference to the character of the effect. In short, it is the character of the effect which must tell us that the effect requires, among its *per se* causes, two essentially different causes that are, by reason of this fact, related as principal and instrumental in the production of the effect. For example, when we know an effect to be the becoming of a work of *art*, we know that its causes must include *artistic action*, action of the artist's mind, as one of its *per se* causes, and as the principal cause subordinating the physical instrumentalities of the artistic making. If we did not know that the thing in becoming were a work of art, if we did not know that this change was truly a "making," we would not have any ground for this inference, from the effect as such, to the existence of artistic action as its principal cause. Now the core of my argument is this: that there is nothing about the character of a natural motion as an effect that requires us to look beyond natural motions as its causes—its *per se* causes, whether instrumental or principal. Hence, it follows that we cannot infer God's existence as a transcendent principal cause of natural motions as effects.

(d) As it was pointed out in the original article, and earlier in this paper, this does not deny that God is involved as an efficient cause in the occurrence of every natural motion— albeit a cause operating analogously to natural motions as efficient causes. It only insists that God's existence as such a cause cannot be inferred from the character of natural motions as the effects of *per se* causes.

g. This concludes my summary of Part II, #1–6 in the previous article, reviewed in the light of the more elaborate and precise analysis given in this paper. The conclusion there given, that God cannot be proved as *causa fiendi*, as the unmoved mover or first efficient cause or highest principal cause of natural motions *as such*, is the conclusion here reached. The fundamental reasons for the conclusion are the same in both presentations, though they are much more explicitly presented here in the light of an adequate account of causes, causation, and natural motion. Furthermore, this paper adds arguments which confirm the main arguments needed for the conclusion, and these confirmatory arguments have also the effect of raising difficulties about understanding the dogmatic truth that God is *causa fiendi*, i.e., an efficient cause of either every or only some natural motions, a cause *per se*, yet either immediate in every case, or immediate in some and mediated in others.

In the light of the foregoing, it will be clear to those who have written me difficulties or objections, how their difficulties are overcome and their objections are answered. All that remains, then, is to deal briefly with the published criticisms by Schwartz (in *The Thomist*, VI, 1, April, 1943). This is almost unnecessary, for a careful reader will see at once that no point raised by Schwartz in any way affects the cogency or validity of the foregoing reasoning, or requires the slightest qualification of the conclusion reached. Nevertheless, I shall now comment very briefly on Schwartz's irrelevancies. In doing so, I shall use the section headings from my own original paper, which Schwartz also uses, and in addition refer to the pages in *The Thomist* containing Schwartz's article.

4. Comment on Schwartz.

a. Of great importance is the fact that Schwartz entirely omits any reference to my #1 in Part II. This, as I have shown, contains the basic analytical distinctions fundamental to the whole course of the subsequent reasoning.

b. #2 (p. 21). I nowhere said that St. Thomas argued for God as the first member in a series, or in temporal succession of causes. I merely said that no one could argue in this way, and that if anyone interpreted St. Thomas as arguing in this way, he would be attributing a false argument to St. Thomas.

(1) Schwartz's remarks are, therefore, irrelevant, except as a defense of St. Thomas where none was needed.

(2) But it should be noted that Schwartz does concede the truth of the argument, namely, that a series of temporally ordered causes need not be finite or have a first member.

c. #3 (pp. 22–31). Schwartz's discussion here is irrelevant for the same reason as before in re #2.

(1) Schwartz fails utterly to see why I introduced the additional distinction (between accidentally and essentially differentiated and subordinated causes), to qualify what I had previously shown to be the case for *any* series of causes. The original argument, that there need be no first member in a series of causes, is not invalidated by the addition of this distinction concerning the way in which successive causes can be related or subordinated *to one another.*

(2) What was said by me concerning essential vs. accidental subordination of causes was utterly independent of my distinction between proximate and remote causes, or causes *per se* and causes *per aliud.* If Schwartz had tried to understand my point in #1, which he omitted, he would have seen that my distinction between causes simultaneous with, and causes not-simultaneous with, their effect is essentially the distinction between causes *per se* and *per aliud* for a given effect. Moreover, everything that Schwartz says about the simultaneity of *per se* causes is true, and that truth is included in and taken account of in my argument. As I have shown, that truth in no way alters the conclusion reached.

(3) What Schwartz says about the "imperfection" of the proofs for God's existence (his pp. 26–27) does not permit a plurality of proofs, if all the proofs have certitude rather than probability. St. Thomas's point in *S.T.* I, 47, 1 ad 3 does not bear on perfect vs. imperfect demonstration; but upon probable vs. certain demonstration. If a demonstration is certain, not probable, there is only one such, whether it be *a posteriori* or *a priori.* Nor need every *a posteriori* demonstration be imperfect, for it can be made by means of real as well as nominal definitions. Thus, the proof that there exists a rational animal is a perfect *a posteriori* demonstration, even though it be made from a multiplicity of effects— the various works of reason. But any proof that God exists will be an imperfect *a posteriori* demonstration, because it cannot use a real, but must use a nominal, definition. Furthermore, the fact that several nominal definitions are used does not create a plurality of logically distinct *a posteriori* proofs. That only happens if the several nominal definitions are absolutely independent of one another. Thus, if one were trying to prove the existence of an Aryan race, and used these two nominal definitions, "white men" and "superior men," the two demonstrations would be

independent, and could, therefore, be only probable at best; as
well as imperfect. But the nominal definitions used in the first,
second, third, and fourth "way" are strictly co-implicative, not
independent. Hence, even if the first four ways were valid proofs,
as stated, they would be merely rhetorical variants of one proof.
Hence, that one *a posteriori* proof, if it were valid as it is not, could
be certain, and yet at the same time it would be imperfect by reason of using a nominal definition.

(4) Schwartz's fourth point (his pp. 27–31) is both irrelevant and
confused, despite the fact that it does contain some truth, which
truth is already taken into account by my argument.

  (a) I do not use the phrase "essentially diverse causes" to signify
causes *per se* for a given effect. That is now sufficiently clear,
but it was sufficiently clear to a careful reader of the original
article. Hence, what I have called "essentially diverse causes"
need not be simultaneous with one another or their effect.
Yet a set of *per se* causes must be. That is the only truth in
Schwartz's reasoning here.

  (b) Schwartz's analysis of *per se* causes is faulty and inadequate. It
is based on St. Thomas's commentary on some passages in
the *Physics*, and not upon a careful and independent study of
all the relevant passages in the *Physics*.

  (c) According to Aristotle, only a motion can be an actual and
proper cause of a motion as an effect. A substance *qua* substance, or the powers or habits of a substance, cannot be
actual or proper causes of a motion as an effect. All of these
are causes *per aliud*—causes responsible for the effect only
through the mediation of operative causes, or actual operations as causes, which, then, are the only causes *per se*, causes
which *require the effect to occur*. Schwartz obviously does not
understand the very passages in Aristotle, concerning which
he cites St. Thomas's inadequate commentary.

  (d) It should be noted that Schwartz also fails utterly to see the
significance of what is the most crucial point in the whole
argument, namely, that causes *per se* have residual effects,
which as motions can, at a subsequent time, operate as *per se*
causes of other effects. He cites an example of this (p. 28),
fire heating water, water heating bed, bed heating body; and
says "The temporal succession is brought about *by the duration of the effect* which subsequently acts as a cause in another
motion" (italics mine). This "duration of the effect" which
permits the motion to act as a subsequent *per se* cause of
another motion is what I have called the "residual effect."

  (e) Furthermore, Schwartz fails to see that though two temporally successive causes may both be causes *per se*, they cannot
be causes *per se* for a given, a single, known effect. A series of
causes, which contains causes *per se*, will contain causes for

different proximate effects. Only the causes *per se* for one and the same effect have to be simultaneous. Schwartz sees this and denies it at the same time, for he argues, without qualification, that causes which are in temporal succession must be causes *per accidens*, which I have called causes *per aliud.* This is both true and false. It is true, if what is meant is that in a temporal succession of causes *all* cannot be *per se* causes for a given effect; all those which are not simultaneous with the effect, cannot be. It is false if what is meant is that in a temporal succession of causes, each efficient cause must be a cause *per accidens* or *per aliud*; for each efficient cause not only can, but must, be a *per se* cause of its own proximate effect, though it will only be a *per aliud* cause of whatever effect is not simultaneous with, but posterior to, it. All of Schwartz's confused thinking and inadequate analysis here flows from his failure (I) to distinguish remote and proximate causes for one and the same effect, and (2) to see that by "essentially diverse causes" I did not mean "causes *per se*" or causes necessarily simultaneous with a given effect.

(f) The rest of Schwartz's reasoning here is invalid. He does not prove that there must be a finite set of causes for a given effect; nor can this be proved on the premise that a cause *per aliud* or *per accidens* must itself have a *per se* cause. His error here is due to his neglect of the crucial fact of "residual effects" which permit every natural motion to have its own *per se* causes, and yet allow these to be an infinite series of causes for any given effect, in which some will be *per aliud* for that effect, and some *per se*. Furthermore, he makes the error of supposing that there can be any argument for a first cause, which is one of a plurality of causes, *except* from the finitude of that plurality. I have already sufficiently demonstrated this error. The fact that every motion must have its own *per se* causes, whether or not this motion is in turn the *per se* cause or *per aliud* cause of a given effect, does not in any way lead to the conclusion that, for the given effect, there must be some first cause. Furthermore, he contradicts himself, for at one place he argues (p. 28) that causes *per accidens* must be in temporal succession, and in another he argues (p. 29) that even causes *per accidens* for a given effect must be finite in number; despite the fact that he has admitted that no temporal succession of causes need be finite. He permits himself to play fast and loose with the notions of cause *per se* and *per accidens*, with the notions of proximate and remote causes, and with the fundamental point about infinite series of successive motions and finite sets of simultaneous actions. All of his contradictions are fully operative in the paragraph at the bottom of his page 29 and at the top of his page 30.

(g) Schwartz is right in connecting the simultaneity of several
     causes with the fact that they are all *per se* causes of one
     effect, and in connecting the temporal succession of several
     causes with the fact that they are *not* all *per se* causes of one
     effect, but with respect to that one effect, some must be
     causes *per aliud*—or in his lanquage *per accidens*. If there were
     no causes *per aliud*, there could be no infinite series of causes
     in temporal succession, regressing from a given effect. If
     there were no causes *per se* for a given effect, there would be
     no necessity for any plurality of causes ever to form a finite
     set. All this is true, without affecting the conclusion, namely,
     that for a given effect, considering all its causes, *every cause
     upon which it depends*, the plurality of these causes need not
     be finite, because though its *per se* causes must be, one of
     these, the first member of the set, can always be the residual
     effect of a *prior* cause, which is *per se* with respect to the ante-
     rior part of the motion which has this residuum, and which
     is *per aliud* with respect to the given effect of which the pos-
     terior part of this motion is a *per se* cause.

(h) Even if Schwartz's reasoning were correct, namely, that there
     must be a first cause on the ground that this is required by
     the principle of sufficient reason, not by the finitude of
     simultaneous causes, the conclusion he reaches thereby
     would be incompatible with dogmatic truth; for the God he
     would then have proved to exist would be a remote or *per
     aliud* cause for some motions as effects, and a proximate or
     per se cause for one or more others. I have already sufficiently
     shown all the difficulties in such a conception of God as
     causa fiendi. Even if God were a *per se* cause immediately of
     some motions and a mediated *per se* cause of other motions,
     the same difficulties would arise. . . . But the difficulties do
     not arise within the area of natural reason or philosophy,
     because God cannot be so proved. They are purely theolog-
     ical difficulties, and do not have to be fully resolved, for the
     action of God as *causa fiendi* is as mysterious and as imper-
     fectly intelligible as the action of God as *causa essendi*.
     Dogmatic faith can tell us *that* God acts in a certain way with-
     out our understanding fully the *what* of that action. But rea-
     son cannot prove *that* God acts in the way Schwartz supposes.

(i) I wish to be sure that it is understood that there can be no
     argument for the finiteness of any plurality of causes except
     from the fact of their simultaneity, which in turn is due to
     the fact that all together are causes *per se* of one and the
     same effect. If causes are not simultaneous, they are not
     causes *per se* of one and the same effect, and if they are not
     causes *per se* of one and the same effect, they need not be
     simultaneous, in which case, the causes upon which the

given effect *depends* at this very moment of its occurrence can be infinite in number, for it is this very infinity which makes it possible to say for every member in the total plurality either that it is the actual effect of some other motion, which is its cause *per se*, or that it is the residual part of a motion which has a cause *per se* in some motion which ceased before this residual effect occurred. Hence the principle of sufficient reason is not violated, for the principle requires *only* that every effect have causes, not that the causes be finite; and that the causes it has be sufficient for the production of the effect.

(j)   The texts from St. Thomas which Schwartz cites are the same texts which I cited. They confirm what I have said, in so far as they speak clearly; and Schwartz can give no contrary interpretation of them. St. Thomas says that in "*causes which do not act simultaneously,* an infinitude of causes is not impossible" (p. 30, italics Schwartz's). The further fact that when causes do not act simultaneously, the non-simultaneous causes, with respect to a given effect, are also *per aliud* causes of that effect, in no way affects the conclusion. St. Thomas's lanquage here is unclear because he fails to see two meanings in his phrase "*per accidens.*" In one of Aristotle's meanings, to call something only "accidentally" a cause is to say it is not cause at all. In another meaning, to call something "accidental" as a cause implies that it is not a cause *per se*, but *per aliud*, albeit an indispensable condition of the effect's occurring. Thus, unless the father of a man is himself created by God, it is not a dispensable condition whether the father was himself generated. True, the generation which is the grandfather's act is only a *per aliud* cause of the generation of the grandson, but it is no less a cause, and indispensable to the becoming of the effect, i.e., the grandson's generation. (The grandson's generation is a *contingent* effect of the grandfather's generative act, precisely because the latter is, with respect to it, only a *per aliud* cause.) The other example St. Thomas uses, of the hand moving the stick to move the stone, shows that the opposite of accidental is *per se;* and hence the opposite of *per se*, which is called "accidental," would be more accurately called "*per aliud.*"

(k)   Furthermore, as I have already pointed, St. Thomas is misled by his own example of the multiplication of the hammers, for the multiplication of the fathers is not like the multiplication of the hammers. In the case of the hammers, it is the multiplication which is entirely accidental to the effect, for the effect would be the same in every way, were it accomplished with one or ten hammers, the ten occurring in a series of substitutions. But that is not true in the case of the generative series. In no sense at all is it accidental that B generates A *only after* C has generated B; for, supposing B not to be created, B could not generate A unless it had been generated by C. Hence, it is false to say in the one case what can be said in the other. The ten hammers, because of the merely accidental character of their multiplication, do reduce to one particular cause, for it would make no difference to the effect's occurring whether one hammer had remained unbroken or whether ten are used. But, omitting the possibility of creation, it does make a great difference to the generation of A, the effect in question, that there can be an infinite number of generative acts prior to the act of his own father; for if there were not, he would not have been generated. It is only true to say that in a series of generative acts, or a series of generators, that these items are only accidentally different, from one another. They reduce, in short, not to *one* particular generator, but rather to one *type* of generator. In contrast, if the action of the sun and the action of elementary bodies were generative causes, as they are not, these would be essentially diverse types of generators. The mention of the sun and the elementary body befogs the issue. For let it be supposed, without referring to "mythical physics," that there are four *per se*, simultaneous, causes of the generation of this man, only one of which is his father's generative act. Now either the rest are also efficient causes or they are not. If they are, then either the generative act by this man's father is itself immediately caused by one of these, or it is an independent cause. It makes no difference, for in any case, if the generative process has a plurality of *per se* causes, we know that that plurality is finite, but unless we know something about the order of these causes to one another, we do not know whether they are dependent or independent, or which is an immediate and which a mediated cause of the generation, and so forth. Furthermore, we know that if any one of the four causes is a "first member" of the finite set, it can itself be a residual effect of some prior cause.

(5) Schwartz's fifth point (p. 31) adds nothing to the previous discussion except more confusion. He starts out saying what is true, namely, that the act of training a dog is not a cause *per se* of the subsequent carrying of the burden. Then he says what is false, namely, that the dog's habitual disposition is a *per se* cause of this operation. This statement is false because it is unqualified. The dog's disposition (or habit) is not an efficient cause of anything. Only an operation can be an efficient cause. The material and formal causes immanent to an operation are, of course, *per se* causes, and it is only *qua* immanent material cause that the habit

is *per se* cause of the operation. But Schwartz forgets that the habit is itself an effect which once became, and that that becoming has a *per se* efficient cause, namely, the acts of the trainer in training. And the habit, in the interval of disuse, is a residual effect of the training. It is in this way that the act of training is both a cause *per se* and a cause *per aliud*, a cause *per se* of the habit's being formed, and a cause *per aliud* of the habit's operation—in both cases an efficient cause. But the habit itself is not an efficient cause, even as a residual effect. Hence, Schwartz's remark that "two things cause *per se*" is analytically confused, for he mentions "being in act" and "the cause of what acts, being in act." But one of these 'being in act' is never an efficient cause, and always a residual effect, whereas the other is always an efficient cause, and may or may not be a residual effect. If not, it requires an efficient cause *per se*. In short, nothing is an efficient cause in virtue of its nature, but only in virtue of its actual operation. And its nature, its powers, and habits, as *per aliud* causes of the effect of its operation are themselves always residual effects of prior efficient causes, generative, or operative in the accidental order. This shows the inaccuracy of analysis in Schwartz's footnote 8 on p. 30. The conclusion he there draws does not follow.

(a) His difficulty throughout this discussion is his inadequate analysis of causes. In one line, he says that the "act of training the dog is *per se* the cause of the dog's being trained, since it is required that someone be training the dog when it is being trained." In another line, he says that "for the dog to be trained does not *per se* require to have come to be trained." But either "be trained" refers to the act of having the trained disposition or it refers to the process of getting the trained disposition. Now in the second case, coming to be trained does *per se* require a trainer, for as Schwartz himself says (fn. 8) "on the part of the effect, that is a cause *per se* without which the effect would not be produced." In the first case, if 'being trained' means the act of having the disposition, which is posterior to getting it, then we are dealing with a residual effect, which does not, as such, have a *per se* cause, though that of which it is the residual effect must have a *per se* cause. . . . The same correction of Schwartz's analysis applies in the case of the man as generated, as generating, and as being a man having the generative power.

(b) But, above all, Schwartz has misunderstood the whole course of my argument, as is indicated by his concluding remark on page 31. I have not been arguing here (my #3) that there can be a "temporal succession of causes *per se* of one effect." That is what Schwartz attributes to me, and he is right in saying that that is impossible. I was arguing that in a temporal succession of causes, including remote as well as proximate causes for a given effect, there can be "essentially diverse causes." What I meant by saying this is now perfectly plain, and would have been plain to a careful reader of the original article. Schwartz converts "essentially diverse causes"—all of which need not be simultaneous—into "causes *per se* for one effect"—and then knocks over a straw man of his own making. And the example I used is a sound example of the point I was making.

d. #6 (pp. 31–34). Schwartz here so completely misstates the argument which I developed at this point, that there is no real need to consider anything he says, except as showing further confusion on his part.

(1) I *did* say that if it were impossible to prove God as one of a plurality of causes for a given effect, then the only remaining possibility would be to try to prove God from an effect of which He is the unique cause. I did *not* say that the *reason* why it is impossible to prove God as one of a plurality of causes for a given effect *is* that God *must* be proved as the unique cause of whatever effect we use to demonstrate His existence. Yet this is what Schwartz makes out my argument to be. He does not see that the fact that God could certainly be inferred from an effect of which He is the unique cause is independent of the fact that it may be impossible to infer God's existence from an effect of which He is in fact a cause, though only one in a plurality of causes. Schwartz does not deny the first of these two facts, but he proceeds as if that fact were the only basis for my argument that it is impossible to infer God as the principal cause of natural motions. My argument turns on the relation of a principal and an instrumental cause to each other, and to their common effect. I nowhere speak of two "ultimate causes" of one effect, each of which is a "total cause" of that effect, but I do, following St. Thomas, speak of the *common* effect of the cooperative active of a principal and an instrumental cause, as flowing from both. But even here it does not flow from both in the same way, for it flows from the instrumental cause immediately and from the principal cause mediately, precisely because these two causes are not ultimate and independent lines of causality, which is what Schwartz erroneously attributes to me. He charges me with saying that "the instrumental cause and the principal cause are independent lines of causality," whereas I say what he says should be said, namely, that "the instrumental is subordinated to the principal cause." This subordination of the instrumental to the principal cause is not incompatible with the fact that the whole effect proceeds from both. It does proceed from both, from the painter's brush immediately, and from the painter's mind and art mediately, for the painter's brush could not produce a work of art except it be the instrument of the painter's art, nor could the painter's art paint except it use a brush or some other instrument for putting paints on a canvas.

(2)   This being so, and what I myself said, it is obvious that Schwartz
      missed the point of my argument. The crux of my argument
      turned on this one fact: that unless the character of the effect
      itself signified that it had to be produced by a principal and an
      instrumental cause in cooperation, as does the artist's work, it
      could not be inferred from the effect that any other than the
      known *per se* causes are at work in producing the effect. Now with
      respect to every natural motion, there are known *per se* causes at
      work, and these are natural motions. If God is also a cause of the
      effect, related as principal cause to the operation of these natural
      agents as instruments, then the character of the effect should
      itself betray the fact that the operation of natural motions as *per se*
      causes for a given motion is insufficient, and that beyond all these
      per se causes a transcendent—non-natural—cause must be
      posited, which cause subordinates natural motions as its instru-
      ments in the production of any natural motion as an effect.

(a)   This was my argument, and Schwartz failed to discuss it.
      Nothing that he said has any bearing on it. To answer it, one
      would have to show that we can know from the character of
      a natural motion, as an effect, that all of the natural motions
      which are its *per se* causes are, at best, only instrumental,
      being subordinate, to God as a principal cause. This I say,
      until the contrary is proved, cannot be shown.

(b)   Hence, I concluded that one cannot infer God's existence
      on the ground that His action must be posited as the princi-
      pal cause of any natural motion, a principal cause subordi-
      nating the known *per se* causes of natural motions, namely,
      other natural motions simultaneous with it.

(c)   In the present paper, I have verified that conclusion, and
      gone beyond it, showing that no "first member" in a set of
      per se causes for a given effect (whether or not that first mem-
      ber be a principal cause, in the strict sense) need be an
      uncaused cause, or unmoved mover—and hence there is no
      inference to God in this way.

(d)   My argument in no sense rested on the authority of St.
      Thomas. The passage I cited from St. Thomas was merely a
      way of saying what could have been said in other words. The
      truth of what was said, in whatever words, is, quite apart from
      St. Thomas, that the science of physics gives us an adequate
      explanation of each natural motion, and in doing so men-
      tions nothing but natural motions as the proximate *per se*
      causes. Hence, if it is a dogmatic truth that God is in fact the
      principal cause of each natural motion, using natural
      motions as instruments, that dogmatic truth can be known
      only by faith, not by reason independently of faith. And
      when it is known by faith *that* God is such a cause, that dog-
      matic position has difficulties for the philosopher, but these

difficulties do not deny the truth of faith. The difficulties are of the sort I have already mentioned, namely, that either God is the principal cause of *some* natural motions, using other natural motions as instruments in producing *this some*, or God is an efficient cause of all natural motions, in which case he is not the *principal* cause of *any*, for a given cause cannot be the *principal* cause of the motion of its instruments, but only of the motion which its instruments produces through subordination to itself.

   (e)   The text cited by Schwartz, from *C.G.*, III, 70 confirms everything I have said. But it must be read in the light of the text I cited, *C.G.*, III, 69.

   (f)   The gist of my argument is contained in #6, b, (3). What has been said in this paper merely expands the analysis therein indicated.

(3) Schwartz's final remarks here are without bearing.

   (a)   Since I do not talk about "ultimate causes," and do not call either the instrumental or the principal cause an ultimate cause, Schwartz's comment is relevant only to his own language, not to mine. If he had understood my argument, he would have known that I could not speak of any known or inferable cause of motion as an *ultimate* cause. Quite the contrary, the whole force of my reasoning was to show that, so far as motion is concerned, we cannot discover, by reasoning from such an effect, an ultimate cause, any first cause *without qualification*.

   (b)   Nor do I anywhere deny the possibility that God may be both *causa movens* and *causa efficiens* in the order of becoming, as well as *causa essendi*. I do not hold that it is impossible or contradictory for God to be both *causa fiendi* and *causa essendi*. Yet Schwartz attributes this to me (pp. 33–34). On the contrary, I only assert that God's existence cannot be proved from *motion* as an effect, but only from *being* as an effect. Even if this be so, it can still be true that motion, as well as being, is a *per se* effect of God's causality. That God is *causa fiendi* may be knowable to faith apart from reason; and it may be known to reason, *after* God is known as *causa essendi*, that God is a *per aliud* cause of natural motions; for if God causes the *existence* of natural things, and the *existence* of their powers and acts, as well as of the natures, God is a cause of the operation of natural powers only in the sense that existence is presupposed by becoming. But to cause the existence of a power is not to cause its operation. To cause the existence of an operation, as an accidental being, is not to cause its becoming. Hence, the fact that the Divine causality is presupposed by the operation of all efficient causes of becoming, which are *per se* causes of their effects, does not tell us that Divine action is a *per se* cause of these effects, according to their becoming. For example, in the sphere of substantial change, God is not a generator, though he does cause the existence of the generator, the generative act, and the generated thing. The *causa fiendi* here is the generative act. The fact that this generative act could not operate causally, as a cause of becoming, unless it itself existed, does not make the cause of its existence the cause of the effect it produces when it operates causally. The point here being made will become clearer in my subsequent discussion of God as *causa essendi*. Here suffice it to point out that Schwartz's remark about my misapplication of the principle of excluded middle is totally unwarranted. I did not say that God had to be either *causa essendi* or *causa fiendi*, and could not be both. I said that in our natural knowledge of God, which is entirely based upon his effects, and not upon a direct knowledge of the Divine nature or operation, we can know *only* that God causes the existence of whatever exists as it exists, but not that God is a *per se* cause of any motion *as such*. *A priori*, it is not impossible that *motion* as an effect could be the sufficient basis for an inference to God's existence; but careful examination of the actual facts shows why no such inference is possible.

5. This completes the first part of my task. What remains to be done is to set forth a valid and tenable proof of God's existence, from being as an effect to God as *causa essendi*. I shall do this in Part IV following. There I will first remove the supposed difficulties and the specious objections which Schwartz has raised to the possibility of such a proof; then I will expound the proof; and finally, I will defend it against such genuine objections as have been brought to my attention.

IV. *God as Cause of Being*

PRELIMINARY REMARKS

If God's existence cannot be proved from the occurrence of natural motions, i.e., if God cannot be proved as a cause required for the occurrence of these motions, then only one possibility remains. Perhaps God can be proved as the cause required by the mode of being (i.e., the contingent existence) of things known to exist.

In my original article, I investigated this possibility, albeit incompletely. In Part II of that article, and in points #7–10, I tried to indicate wherein the possibility of such a proof is suggested by St. Thomas. The central insight is contained in St. Thomas's notion that 'being is the *proper effect* of God.' As I shall show presently, there can be no question that "proper effect" means that *only* God can efficiently cause being, that being, or existence, is the effect of no other efficient cause, and hence that God is the unique and exclusive cause of the existence of His creatures. Only one text in St. Thomas—as against many to the contrary— *seems* to say that creatures can cause being, but that text, as we shall see can either be given another interpretation, or it contradicts the truth of what is said elsewhere.

I devoted points #7–10 in Part II to a consideration of St. Thomas's views on the causation of being, in order to show that the proof of God's existence that I was about to propose had some basis in Thomistic teaching, though, so far as I know, none in the writings of Aristotle. This discussion was in no sense an argument *from* authority. Rather it was an argument *about* the authority of St. Thomas. Whether or not there is a valid proof for God as *causa essendi*, which rests upon the uniqueness of God as such an *efficient* cause, is a question which can be solved only by examining every step in the reasoning proposed. If there is a valid proof of this sort, and the authority of St. Thomas is against it, so much the worse for St. Thomas. If there is no valid proof of this sort, and the authority of St. Thomas seems to favor one, again so much the worse for St. Thomas. But I tried to show two things: (a) that the authority of St. Thomas favored such a proof; and (b) that the proof was itself valid. I did both of these things incompletely in the original article, and I shall now try to do both completely.

It is absolutely important, for an understanding of the original article and the present work, to see that these two things are independent. They would be independent even if St. Thomas had explicitly stated the proof of God as *causa essendi* through the premise that *only* God can efficiently cause being. This he did not do. The Fourth of the Five Ways cannot be so interpreted, though it is suggestive in this direction. As written, it is far from being adequate or explicit reasoning. Furthermore, St. Thomas nowhere proves the proposition that 'being is the proper effect of God,' though he provides us with all the materials for making such a proof. The reason St. Thomas fails to prove this proposition is that he supposes God's existence to be proved quite apart from it, and then reaches this proposition as a consequence from knowledge of God's nature. Since this proposition must be proved before we can conclude that God exists, the proposition must be stated in its negative form: 'No contingent being can cause the being of anything.' St. Thomas provides us with the materials for proving this proposition. Hence, I say that the authority of St. Thomas is favorable to what I shall show to be the only valid proof of God's existence, but the showing that this proof is valid is absolutely independent of any discussion of St. Thomas's authority, favorable or unfavorable. The only way in which a proof can be shown to be valid is by an explicit statement of *all* its premises, and an examination of the grounds upon which each is capable of being affirmed as true.

The critics of my original article fell into three groups: (1) those who thought the proofs from motion were valid, but that the proof of God as *unique causa essendi* was also valid, and distinct from the others as a proof; (2) those who thought that the proof I proposed was the one valid proof, and that the "five ways" were merely five ways of expressing this one proof; and (3) those who defended the proofs from motion and denied that God could be proved as *causa essendi* in any other way than he could be proved as *causa fiendi*, namely, as a first or highest or most universal cause of the given effect (i.e., being) but not as the sole efficient cause of such an effect, these critics arguing that with respect to being, as with respect to motion, God works through intermediary or instrumental causes.

Against the first group, I have already sufficiently argued in Parts II and III *supra*. Since they agree that God can be proved as the *sole* cause of being, which is His *proper* effect, I have no further argument with them here.

Against the second group, I wish only to say that I cannot find the grounds for reading Q.2, A.3 as they do, nor have they succeeded in showing precisely how the actual words in which the "five ways" are stated can be so interpreted. But this issue seems to me totally unimportant, for it has no bearing on philosophical truth, but only on the "perfection" of St. Thomas's writing—his writing, not his thinking. I disagree with these critics only if they think that it makes no difference whether the proof be formulated from motion as the effect, or from contingent being as the effect, requiring God as cause. I have shown that no inference to God can be made validly from motion as the effect; more precisely, I have shown that from motion as the effect, no inference can be drawn to any unmoved mover or uncaused cause or first efficient cause. Hence if, quite apart from their desire to defend the perfection of St. Thomas's written words, these critics do agree that the only proof of God's existence is based upon an effect which *only* a necessary being can cause, then I have no further argument with them.

The third group consists of Schwartz. I have already argued against the first part of his contention, namely, that from the facts of motion, the existence of an unmoved mover, a first efficient cause operating through intermediary or instrumental causes, can be proved. I shall now argue against the second part of his contention in a twofold manner: first, by showing that the authority of St. Thomas supports the notion that *only* God is an efficient cause of being; and second, quite apart from the authority of St. Thomas, by showing that the proof proposed is valid. If Schwartz were right about St. Thomas, then St. Thomas would be opposed to the only valid proof. If Schwartz were right about the facts, then there would be no valid proof of God's existence.

Two more things must be mentioned here. (1) In my original article, I myself proposed difficulties about the one proof that seemed possible. I can now over-come all of those difficulties. (2) I have already indicated how this can be done in several memoranda which I have written and circulated among some of my correspondents. Some of those have raised new problems or difficulties, which I myself would not have raised. These questions or difficulties must, of course, be answered.

I shall, therefore, divide the present discussion into three main sections, A, B, and C. In A, I shall deal with the authority of St. Thomas, and there I shall argue against Schwartz's interpretation of St. Thomas. In B, I shall consider the proof itself, first removing my original difficulties about it, and then perfecting the statement of it so that its truth is plain. In this connection, I shall also point out Schwartz's misunderstandings of my original discussion of difficulties. In C, I shall present and try to meet new difficulties or objections that have been raised by those who really understand the proof I am proposing.

A. The Meaning of the Proposition 'Being Is the Proper Effect of God' in the Thought of St. Thomas

1. My interpretation of the thought of St. Thomas depends upon the following texts.

a. *S.T.*, I, 8, 1: "God is in all things, not indeed as part of their essence, nor as an accident, but as an agent is present to that on which it acts. For every agent must be joined to that on which it acts immediately, as well as reach it by its power; for it is said in the *Physics* (VII, 243a4) that the moved and the mover must be together. Now since God is being itself through His essence, it is necessary that created being be His proper effect, as to ignite is the proper effect of fire itself. This effect God causes in things not only when they first begin to be, but also as long as they are conserved in being; just as light is caused in the air by the sun as long as the air remains illuminated. Therefore, as long as things have being, so long must God be present to them in the way in which they have being."

(1) This shows that St. Thomas conceived God as an *efficient*, not a formal or a material, cause of the being of creatures, for he com-pares God as cause of being with efficient causes of motion, i.e., of combustion and illumination.

(2) It shows also that as an efficient cause of the being of things, God is an immediate cause, even as the mover is the immediate cause of the motion with which it simultaneously acts. Fire does not *ignite* the combustible through intermediary or instrumental causes. It is the direct and immediate agent of its proper effect. So God is the direct and immediate agent of contingent being as His proper effect. (The point of these comparisons is not affected by the truth or falsity of St. Thomas's *Physics*.)

(3) It shows, above all, that this truth is not affected by the problem
of whether things ever began to be. The character of the Divine
causality, efficiently causing the being of things, is the same at the
moment of their *initiation* and at the moment of their *conservation*. St. Thomas obviously does not think that the endurance of
things in being is a residual effect of God's causing them to be
initially. If that were so, he would have said that the proper effect
of God's action is the *initiation* of contingent beings, and that
God's action is not required for their endurance in being, any
more than the continued motion of the mover is required for the
residual motion of the moved. He is saying, on the contrary, that,
unlike the sphere of motion where there are residual effects,
there are no residual effects in the sphere of being. The effect
cannot outlast the actual action of the efficient cause. (Again, it
is unimportant whether illumination can ever be a residual
effect.)

(4) It follows, therefore, that if one uses the word "creation" to mean
"efficient causation of caused (or contingent) beings," the meaning of the word is not altered when we use the phrases "creation
in time" and "eternal creation," For the first of these phrases only
adds a note which can be subtracted, namely, that God *initiates* as
well as *conserves* contingent beings; whereas the second of these
phrases subtracts that note (i.e., of *initiation*), but leaves the
other note (i.e., the continual action of the Divine causality so
long as contingent things exist). Now since the initiation of
things (creation in time) can neither be proved nor disproved,
according to St. Thomas (vd. *S.T.*, I, 46, 2), a philosophical, as
opposed to a dogmatic theological, use of the word "creation"
must abstract its meaning from the note of *initiation*, which is
accidental to the meaning of "creation" as signifying "efficient
cause of contingent being." Hence, we can conclude that, on the
philosophical level, the statement that "being is the *proper* effect
of God" is strictly equivalent to the statement "*Only* God can create beings."

b. *S.T.*, I, 19, 5 ad 3: "Since God wills effects to come from causes, all
effects that presuppose some other effect do not depend solely on the
will of God, but on something else besides, but the first effect depends
on the Divine will alone:' This text must be read in conjunction with
another text, viz., *S.T.*, I, 45, 5, which is as follows:

Now to produce being absolutely, not as this or that being,
belongs to creation. Hence, it is manifest that creation is the
proper act of God alone. It happens, however, that something
participates the proper action of another, not by its own power,
but instrumentally, inasmuch as it acts by the power of another.
And so some have supposed that although creation is the proper
act of the universal cause, still some inferior cause acting by the
power of the first cause, can create. . . . But such a thing cannot

be, because the secondary or instrumental cause cannot participate the action of the superior cause, except inasmuch as by
something proper to itself it acts dispositively to the effect of the
principal cause. If therefore it effects nothing, according to what
is proper to itself, it is used to no purpose, nor would there be
any need of certain instruments for certain actions. Thus, we see
that a saw, in cutting wood, which it does by a property of its own
form, produces the form of the bench, which is the proper effect
of the principal agent. *Now the proper effect of God creating is what is
presupposed to all other effects, and that is absolute being.* Hence, nothing else can act dispositively or instrumentally to this effect, since
creation is not from anything presupposed, which can be disposed by the action of the instrumental agent. So, therefore, it is
impossible for any creature to create, either by its own power or
instrumentally. And above all it is absurd to suppose that a body
can create, for no body acts except by moving or touching; and
thus it requires in its action some pre-existing thing, which can
be touched or moved, which is contrary to the very notion of creation." (Italics mine.)

(1) Now, in the first place, it should be observed that this text precedes the discussion (in I, 46, 2) of whether God's creative activity involves *initiation*. That initiation is involved, is a matter of
dogma (vd. I, 46, 3), but not known by reason. Furthermore,
whether it is or not fails to alter the sense of the foregoing passage. St. Thomas is not saying that there are no instrumental
causes in creation *if* creation involves initiation. He is saying that,
whether or not creation involves initiation, there are no instrumental causes. Only God creates.

(2) In the second place, his reason for saying this is plain. Creation,
or the causation of being, is radically distinct from motion or
change of any sort, accidental or substantial. For "what results
from movement or change results from something pre-existing"
(*S.T.*, I, 45, 3). Any action by a natural agent presupposes a pre-
existent potentiality. (Vd. *ibid.*, 45, 6, ad 3). Now whatever causes
an effect by an operation distinct from its own essence must act
on something pre-existing. It must move or change in order to
cause a movement or change. But, according to St. Thomas, "creation signified actively means the Divine action, which is God's
essence" (*ibid.*, 1, 45, 3 ad 1), and hence "God by creation produces things without movement" (*ibid.*, *corpus.*). All of these points
help us to understand what it means to say that creation is *ex
nihilo*, which means that created things are *not* produced from
anything pre-existent; it does not mean that they are produced
from nothing, as from a pre-existent material cause. (Vd. *ibid.*, 1,
45, 1, ad 3).

(3) All of these points hold for "eternal creation" as well as for "creation in time." Though it is more difficult for the imagination to

grasp *exnihilation* without imputing *initiation* there is no analytical reason for combining *exnihilation* and *initiation*. Strictly speaking, exnihilation is beyond the power of the imagination to grasp in any way, except by remote and inappropriate metaphors, i.e., by comparison with motion and change. (Vd. *ibid.*, I, 45, 2 ad 2). Strictly speaking, "exnihilation" means only this: that that which needs a cause for its existence so long as it exists is caused to exist by a cause which does not reduce a pre-existent potentiality to act. Existence as a caused act is, in short, the act of no passive potentiality whatsoever. Hence, no natural agent can efficiently cause existence, even instrumentally.

(4) The foregoing is confirmed by St. Thomas's discussion of annihilation.

    (a) "That God gives existence to a creature depends on His will; nor does he preserve things in existence otherwise than by continually pouring out existence into them, as we have said. Therefore, just as before things existed, God was free not to give them existence, and so not to make them; so after they have been made, He is free not to continue their existence; and thus they would cease to exist; and this would be to annihilate them" (*ibid.*, I, 104, 4). Furthermore, "God does not cause a thing to tend to non-existence, for the creature has this tendency of itself, since it is produced from nothing. But indirectly God can be the cause of things being reduced to non-existence, by withdrawing His action from them" (*ibid.*, ad 1); and "if God were to annihilate anything, this would not imply an action on God's part; but a mere cessation of His action."

    (b) Now, that which is exnihilated is annihilable, whether or not it was ever initiated. What makes it annihilable is not that it once began to be, but that its being is the result of exnihilation. Hence, even if there were no truth in the phrase "before things existed," it would still be true that contingent beings are annihilable by God, and this means that, even if they are not initiated in being, they are exnihilated by God, and by God's action alone.

    (c) Furthermore, only God can annihilate things, by ceasing to cause their being, by ceasing to exnihilate them. St. Thomas never suggests that created things or natural agents can cooperate with God, or serve as God's instrumental causes, in the annihilation of things. Hence, neither can they serve in the exnihilation of things.

(5) The foregoing is also confirmed by *C.G.*, II, 6,15, 17–21, and by *S.T.*, I, 65, 3, 4; and 66, 1.

    (a) In 1, 65, 3, St. Thomas denies that even the angels can serve as instrumental causes, as media, in the production of corporeal things, i.e., not their initiation in time, but their exnihilation so long as they exist. "The thing that underlies all other things belongs properly to the causality of the supreme cause. Therefore no secondary cause can produce anything, unless there is presupposed in the thing produced something that is caused by the higher cause. But creation is the production of a thing in its entire being, nothing being presupposed either uncreated or created. Hence, it follows that nothing can create except God alone, Who is the first cause." And he explains this by saying: "The production of finite things, where nothing is presupposed as existing, is the work of infinite power, and, as such, can belong to no creature" (*ibid.*, ad 3).

    (b) "Nature produces effects in act from being in potentiality; and consequently in the operations of nature potentiality must precede act in time, and formlessness precede form. But God produces being in act out of nothing" (I, 66, 1, ad 2).

    (c) Both of these texts remain unaltered in significance whether creation does or does not involve *initiation*.

  c. It is important to observe that St. Thomas distinguishes between annihilation (or annihilability) and corruption (or corruptibility). The corruption of a thing in the course of natural processes is not its annihilation. Hence, the generation of a thing is not its exnihilation. Natural causes are operative in the occurrence of generation and corruption, but this does not mean that they are cooperative in the exnihilation of things, or would be cooperative in the annihilation of things, did this occur.

    (1) In *S.T.*, I, 65, 1 ad 1—which, in my original article was, as the result of typographical error, mis-cited as 1, 65, 9 ad 1—St. Thomas says: "What is created will never be annihilated, even though it be corruptible."

    (2) This text must be read in connection with *ibid.*, I, 104, 4, in which St. Thomas affirms that nothing will be annihilated by God. He does not say that nothing is *annihilable* by God, for if that were so, then nothing would be *exnihilable* either. But his reasoning here is unclear; for he seems to say, on the one hand, that the very nature of things proves that they are not annihilated; and, on the other hand, he says that it is due to the goodness of God that he does not annihilate them, for their annihilation, as their exnihilation, is within God's freedom. Cf. *ibid.*, I, 104, 3. It is certainly not true to say that the angels are, by nature, not annihilable, because by nature they are incorruptible; nor is it true to say that corporeal things are by nature not annihilable, because matter is, by nature, incorruptible.

    (3) The truth, which is not clearly expressed in this passage, should be stated as follows. That which is in itself incorruptible, such as angels and human souls, is in itself annihilable, and here the fact of incorruptibility of nature merely *suggests*—does not prove—

that God will not in fact annihilate that which he created to be incorruptible. On the other hand, that which is in itself corruptible, such as all bodies are, living or non-living, celestial or terrestrial, is not annihilable *because* corruptible, for that would mean that every instance of a body's corruption would be an act of annihilation on God's part. Hence, here we must say that corporeal substances are annihilable only with respect to that which is incorruptible in all of them, namely, their matter. Here, then, we see that God will not annihilate the whole material order of being, as such, for he created it as incorruptible by nature. This is confirmed by what St. Thomas tells us in the treatise on the end of the world, for the elemental bodies will endure forever, even after the final conflagration. Vd. *S.T.*, III, Sup., 91.

(4) The significance of this is very great, indeed; for according as we locate the annihilability of things, so also must we locate their exnihilability. Hence, we see. that the objects of God's creative action are precisely the things He is free to annihilate, and these are: (1) the angels; (2) human souls; (3) the whole order of material being as such, and not particular bodies as such, for these are the work of generation, not the work of creation or exnihilation.

(a) This is confirmed by what is said in *S.T.*, I, 69, 2. "In the first days, God created all (corporeal things) in their origin or causes, and from this work He subsequently rested. Yet afterwards, by governing His creatures, in the work of propagation, He worketh until now. Now the production of plants from out of the earth is a work of propagation, and therefore they were not produced in act on the third day, but in their causes only." Cf. *S.T.*, I, 45, 8, *per contra*.

(b) Vd. also I, 73, 1, ad 3, where St. Thomas says: "Nothing entirely new was afterwards made by God, but all things subsequently produced had in a sense been made before in the work of the six days. Some things, indeed, had a previous existence materially, whilst others existed not only in matter, but also in their causes, as those individual creatures that are now generated existed in the first of their kind." Also *ibid.*, I, 73, 2 ad 1: "God worketh until now by preserving and providing for the creatures He has made, but not by the making of new ones." And *ibid.*, I, 73, 3, ad 3: "In the first six days, creatures were produced in their first causes, and after being thus produced they are multiplied and preserved, and this work also belongs to the Divine goodness." And in *ibid.*, ad 4: "The good mentioned in the work of each day belongs to the first institution of nature, but the blessing attached to the seventh day to its propagation." Cf. *ibid.*, I, 74, 2.

(c) Throughout the foregoing passages, St. Thomas is proceeding on the dogmatic truth of a beginning of the world. But

the philosophical truth remains the same, even if the dogmatic truth be not affirmed. And that philosophical truth
consists in a clear distinction between the work of God and
the work of creatures—the work of God being the exnihilation of the whole material world, the work of creatures in
the corporeal order consisting in the generation of new individuals, and in their accidental variations. Now since, when
we omit the note of initiation from creation, exnihilation
becomes identical with God's conservation of things, it follows that the multiplication of creatures, through the work
of generation or propagation, must be distinguished from
the conservation of creatures, which is the work of God
alone. Hence, what is being said in these texts is: (1) The
work of initiation belongs to the six days. (2) The work of
conservation is the Divine action wherein God worketh until
now as sole cause. (3) The work of propagation, multiplication, accidental variation, is the work of natural agents,
whose work God governs.

(5) This explains how we must understand what St. Thomas means
when he says that "to produce being absolutely, not as this or that
being, belongs to creation . . . which is the proper act of God
alone" (*S.T.*, I, 45, 5). That statement does not mean that creation is the production of being without any distinctions of mode
or grade of being whatsoever. If that were what it meant, then it
could not be said that the distinction of things comes from God.

   (a) But it is clear from I, 47,1 that the distinction and inequality
   of the angels is directly caused by God. "What can be caused
   only by creation is produced by God alone, viz., all those
   things which are not subject to generation and corruption"—which we must interpret to mean (1) the angels, (2)
   human souls, and (3) the whole material order as such.

   (b) Furthermore, in the subsequent article, St. Thomas tells us
   that in the material order, the formal inequality of things,
   according to the hierarchy of the true species, is due to the
   Divine wisdom. God creates the true species, whether in act
   or in their causes, but he does not create the generable and
   corruptible members of these species. "In things generated
   and corruptible, there are many individuals of one species
   for the preservation of the species." Cf. *ibid.*, I, 74, 1, 2, 3.

   (c) But unless the matter, which is presupposed by generation
   and which is annihilable as it is exnihilable, is caused to exist
   by God, there would be no existing individuals to generate
   other individuals. Hence, the preservation of a species has
   two causes: one is God, who preserves the being of the whole
   material order; the other is the individual member of the
   given species who generates another, and whatever other
   natural agents cooperate with the propagator in the work of

generation. Here we see at once that the word "preservation" is ambiguous, for it has the sense in which God preserves the being of the whole material order, and the sense
in which acts of generation preserve a species. There is some
truth, therefore, in saying that creatures participate in the
work of "preservation," but when the ambiguity in the word
is noted, it will also be seen that creatures do not participate,
as efficient causes, in God's work of preservation, which is
the act of exnihilation, not the act of generation.
Furthermore, what God preserves directly is the whole material order of being; and this is not inconsistent with saying
that God *indirectly* preserves the various species of material
things *through* governing the activity of such things in their
work of propagation, or multiplication of individuals. The
object of the Divine action is not the same in both cases, nor
is the Divine action the same in both cases. In the case of the
whole material order of being as object, the Divine action
cannot be instrumentally assisted by the operation of any
material thing in any way; but in the case of a given species,
the Divine action can be instrumentally assisted by generative acts on the part of corporeal things.

(6) One further qualification must be added. Neither the substantial forms or accidents of things, nor the formless matter
which enters into their composition, are, strictly speaking, created by God or sustained in being by God.

(a) *S.T.*, I, 45,4: "To be created properly belongs to whatever
being belongs, which, indeed, belongs properly to subsisting
things, as in the case of separate substances, or composite
substances, i.e., material substances. For being belongs to
that which has being—that is, to what subsists in its own
being. But forms and accidents, and the like, are called
beings, not as if they themselves were, but because something is by them. Hence, according to the Philosopher, accident is more properly said to be *of a being*, rather than *a
being*. Therefore, as accidents and forms and the like non-
subsisting things are said to co-exist rather than to exist, so
they ought to be called *concreated* rather than *created*;
whereas, properly speaking, created things are subsisting
things." Vd. ad 2: "Creation does not mean the building up
of a composite thing from pre-existing principles; but it
means that the *composite* is created so that it is brought into
being at the same time with all its principles." Nor can it be
said that "matter alone is created, but that matter does not
exist except by creation; for creation is the production of the
whole being, and not only of matter" (*ibid.*, ad 3). Cf. *ibid.*, I,
45, 8; and I, 104, 4, ad 3.

(b) *S.T.*, I, 66,1: "To say that matter preceded, but without form is to say that being existed actually, yet without act, which is a contradiction in terms. . . . Hence, we must assert that primary matter was not created altogether formless, nor under any one common form, but under distinct forms."

(c) Hence, we see that the object of the Divine action in creation is not the form as such, nor the prime matter as such, but the subsistent composite as such. But the composite substance is also the term of an act of generation; and it is corruptible, yet when it is corrupted, nothing is annihilated by God. Hence, we know that this particular composite substance, which is corruptible, cannot be the effect of God's exnihilation. What is it, then, which God causes to exist—in the order of material or corruptible things? The answer must be that he causes the co-principles of the being of composite substance to exist—prime matter, substantial forms. In this way, He causes what is common to the being of all material things, but does not directly and solely cause the existence of this particular thing which is generated and which is corruptible.

(d) This interpretation is confirmed by what is said in *S.T.*, I, 45,5 ad 1. "An individual man is not the cause of human nature absolutely . . . but he is the cause of human nature being in the man begotten; and thus he presupposes in his action a determinate matter whereby he is an *individual* man" and, it can be added, he presupposes a form whereby he is *specifically* a man. And St. Thomas concludes: "From which it evidently appears that no created being can cause anything unless something is presupposed, which is against the very idea of creation." And in *ibid.*, I,45,8 ad 4: "The operations of nature take place only on the presupposition of created principles." Now the operations of nature are generation and accidental change or motion. These operations presuppose prime matter, substantial forms, and accidental forms, which are the created principles.

(e) The foregoing leads us to the following alternative conclusions. Both must be mentioned. Neither by itself is an adequate rendering of St. Thomas's thought. These two conclusions follow from the alternative possibilities: (1) that creation involves initiation, (2) that creation does not involve initiation.

(1) *On the assumption that the material world had a beginning, an absolute initiation:* God created composite substances, by concreating prime matter together with several distinct substantial forms. This was the accomplishment of the six days, however that work be interpreted. Thereafter, in time, the operations of nature, presupposing the principles of material being created in the

original substances, produced the multiplicity and variety of individual things by acts of generation and the accidental motions. On this assumption, God preserves the whole material world in being by directly causing the co-existence of these principles of material being at every moment that any or all material things exist. But He does not *directly* preserve corruptible individuals from corruption, nor accidentally changeable things from accidental change. Thus, the Divine action in conserving the being of material things is continuous with the Divine action in initiating them, and it is not to be confused with natural action in generating or changing material things. The latter always; and at every moment, presuppose the former. And the effect of the natural action is always motion (accidental change or generation: whereas the effect of the Divine action is always being or existence, for being is pre-supposed in becoming and is not reducible thereto. Furthermore, this fact does not permit us to say that God is a cause of natural motions unless what we mean is that God is the cause of the principles underlying natural motions; but that is tantamount to saying that God is a cause of the being which becoming presupposes. Hence, the effect which God directly and exclusively causes is being, not motion. This has an obvious bearing on the proof of God's existence from effects. Those who claim that God is a cause of motion, *because* He is the cause of those *existent* principles without which motion could not *occur*, or mobile beings *exist*, fail to see that God is related to motion as *causa essendi*, not as *causa fiendi*.

(2) *On the assumption that the material world did not have a beginning or an absolute initiation, but that natural things in motion have been everlastingly*: This assumption does not, according to St. Thomas, demand the denial of God's creativity. Hence on this assumption we must understand God's creative action as identical with, or nothing but, what on the first assumption we called God's preservative action which, on the first assumption, is continuous with God's initial creative action. On this assumption, God at every moment of the material world's existence causes its existence by the exnihilation of the principles of its existence. Should God at any moment cease from this action, the individual substances existing at that moment would be annihilated, and hence natural motions and generations would also cease. Looking at this truth from the point of view of an individual composite substance at this moment, we can

see that it is capable of ceasing to be in two quite distinct ways: (1) by the action of corruptive causes, in which case, its matter will not cease to be, but will only undergo a *transformation*; and (2) by Divine annihilation, which is the cessation of God's creative causality, in which case, its matter will cease to be absolutely.

(f) On both of the foregoing assumptions, one point remains the same. To say that God is the cause of the principles of motion is not to say that God causes particular motions to occur, whether or not in fact He does. A proper *causa fiendi* is that which, through its action, requires a particular motion to occur. But God, in causing the principles of motion to exist, does not by that act require any particular motion to occur. So long as it is understood that God is the cause of motion in the sense that He causes the existence of the underlying principles which every particular motion pre-supposes, His action will be understood as *causa essendi.* Acts and potencies have to exist. The causes of motion, which are truly *causa fiendi*, cause neither the acts nor the potencies to exist, but only cause a particular act to be the actualization of this particular potency. I have not denied that God may be a *causa fiendi* in this sense, just as natural agents are; and if He is, God and natural agents are only analogically the same as *causa fiendi.* I have only asserted that we cannot infer that God is even analogically a *causa fiendi* from the occurrence of any known natural motion (miracles excepted). And this assertion is not incompatible with my present statement that the existence of motion depends upon the existence of its principles, the formal and material causes which enter into the composition of material and mobile beings; and hence that, if these principles require God as the cause of their existence, motion requires God as cause of its existence; in which case our inference is to a *causa essendi*, not to a *causa fiendi*; and it is based upon *existence* as an effect, even though that be the existence of motion in the world. There can be no excuse for confusion on this point. Suppose that God is both *causa essendi* and *causa fiendi*, and suppose motion to be the effect in both cases. Then as *causa essendi*, God efficiently causes the formal and material causes of motion, i.e., causes the existence of potencies and acts, in which case the effect must be precisely described as "the *existence* of motion." And as *causa fiendi*, God either alone (as in miracles) or in coop-eration with natural agents as instrumentalities, efficiently causes the reduction of a pre-existent potency to act, in which case the effect must be precisely described as "the *occurrence* of *this* motion." The effect which is described as the occurrence of a motion is the effect from which we cannot infer that God exists: This effect is not God's *proper* effect; according to our understanding of its nature, it does not require God as efficient cause *per se*.

d. Three texts remain to be examined. It will now be seen that they confirm the interpretation of the texts already reviewed.

(1) The first of these is *S.T.*, I, 104, 1. "Both reason and faith bind us to say that creatures are kept in being by God. To make this clear, we must consider that a thing is preserved by another in two ways. First, indirectly and accidentally, thus a person is said to preserve another by removing the cause of its corruption, as a man is said to preserve a child, whom he guards from falling into a fire. In this way God preserves some things, but not all; for there are some things of such a nature that nothing can corrupt them, so that it is not necessary to keep them from corruption. Secondly, a thing is said to preserve another *per se* and directly, namely, when what is preserved depends on the preserver in such a way that it cannot exist without it. In this manner, all creatures need to be preserved by God. For the being of every creature depends on God, so that not for a moment could it subsist, but would fall into nothingness; were it not kept in being by the Divine action." And in ad 4, it is said: "The preservation of things by God is a continuation of that action whereby He gives existence, which action is without motion or time."

(a) Now, in the first place, we see that in one of the two ways in which God preserves the being of things (i.e., in a direct or *per se* manner), no corporeal thing can preserve the being of another, for no action of a corporeal thing is "without motion or time."

(b) In the second place, we see that incorruptible beings can be preserved in being in only one way, whereas corruptible beings can be preserved in being in two ways: (1) by a cause that operates directly and *per se*; (2) by a cause that operates indirectly and accidentally. (I have changed the order of St. Thomas's enumeration of these two senses.) This second mode of preservation consists in counteracting the operation of corruptive causes. But corruptive causes, like generative causes, consist in the motions of natural agents. Hence, when God preserves the being of corporeal substances in the second way, He must act through the mediation of natural causes which counteract other natural causes—unless, of course, God performs a miracle. It follows, then, that only preservation in the first sense is identical with God's direct exnihilation of things; and here the being of things is the proper effect of God's action, and He is the exclusive cause of this effect. It is only preservation in the first sense which can be called "continuous with God's creative action" in that sense of "creation" which involves *initiation*; for just as generation is not exnihilation, so the prevention of corruption through the operation of natural causes is not exnihilation.

(c)   Moreover, if we say, as St. Thomas does, that the generator does not cause being, but only becoming, we cannot say that the preserver in the second sense—opposing corruption—causes being. Preservation in the second sense is no more the causation of being than is generation. "Every effect depends on its cause, so far as it is its cause. But we must observe that an agent may be the cause of the *becoming* of its effect, but not directly of its *being*. This may be seen in both artificial and natural things: for the builder causes the house in its *becoming*; but he is not the direct cause of its *being*. For it is clear that the *being* of the house results from the putting together and arrangement of the materials, and above all from their natural qualities. . . . The *being* of a house depends on the nature of these materials, just as the *becoming* of the house depends on the action of the builder. The same principles apply to natural things; for if an agent is not the cause of a form as such, neither will it be directly the cause of the *being* which results from that form, but it will be the cause of the effect, in its *becoming* only. . . . When two things are the same in species, one can be the cause of this form's being in this matter—in other words, the cause that *this matter* receives *this form*. This is what it means to cause becoming, as when man begets man, or fire causes fire" (*ibid.*).

(1)   In objection 2, it is pointed out that the house continues to exist, or the son continues to exist, after the house-builder or the generator ceases to act. "Much more, therefore, can God cause His creature to continue in being, after He has ceased to create it." To which St. Thomas replies, "God cannot grant to a creature to be preserved in being after the cessation of the Divine influence, as neither can He make it not to have received its being from Himself. For the creature needs to be preserved in being, in so far as the being of an effect depends on the cause of its being. So there is no comparison with an agent that is not the cause of *being*, but only of *becoming*." This has a bearing on the matter of residual effects. St. Thomas is here saying that being, unlike motion, is never a residual effect. He recognizes that a motion may cause a motion, and that the caused motion may continue after the causing motion has ceased, its continuance being the continuance of the act by which the potentiality was actualized. Thus, the hot water does not cease to be hot when the fire ceases to heat it; nor does the moving ball cease to move when the ball which moved it ceases to move. In the order of

nature, residual effects of this sort are the rule, rather than exception. What St. Thomas was dealing with here, without knowing it, is the principle of inertia. We can, therefore, ignore the mythical physics by which he tries to explain residual effects, or which leads him to deny that illumination can be a residual effect of the action of a source of light, such as the sun.

(2) But the fact that there is no real comparison between the order of motion and the order of being, i.e., the fact that there is no cause of motion which must continue to act in order for its effect to continue to be in act for some period of time, however short, does not invalidate St. Thomas's point that in the order of being, "the *being* of a thing cannot continue for an instant after the action of the causal agent has ceased." In short, existence, which is not the reduction of a pre-existent potency to act, is not an act which can post-exist its active cause. Only those acts of matter, substantial or accidental, that result from motion or from reduction of potency to act, can post-exist the activity of the efficient cause. Generation is certainly a change, in the sense that it is a reduction of potency to act; and certainly here the first act, which terminates the process of generation, continues to be the act of the matter which underwent generative transformation *after* the efficient cause of the generation, the generative act, has ceased.

(3) Involved here is another point that must not be overlooked. St. Thomas speaks of the materials out of which the house as made, and the accidental form which arranges those materials, as causes of the being of the house, *not its becoming*. But it is clear that neither is *efficient* cause of the house's being; the stone, rock, etc. are the *material* cause of the house's being, and the artificial arrangement the *formal* cause. In general we can say that a substance is the material cause of the being of its accidents, and here we do not have to ask about an efficient cause of the accident's being, since, strictly speaking, it does not subsist, but is *of a being*. Hence, whatever efficiently causes the being of the substance also efficiently causes the being of the accident. Similarly in the sphere of natural, as opposed to artificial things, the generator, like the house-builder, is only a cause of becoming. The prime matter and the substantial form are causes of the substance's being; but again they are neither of them efficient causes. The prime matter is a material cause of the substance's being, and the substantial form is the formal cause. Thus, St. Thomas fre-

quently says: "The substantial form gives being simply"
or "the substantial form gives substantial being" (I, 76,
4). But clearly he does not mean that the substantial
form "gives being" in the same sense that he says God
"gives being" in I, 8, 1. There he says that God is not *in*
the things He causes as part of their essence, but as an
agent is present to that on which it acts. Now a substantial form is not an agent. It is an act *of* matter, but it does
not act *on* matter, for nothing can act unless it subsists,
and a substantial form does not subsist. Hence, we must
conclude that a substantial form "gives being" only as a
formal cause, just as prime matter gives being as a material cause. But this leaves the question: What is the efficient cause of the being of a corporeal substance? It is
not the generative act, for that is only the efficient cause
of its becoming. It is not the prime matter or substantial
form, for though these are causes of the substance's
being, they are its formal and material causes. Hence,
the only agent which could be the efficient cause of the
being of this existing substance is either another substance or God.

(4) Considering "another substance," we find these two
alternatives. Another substance can be one of two sorts:
(1) either it is a substance of the same species; or (2) it
is a substance of diverse species. The former is what St.
Thomas understands by a "univocal generator." But we
have already seen that the action of the univocal generator is never more than the efficient cause of another
substance's *becoming*, according to St. Thomas. The only
other possibility is what St. Thomas understands by an
"equivocal generator" —i.e., "an agent which does not
produce an effect of the same species as itself; thus the
heavenly bodies cause the generation of inferior bodies
which differ from them in species" (*ibid.*, I, 104, 1). Now
here St. Thomas *wrongly* supposes that he has a solution.
He says: "Such an agent can be the cause of a form *as
such*, and not merely as existing in this matter.
Consequently it is not merely the cause of *becoming*, but
also the cause of *being*" (*ibid.*). Now the principle of the
reasoning here is correct, but the facts are wrong, for
they are based on a mythical or, at least, erroneous
physics. The scientific errors are to be found in *S.T.*, I,
45, 8, ad 3; 71, 1, ad 1; 73; 1, ad 3.

(a) The true principle is this: if anything efficiently
causes the form *as such*, and not merely the occurrence of the form in this matter, it is a cause of
the *being* of the substance, and not merely of its

becoming.

(b) The errors in fact are as follows. *First,* that the heavenly bodies are superior bodies, which is based on the metaphysical, as well as the scientific, error of supposing that there are any incorruptible bodies, any incorruptible yet changing material substances. On the contrary, the heavenly bodies, being inanimate, are inferior in grade of being and of action to the lowest form of living thing, the unicellular specimen of plant-life. The least perfect living substance is essentially superior to the sun and stars, and has modes of operation, which by their immanence and by the impassibility of the operative powers, are superior to the actions of the sun or other heavenly bodies. *Second,* that an inanimate substance can be a generative cause of a living thing, *even equivocally,* unless what is meant is that the action of the sun or other bodies is an efficient cause *disposing* matter for generation, or otherwise affecting the material causes involved in generation. Strictly then, it is not a generative cause at all, for in a strict meaning, only living things have vital powers, of which generation is one. Hence, nonliving things do not have generative powers; and so the celestial bodies, as non-living, cannot be efficient causes through generative action. *Third,* St. Thomas himself says that "the heavenly bodies inform earthly ones by movement, not by emanation" (*ibid.,* I, 65, 4 ad 3). This is said in answer to an objection that "spiritual substances have more power of causation than the heavenly bodies. But the heavenly bodies give form to things here below, for which reason they are said to cause generation and corruption." Now in that article, St. Thomas argues that "corporeal forms are not from the angels but from God." *A fortiori,* corporeal forms of terrestrial bodies are not from celestial bodies, but from God. And the fact that St. Thomas says that the heavenly bodies cause the forms of earthly ones, not by emanation, but by movement, indicates that if they are efficient causes at all, they are causes of becoming, not of being. This, according to St. Thomas, is true even of the angels. They are only efficient causes of becoming in the material order, not of being. *Therefore,* we must conclude two things: first, that the heavenly bodies are in no sense efficient causes of being, for even less than the angels are they agents which cause the form as such; and second, that even as efficient causes of becoming, they are only causes of accidental change and not of generation. This does not deny that the action of the sun is not involved in the life of living things; but it is involved in the same way that salt is, or oxygen, or water, namely, in the order of material causality, with respect to accidental changes in the matter that is the matter involved in substantial change, whether that be generation, or aggeneration, i.e., digestion. (The heating of food does not *digest* it, but prepares or disposes the matter for the animal's digestive action.) Inanimate bodies are never efficient generative causes of living things; and no corporeal substance is, in any sense, an efficient cause of the being of any other substance.

(5) Hence, eliminating the scientific errors made in the fourth paragraph of the *Respondeo* in I, 104, 1, we come to the conclusion St. Thomas should have reached from all his other principles and premises, namely, that only God is the efficient cause of the being of any corporal substance, and that God is the efficient cause of being in this order through causing the existence of the formal and material principles of each thing's being, i.e., through efficiently causing that which is the material and the formal cause of the corporeal substance's being.

(a) Now when Article 1 of Q. 104 is thus corrected, Article 2 must be corrected accordingly. That article seems to say that created things act as intermediate or instrumental causes cooperating with the Divine action in the causation of being. But, recalling Article 1, St. Thomas points out that this action can take place in two ways: "first, indirectly and accidentally, by removing or hindering the action of corruptive causes; and second, directly and *per se*, by the fact that on the cause depends the other's being." Then he says: "And in both ways, a created thing keeps another in being."

(1) Now there is no difficulty at all about the first way here mentioned; for, as we have seen, to work against the action of corruptive causes is not to withhold a thing from annihilation. Hence, this sort of 'preservation action' properly belongs to natural agents, and hence God uses them as instrumental causes for achieving this sort of "preservation" under the operation of His Providence.

(2) Nor is there any difficulty about the second mode of preservation, if the natural causes meant are nothing but formal and material causes, rather than efficient, causes of the thing's being.

(3) If, however, as his text suggests, he supposes that created things, such as the heavenly bodies, can be instrumental efficient causes of being, then his error is due to the same mythical astronomy or physics that I have already pointed out in Article 1. That this is so will be seen from the second paragraph of the *Respondeo*. It follows, therefore, that if we eliminate these scientific errors on St. Thomas's part, the remainder of the text of I, 104, 2, like the corrected text of I, 104, 1, can have only one true interpretation, namely, that no created thing can be an efficient cause of the being of another created thing, though such created principles as prime matter and substantial form can be the material and formal causes of the being of corporeal substances. Hence, the only instrumental causes used by God in the direct and *per se* preservation of being, which is a continuation of His creative action, are material or formal causes. There are no efficient instrumental causes of being. And so it follows that, in the order of efficient causality, only God is a cause of being, either in initiating being, or in preserving being, whether or not initiated.

(4) Objection 3 here argues that all created causes cause only the *becoming* of their effects, for they cause only by moving, as is stated in Q. 45, A. 3. In answering this objection, St. Thomas admits the premises completely, and then says that sometimes the "preservation" of the effect, in the order of becoming, is due to the continued action of the same cause which caused it to become. The example given here is that of the action of the sun as an illuminating cause. This, as, we have seen, is just more bad physics on St. Thomas's part, for it ignores the principle of inertia and the plain facts about residual effects in the sphere of natural motions. Luminous reflecting surfaces retain light after the source of light has ceased to act.

(b) The present discussion gives a much sounder reso-

lution of the "apparent" contradiction between
104,1,2 and the rest of the passages on God's causation of being, than the resolution given in the original article. In the original article, I failed to note
the scientific errors which caused all the trouble,
and so I could find no resolution for the "apparent"
contradiction. Hence, I was forced to suppose it was
real. But now I see that there is no philosophical
contradiction at all, but only a conclusion based on
false premises about the "powers" and "actions" of
the heavenly bodies. If those false premises are
removed, and the conclusion is altered accordingly,
the conclusion will be that only God is efficient
cause of the being of things in a *direct and per se manner.* And this conclusion conforms to St. Thomas's
position in all of the other passages which we have
so far considered. Since no one, except perhaps
Schwartz and persons like him, would confuse the
authority of St. Thomas's philosophical doctrine
with the mythical astronomy which he accepted in
his day, no one would say that this conclusion violates St. Thomas's philosophical teaching in any
way. Hence, the philosophical authority of St.
Thomas can be cited as favoring this interpretation
of the proposition 'being is the proper effect of
God'—namely, that *only* God is the efficient cause of
the being of created things, which Divine action
proceeds without *efficient* intermediaries or instruments, whether in an original initiation of created
being, or in the withholding from annihilation of
co-eternal created being.

(2) The final text to be cited is that of *Quodlibetum,* XII, Q.4, A.5,
wherein St. Thomas says: "the proper effect of God is being, and
no cause gives being except inasmuch as it participates in the
Divine operation."

  (a) The same interpretation applies to this passage, as applies to
  S.T., 104, 1, 2. If by "giving being" is meant an efficient causation of existence, the no cause except God "gives being."
  For if "giving being" means "creation" in either of its two
  senses—i.e., with or without the note of *initiation*—then the
  authority of I,45,5 warrants us in saying that St. Thomas
  would hold that only God gives being, and that no other
  cause even participates in this Divine operation.

  (b) If, however, "giving being" means an indirect and accidental
  preservation of being—i.e., opposition to corruptive
  causes—rather than the direct and *per se* preservation of
  being, which is identical with exnihilation apart from initia-

tion, then natural agents, i.e., created causes, can participate in the Divine operation, working as instruments of the Divine Providence in preventing the corruption of corruptible things, or preventing the alteration of alterable things, etc.

(c) And if by "giving being" is meant the formal or material causation of being, then created principles or causes "give being" precisely because God creates them to achieve this effect. Cf. here I, 104, 1, ad 1.

(d) Only one thing is definitely excluded, *as impossible.* If a thing is understood to participate in Divine being, which is Pure Act, by reason of its own actuality, then as thus participating in Divine being, no created thing causes being, in the sense of causing anything's form or existence. For the acts of any created substance are either its first act or its second acts. But by its first act, which is its essence, no created substance causes anything in any way. And by its second acts, which are its operations, created substances are only efficient causes of becoming, not being, whether coming to be simply (generation) or coming to be such and such (accidental change). But as St. Thomas himself points out, the house-builder and the man generating are not causes of being, but only of becoming. Certainly, then, the sun which heats, or bleaches, or reddens, or illuminates, or is involved in photosynthesis through the action of chlorophyl, is only an efficient cause of becoming *such and such,* and not of being. The fact that the accidental effect, like the substantial effect, may endure after the action of the cause has ceased, cannot be interpreted to mean that these efficient causes are, after all, causes of the being of the residual effect, as well as of its becoming. If that were so, then the generating father would be the cause of the "persistence in being" of his generated son, which he most certainly is not. The persistence in being of the son has two causes: one is God, who causes the existence of the principles of every substance's being; the other includes whatever natural agents are opposing corruptive causes, in short, whatever natural agents are, in the sphere of motion, causing the health of the living thing. What is true of residual effects in the sphere of substantial change is equally true of residual effects in the sphere of the accidental motions. Hence, the generative cause or the cause of the accidental motion does not cause the "continued being" of the effect.

e. This concludes my interpretation of Thomistic texts bearing on the interpretation of the proposition 'being is the proper effect of God.' I think I have shown that, once certain scientific errors about the character and action of the celestial bodies are expunged, the philo-

sophical doctrine of St. Thomas, freed from these entirely adventitious errors, is absolutely clear in the position it takes, namely, that
only God efficiently causes the being of anything which needs an efficient cause for its being. The truth of this position is unaffected by the
alternatives of "creation in time" and "eternal creation." The truth of
this position can, therefore, be stated by the proposition 'Only God
creates' in which the meaning of the word "creates" completely prescinds from the notion of an original initiation of things.

The fact that this is St. Thomas's position does not, however, prove the existence of God, nor is it sufficient warrant for saying that this is what St. Thomas
had in mind in his "Five Ways," all of which are proposed antecedent to the
affirmation that being can be caused by God alone. It merely suggests the possibility of a proof in which the *a posteriori* reasoning goes from being as a *proper
effect* to God as *sole cause*. Whether that proof can be validly made without begging any questions about God's nature and God's action in the course of proving God's existence is a problem I shall deal with presently. Now I wish to turn
to Schwartz's criticism of my original article, with respect to matters covered
by the foregoing discussion, and show how completely Schwartz missed the
point of, or misrepresented, my argument, and also how untenable is his
interpretation of the texts in St. Thomas relevant to the proposition that
'being is the proper effect of God.'

2. Schwartz's Misinterpretations and Errors

NOTE: The discussion just completed is a more adequate consideration of the relevant texts in St. Thomas's writings than it was possible to present within the brief
scope of the original article. But the main point which was made in the original
article, Part II, #7–9, is completely confirmed by this more thorough examination
of Thomistic texts; namely, that God is the only efficient cause of being, the only
agent which conserves things in being in a *direct* and *per se* manner.

But the present discussion makes one important advance over the previous
one, with regard to the interpretation of *S.T.*, I, 104, 1, 2. Where before I thought
there were passages here that either really or apparently contradicted earlier passages in Part I of the *Summa*, the contradiction being on the level of philosophical doctrine, I now see that all the difficulties in I, 104, 1, 2 arise from the false
astronomy and physical science which St. Thomas accepted. The falsehoods
which he accepted as true could not help but distort the face of his philosophical
doctrine, but once they are removed, the surface blemishes also disappear.

Schwartz omits any discussion of points #7 and #8, and considers only #9. His
criticism of #9 occurs, in his article, on pp. 34–40. He makes three points, and at the
end of the third enters into a lengthy disquisition. I shall proceed by considering his
three points, and exposing the errors therein as well as in the lengthy disquisition.

  a. Schwartz's first two points (pp. 34–35) rest upon a total misunder-
      standing of what I tried to do in my article, Part II, #7–9. He charges
      me with arguing from authority. In this section of my original work I
      did not try to prove that "preservation in being is a known effect

which is the proper effect of God." In fact, I did not try to prove that proposition anywhere in my entire article. If I had been able to prove that proposition—as I now think I can—I would have concluded the original article by saying that I knew a valid proof of God's existence, which unfortunately I was unable to do at the time. Quite contrary to Schwartz's misreading, my only aim in #7–9 was to show *that the authority of St. Thomas favored the possibility of a proof of God as causa essendi*, where there was none in the field of the causation of motion, *because it was St. Thomas's philosophical, position that only God efficiently causes being in a direct and per se manner*.

(1) Hence, the fact that I did not myself here demonstrate the proposition is quite irrelevant; because all I tried to do was to show that St. Thomas held it; and if to show that is to argue from authority, then all scholarly work which is concerned not with the truth about things, but with the truth about authors, consists in arguing from authority. I should think it would be more accurate to say that an argument about what an author's position is, an argument about the interpretation of his texts, is an argument *about* his authority, not *from* it.

(2) Schwartz's second point here is equally irrelevant. Since I am not arguing *from* the authority of St. Thomas, but only *about* it, there can be no violence done by the fact that I charge St. Thomas with error on certain points. Certainly, in the *critical* interpretation of a writer's thought, it cannot be amiss to point out inadequacies of statement, factual errors, or inconsistencies, whether real or apparent. The fact that I find St. Thomas's writings inadequate on many difficult philosophical points, that I find many factual errors due to the antiquated "empirical science" of his day, that I also find inconsistencies,—these facts mean to me only that St. Thomas was a finite and fallible man. Though I regard him and Aristotle as the two philosophical writers who are most worthy of study, I have never been able to regard either of them as infallible or perfect.

Since I never argue from authority, since I never cite them in the course of an argument except on propositions which I am able to prove independently, the fact that I find all these flaws and defects in their writings has no bearing on my reference to them. And certainly, when the only problem under consideration is what St. Thomas thought, *not what the truth is*, then the fact that "in the very act of determining the basic teaching of St. Thomas, Mr. Adler accuses him of contradicting himself" (Schwartz, p. 35), does not warrant condemnation of my procedure. In determining the basic teaching of a philosopher, should one ignore errors or inconsistencies that appear on the surface of his work? I admit that a real contradiction is shocking, but even the best philosophers make them. But whether I was right in my original interpretation, that there was a real contradiction between, I,

104, 1, 2 and many other passages of Part I of the *Summa,* or whether I am now right that the difficulties in I, 104, 1, 2 are due to scientific errors about the nature and action of the heavenly bodies, makes absolutely no difference to the main point. That point is that any careful reader will find difficulties in I, 104, 1, 2, if he reads these articles in the light of I, 8, 1; I, 19, 5 ad 3; I, 45, 5; I, 65, 3, and other texts which I have already cited and discussed. The only person who will not see these difficulties is one who is completely blinded by the idolatrous worship of *Divus Thomas.*

b. Schwartz's third point is so outrageous that it can only be attributed to the fact that his dominant desire as a critic was to refute and denounce, rather than to understand and think. I shall quote it in full, for it deserves to be completely exposed—not for the sake of philosophical truth, but for the sake of throwing some light on "the authority of Schwartz." I must admit that I am tempted to say of Schwartz what St. Thomas said of a certain work—"That book has no authority, and it can be despised with the same facility as it was written" (*S.T.,* I, 77, 8 ad 1). But, unfortunately, under the present circumstances, I must go further.

Schwartz writes: "There is no authority whatsoever in St. Thomas for the proposition that God is a unique cause of conservation of being. The one citation which Mr. Adler gives for this opinion (*Summa Theol.,* I, 65, 9, ad 1) is unfortunately incorrect; there are only four articles in question 65 of the first part."

(1) Let me deal with the second of these two statements first. In my article, the reference to *S.T.,* I, 65, 9 ad 1 occurred in the opening paragraph of #9 on p. 206. The citation is given as follows in a parenthesis: "Vd. *Sum. Th.,* I, q. 65, a. 9 ad 1 on annihilation and corruption." The typographical error, which Schwartz himself could have corrected by examining the answer to the first objection in each of the four articles of question 65, was the substitution of "9" for "1." Now if we turn to I, 65, 1 ad 1 we find the following statement: "All creatures of God in some respects continue for ever, at least as to matter, since what is created will never be annihilated, even though it be corruptible." As I have already shown, a fuller understanding of this sentence requires the consideration of I, 104, 3, 4. But that is not the point. The point is that the text cited was not cited for its bearing on the proposition that "God is the unique cause of the conservation of being." If Schwartz had considered #7 which opens this discussion in my article, instead of beginning with #9, he would have been able to find a typographically accurate and an analytically adequate citation of the relevant texts.

The opening paragraph of #7 says that "the *only way* in which God can be proved is as *causa essendi.*" I say this on my own authority, indicating that I am compelled to this conclusion by the preceding analysis in #1–6. I then go on to say that "this is confirmed by St. Thomas's insight into the character of *being* as an effect." It is here that I cite all the passages in which St. Thomas presents and analyzes the proposition that 'being is the proper effect of God.' My citation, in #7, a, is as follows: "Vd. *Sum.Th.*, I, 8, 1; 19, 5, ad 3; 45, 5; 65, 3; 104, 1; *Con. Gen.* II, 6, 15, 17–21." This enumeration of texts is not complete. I have expanded on it in this present work. But it is certainly sufficient for supporting my contention that St. Thomas does conceive God as the sole efficient cause of the being of created things.

(2) This brings us to the first of Schwartz's two statements. Do the texts cited in my #7, a, support the position that St. Thomas understood 'being is the proper effect of God' in such a way that it meant, not only that God alone creates (*ab initio*), but also that God alone creates (*non ab initio*), or in other words, that God alone conserves being in a direct and *per se* manner? Schwartz answers this question by a flat negative: "there is no authority whatsoever in St. Thomas for the proposition that. . . ." Let us consider this issue.

(a)   The only text which Schwartz can cite on his side is I, 104, 2, where St. Thomas said that created things conserve being in both ways: (a) indirectly and accidentally, and (b) directly and *per se.*

(b)   Against that citation, I argue now, as I argued then, in a twofold manner. First, I argued that all the other texts I had cited, in #7, a, stood against the one passage in I, 104, 2. Second, I argued that the weight of St. Thomas's authority being on the opposite side, this discrepant passage must be dismissed. I originally dismissed it as contradictory. I now dismiss it as based upon the scientific errors which I have pointed out in the body of I, 104, 1, errors concerning the nature and action of the heavenly bodies, both as generators and as "causes of being." There is obviously no need to argue against St. Thomas's statement that created things conserve beings "indirectly and accidentally" for such "preservation" does not consist in the causation of being as such, but merely in the operation of certain causes, in the sphere of motion, which oppose the action of other causes, working for corruption. But if it is not true that any created thing conserves being "directly and *per se,*" then St. Thomas's position must be that only God conserves being "directly and *per se,*" just as only God creates *ab initio.*

(c)   I need not repeat here what I have already fully shown, namely, the scientific errors which led St. Thomas wrongly to suppose that the heavenly bodies conserve the being of inferior bodies "directly and *per se.*" But it is worthwhile to call attention here to the way in which I argued in my original

paper, because Schwartz entirely ignored the explicit arguments I advanced for insisting that what St. Thomas said in
I, 104, 2 was erroneous, whatever be the cause of his error. I
presented my arguments on this point in #8 which Schwartz
does not discuss. There I pointed out that, on the philosophical level, it is necessary to proceed with a notion of creation *non ab initio.* And in a long, and carefully written
footnote (fn. 19) which Schwartz entirely ignored, I showed
that when the word "creation" is used with a meaning which
prescinds from the note of *initiation,* the meaning of "creation" is identical with the meaning of "preservation"—not
in both its senses, but only when it is qualified by the words
"directly and *per se.*"
Furthermore, I pointed out that this is the meaning of St.
Thomas's statement that God's action preservatively is a continuation of God's action creatively; for St. Thomas's statement uses the word "creation" with a meaning that includes
initiation. Hence if we subtract that note (i.e., initiation), we
would not say, on the philosophical level, that God's preservative action is continuous with his creative action. Rather
we would say "identical with"—for if God does not initiate
being, then His total action and *per se* cause of being is the
same, whether it is called "creative," or "conservative." From
this it follows that St. Thomas's flat and unqualified statement that "Only God creates" is strictly equivalent to an
equally flat and unqualified statement that "Only God conserves."

(d) This was the way in which I showed, in my original article,
that the authority of St. Thomas—in all passages other than
I, 104,—favored the position that no created thing conserves
being in a direct and *per se* manner; or, in other words, no
created thing efficiently causes the being of anything, since
to act preservatively in an indirect and accidental manner,
which it is possible for created things to do, is to work in the
sphere of motions, one moving cause opposing the corruptive action of another. Since Schwartz does not consider
these arguments of mine at all, his first statement in his paragraph 3 quoted above, is unwarranted, just as his second
statement is an outrageous misrepresentation.

c. The foregoing completely disposes of the three points which Schwartz
offers as a criticism of what I tried to accomplish in #7–9 of Part II of
my original article, a criticism that is *prima facie* invalidated by the fact
that Schwartz ignores what is said in #7–8, and said as a foundation
for what is said in #9. But Schwartz goes on, after his third point, to
try to argue positively that the authority of St. Thomas favors the
opposite position, viz., that created things are efficient causes of
being, that some of these conserve the being of others directly and *per*

se. In the course of this argument (his pp. 35–40) Schwartz makes many errors, which I shall now point out.

(1) On p. 35, Schwartz cites I, 45, 5, in which St. Thomas argues that only God creates. On p. 36, he cites, I, 104, 1 ad 4, in which St. Thomas says that God's conservative action is a continuation of God's creative action and that like it, it takes place without motion or time. And he goes on (p. 37 top) to say that this means that "there is no distinction on the part of God between the efficient cause of a thing in the order of production and in the order of conservation." With all of this I agree. But what Schwartz fails to consider here crucially affects the understanding of these points. He fails to consider the two meanings of "creation," that is, *creation ab initio* and *creation non ab initio.* He fails cognize the significance of the fact that the philosopher cannot prove the fact of *creation ab initio;* nor disprove it. He fails to see that that compels the philosopher to proceed with the other meaning of creation, i.e., *non ab initio;* for to assume initiation is to assume God's existence. And failing to see all these points, he fails to see that, when creation *non ab initio* is assumed, the meaning of I, 104, ad 4 is altered, especially in the light of I, 45, 5. That alteration in meaning, as I have already shown, consists in the real identity of *creation* and *preservation,* which leads to the conclusion that, since only God creates (I, 45, 5) whether *ab initio* or *non ab initio,* only God conserves being directly and *per se,* for creation *non ab initio* is identical with conservation directly and *per se.* Furthermore, Schwartz fails to appreciate the significance of St. Thomas's statement that conservation directly and *per se* is an action which takes place "without motion and without time." Now if any created thing, especially any body, conserved being directly and *per se,* its action would be the continuation of an action whereby it gave being, or identical therewith; in either case, the action would be "without motion and without time." But no body can act "without motion and without tine," as St. Thomas himself says in I, 65, 4 ad 3. Hence it must follow that no created thing, and certainly no body, can *per se.* Hence the text which Schwartz cites from St. Thomas (middle of his page 36), which is from I, 104, 2, cannot be interpreted to mean that natural agents are as agents efficient causes of being, not oven inferior or instrumental efficient causes of being, acting in a direct and *per se* manner in the conservation of being. It can be interpreted to mean only that formal and material causes, i.e., the created principles of being, are inferior causes instrumental to God's efficient causality in the conservation of being; or it can be rejected as an error on St. Thomas's part, due to the scientific errors made in I, 104, 1, concerning the action of the heavenly bodies. In short, Schwartz's statement that "there are secondary causes of the preservation of being" (p. 36) is true on two inter-

pretations, and false on a third. It is true if it means that there are formal and material causes which are direct and *per se* causes of the being of corporeal substances, and that these are inferior causes, instrumental to the Divine action as the efficient *per se* cause of being. Here it is worth examining St. Thomas's remark on forms as causes of being: "*Being* naturally results from the form of a creature, *given the influence of the Divine action*" (I, 104, 1 ad 1): This is said in answer to an objection which claimed that the immanent form is quite sufficient as the cause of being, and the conservation of being, in the creature composite of matter and form. Clearly, the formal cause is only instrumental; and without the Divine action as efficient cause, would not suffice to cause or conserve being. In the second place, it is true if it means that there are secondary causes of the preservation of being, operating in an indirect and accidental manner; such a secondary cause, according to St. Thomas, is the action of salt which works against the corruption of meat (I, 104, 2). But this is not action "without motion or time." If, however, in the third place, it means that there are secondary causes, or natural agents operating instrumentally as *efficient* causes, of the being of created things, then it is absolutely false; for no natural agent either "gives being" efficiently, or "conserves being" efficiently in a direct and *per se* manner, and so it cannot be used by God instrumentally; even as no natural agent can be used by God instrumentally in creation *ab initio* (vd. I, 45, 5).

(2) On p. 36, Schwartz makes the false statement that "in the teaching of St. Thomas, the conservation of things is proper to God only in respect of the conservation of immaterial things." I mention this, even though it is false, to show that Schwartz agrees with my meaning of the word "proper" when I speak of being as God's "proper effect." For what he is saying here, though it is false because of his "only," is that in the case of immaterial things, the conservation of their being is proper to God in the sense that God alone is the conservative *causa essendi*. Here there are no secondary or instrumental causes of being. Furthermore, here there are no secondary or instrumental causes which conserve being in an indirect and accidental manner, because immaterial things are incorruptible, and do net need such "preservation." (What Schwartz has done here is to argue *from* the fact that, with respect to immaterial and incorruptible things, there is no need for *indirect* or *accidental* preservation, *to* the fact that *only* such beings need the *direct* and *per se* preservation which is by God's action.

   (a) I have already shown that what is true of God's action with respect to immaterial things is equally true of God's action with respect to corruptible substances. Hence either Schwartz's interpretation of I, 104, 2 is wrong; or if it is right, then St. Thomas is wrong, due to scientific errors already pointed out.

(b) But here he makes anther error, namely, that of confusing "necessity" with "incorruptibility." This purely verbal error is also made by St. Thomas, but even though it is verbal it is worth correcting. If the word "necessary" is used for both God and for angels and souls, it is used ambiguously; for as said of God it means the identity of essence and existence, and hence uncaused being, being which is neither exnihilated nor annihilable; but as said of any creature, whether angels, or souls, or even prime matter, it means only "naturally incorruptible" for such beings are all caused beings, according to St. Thomas. They are all exnihilated, whether or not *ab initio*, and they are all annihilable by nature, though their natures signify to us that God will not annihilate them, even though He can. A careful reading of Objection 1 in I, 104, 1, and the answer thereto, shows the ambiguity, especially when the reading is done in the light of the *corpus* itself, where St. Thomas repeats his fundamental proposition about the identity of essence and existence in God alone; and also when understood in the light of I, 104, 3, 4, on annihilation and annihilability. Hence it is absolutely false to say of immaterial beings that "they cannot not-be." If it were absolutely impossible for them not to be, God could not annihilate them, and God's exnihilation of them would not be a free act. The truth here should be more carefully expressed by the statement that angels and souls do not perish through the operation of natural causes, which simply means they are by nature incorruptible. There is certainly no point in continuing St. Thomas's ambiguous use of "necessary" simply because he followed Aristotle's error here, an error which was due to Aristotle's failure to understand necessary being as due to the identity of essence and existence. What applies to the word "necessary" holds also for the word "contingent." Since "contingent" does not mean "naturally corruptible" but, strictly, "caused being," it is false to say that immaterial substances are "not contingent" because they are by nature incorruptible.

(c) The rest of Schwartz's discussion here is totally irrelevant, for certainly nothing that I said in my original article could be construed as meaning that I thought God's existence could be proved from the existence of incorruptible beings. In the first place, I am far from sure that there is any *purely philosophical* proof of the existence of angels. Hence one could not argue *a posteriori* from an effect not itself known to exist, either by evidence or demonstration. In the second place, although I do think there may be a philosophical proof of the self-subsistence of the soul as an incorruptible being, I do not think that the proof of God as *causa essendi* is any different whether it be made from the existence of souls as caused and contingent beings or from the existence of bodies as caused and contingent beings; in either case the proof is from the known existence of a being which needs a cause for its being. And in the third place, I certainly did not, nor do I now, think that the "third way" is valid reasoning; and no proof which I would ever propose as possibly valid would consist in a restatement of that argument in St. Thomas. (By the may, Schwartz refers here, on his page 37, to the "Second Way," which has nothing to do with the distinction between necessary and contingent beings; but that is probably a typographical error.) The only relevant truth in the Third Way is the distinction between necessary and contingent beings, but this truth is obscured by St. Thomas's use of the word "necessary" for both merely incorruptible substances and for God.

(3) On pages 36–37, Schwartz tries to defend what I have called a contradiction in St. Thomas—whether it is or not makes no difference here—by saying that the following two statements are not contradictory, and that my thinking so results from the application of "the law of excluded middle in an uncritical fashion." The two statements are: *first*, that God alone conserves being; and *second*, that creatures, as well as God, conserve the being of things. Now I shall show that, on one interpretation of these two statements, they are flatly contradictory; and that on another, they are not.

(a) They are contradictory when they are interpreted as follows. Let the first statement mean: "God alone is an efficient cause of the being of anything, whether the causation of being be *ab initio* (i.e., creation with both notes) or whether it be *non ab initio* (i.e., creation without the note of initiation, and hence identical with "conservation directly and *per se* through efficient causality"). Let the second statement mean: "Creatures, as well as God, are agents efficiently causing being, i.e., conserving being in a direct and *per se* manner, albeit in a manner that is secondary and instrumental to God's action in causing being and conserving it." When the two statements are thus interpreted, they are flatly contradictory, as is formally shown by the contradiction between "A alone is B" and "C as well as is A is B." The contradiction occurs, of course, only if the symbol "B" is used univocally in the two statements; for "as well as" means "not alone," and hence we have "A alone is B" and "Not only A is B." I am not here arguing that this contradiction occurs in St. Thomas. It makes no difference whether it does or not, If it does, the truth isn't affected; only St. Thomas is. I am arguing only that what I called a contradiction is a contradiction.

(b) But the two statements need not be contradictory, for the predicate may not be univocally expressed. Thus, if in one statement using "B" the symbol "B" means X, and if in another using "B," the symbol 'B" means Y, then these two statements "A alone is B, i.e., X" and "Not only A is B, i.e., Y" are not contradictory, but quite compatible. Now the two statements Schwartz presents can be so interpreted. Let the first statement mean: "God alone is an efficient cause of the being of anything, i.e., the only efficient cause of a direct end *per se* conservation of things." And let the second statement mean: "Form and matter are also causes of the being of things, in the sense that they are immanent , formal and material, not extrinsic efficient, causes of a thing's conservation in being, albeit as such, i.e., as formal and material causes, they are direct and *per se* causes." This statement does not contradict the first statement. Or let the second statement mean: "Created things, whether heavenly bodies, elemental bodies, or other bodies, preserve the being of things *in an indirect and accidental manner,* and in such causality they are efficient causes which as motions work against the corruptive influence of other motions." This statement does not contradict the first statement.

(c) Hence if one wishes to save St. Thomas from contradiction one must give a non-contradictory interpretation of the two statements; or if there are some words in St. Thomas which militate against the non-contradictory interpretation of these two statements, one must find an explanation of the contradiction. Either it is due to philosophical error on St. Thomas's part or to scientific error, Now I have done both things: I have shown grounds for making the non-contradictory interpretation of these two statements; and I have also shown the scientific error on St. Thomas's part which may have led him, in one place, to fall into a contradiction, a contradiction which can, however, be expunged from his philosophical doctrine along with his scientific errors. Schwartz does neither. He fails to reject the scientific errors; and he fails to see the possible non-contradictory interpretations. What he does do, instead, is to embrace a contradiction. He is willing to accept the statement that the heavenly bodies can be "the cause of the form (of inferior bodies), according to the ratio of such a form, and not only according as it is acquired in this matter; and *therefore it is the cause, not only of the becoming (fiendi), but of the being* (the quotation is from I, 104, 1; the italics are by Schwartz).

(1) Now I say that this statement, on which Schwartz hangs his case, is both contradictory of other statements in St. Thomas and is also false in itself,

(2) The contradiction will be found in I, 65, 4, where St. Thomas argues that not even angels can cause the forms of corporeal substances in a manner that is not merely the reduction of a potency to act. The forms of corporeal things result either from emanation or from movement. Vd. *ibid.*, and esp. ad 4. If they result from movement, then the form is not caused according to the ratio of such a form, but only according an it is acquired in this matter. Now, according to St. Thomas, the action of angels and of the heavenly bodies do not cause the forms of corporeal things "by emanation." Hence the contradiction is clear.

(3) Furthermore, the proposition which Schwartz thinks is true is false as a matter of fact. As a matter of fact, the heavenly bodies do not cause the generation of imperfect living things by the putrefaction of inanimate matter. The Thomistic statement in I, 104, 1, which Schwartz relies on, would be true only if the Thomistic account of certain generations were true.

(a) In I, 71, 1 ad 1, St. Thomas says that in the case of "animals generated from putrefaction, the *formative* power is the influence of the heavenly bodies." This is false as matter of scientific fact, not as a matter of philosophical doctrine. In I, 73, 1 ad 3, he repeats this error, speaking of animals "produced by putrefaction by the power which the stars and elements received at the beginning."

(b) And the error is crucially revealed in I, 45, 8 at 3. Here the objector says that, since some animals are generated by putrefaction, and since in these cases, the generative cause is *unlike* the generated thing *in* specific nature, hence "the form of these is not from nature, but by creation." And St. Thomas replies: "For the generation of imperfect animals, a universal agent suffices, and this is to be found in the celestial power to which they are assimilated, not in species, but according to a kind of analogy.... However for the generation of perfect animals, the universal agent does not suffice, but a proper agent is required, in the shape of a univocal generator."

(c) This last passage is significant for three reasons. In the first place, it repeats the scientific error. In the second place, it shows that the so-called "equivocal generator" operates only in the generation of some, not all, forms of life, i.e., only those falsely supposed to arise from putrefaction. And in the third place, it shows that the so-called superior body (i.e., the celestial body) is a "formative influence" only when it acts as an "equivocal generator." Hence if as a matter of fact, the heavenly bodies are never equivocal generators, in the sense demanded by generation through putrefaction, neither are they "formative influences"—that is, neither are they ever the "cause of a fern according to the ratio of such a form, and not only according as it is acquired in this matter."

(d) Hence the scientific error being corrected, the statement on which Schwartz rests his case is without foundation, for it is not a philosophical statement. It is not capable of being proved by reduction to first principles. It is not self-evident. It is merely en empirical statement, which happens to be wrong as a matter of fact. Hence if Schwartz wishes to insist that no one can accept St. Thomas's philosophy who does not also accept his scientific errors, he can also insist that the authority of St. Thomas is on his side here. But he can do that only at the peril of generating a basic philosophical contradiction within the pages of the *Summa*.

(4) There are still other difficulties with Schwartz's position, considered as he himself intends it.

(a) In the first place, not even God can create a corporeal form as such; for as we have seen, corporeal forms are concreated or caused only in connection with the causation of the matter of which they are forms, Hence the celestial bodies cannot be the causes of corporeal forms as such; for they are not, according to St. Thomas, causes of the terrestrial matter as well and conjunctively. Hence they cannot be causes of the forms as such, if they are not also causes of the matter.

(b) In the second place, Schwartz's argument comes to this: that the only created agent which is a cause of being, through being a cause of the form in other bodies, is a "universal cause"—in the sense of "equivocal generator." Only what is called an "equivocal generator" conserves being in a direct and *per se* manner; the univocal generater does not, i.e., the generating man is only the cause of the becoming of his son, not of his being, either productively or conservatively. Now the only reson which can be given why univocal generators cannot do what equivocal generators can do is the false fact that this is what equivocal generators do do in the case of animals generated by putrefaction. There is nothing in the nature of the distinction between equivocal and univocal generators that requires this to be so, as a matter of reason. It is only a matter of fact, and the fact is false. Furthermore, God is also called a "universal cause"—for Schwartz, He is simply "the most universal cause of the being of things." Hence if to be a universal cause, with respect to any particular effect, is also to be an equivocal cause, then God is an equivocal cause of being. But this is false. God is an analogical cause of being, not an equivocal cause of being, and this statement is true as a matter of reason, not as a matter of fact; for the being which God causes, participated being, is not called "being" equivocally when compared with the being of God, its cause. The sun is called an "equivocal cause" because its nature is supposed to be either specifically or generically different from the nature of the living thing it generates. But God does not differ from created things in nature, but in being, and this difference is involved in the analogical sameness of God and creatures; it is not the sort of difference which is involved in "equivocation."

(c) In saying all this, I by no means accept the very inadequate and confused Thomistic account of the univocal, equivocal, and analogical. I am merely using the "traditional opinions" dialectically with respect to Schwartz, who claims to be a Thomist, in a sense in which I do not and would not make any such claim. Furthermore, in this connection let me say that the two quotations from St. Thomas's Commentary on the *De Trinitate* of Boethius, which Schwartz appends to his article for my edification (his pp. 47–48) are totally irrelevant to the issue. Schwartz's position is not saved from error or contradiction by the supposed distinction between logical and natural genera, nor by the supposition that the celestial bodies are incorruptible, and hence net in the sane natural genus with terrestrial ones. For one thing, the fact is false: the heavenly bodies are not incorruptible. For another thing, the distinction is itself false, quite apart from the fact. I have elsewhere proved (in my forthcoming work on analogy) that the Thomistic "theory" of logical vs. natural genera is without any foundation, and involves basic confusions. There are no "logical genera," such as 'substance' predicated of angels and corporeal things. (All the Thomistic, *not* Aristotelian, errors about "natural" and "logical" genera, about definitions given by the logician vs. definitions given by the Natural Philosopher, and about the so-called "analogy of inequality," are plainly exhibited in a recent series of articles by W.A. Van Roc, "A Study of Genus," in *The Modern Schoolman*, XX, 2, 3, 4.)

But this matter need not be argued here. It has no bearing on the present issue whatsoever; for even if it were true that celestial bodies are incorruptible; even if, for that reason, they were diverse in genus from terrestrial bodies, it would still not be true that they are "equivocal generators." They are not generators at all; nor do they in any way efficiently cause being or conserve it in a direct and *per se* manner. It is not even true that in the sphere of accidental effects, (such as causing illumination), the sun operates differently from other natural agents, as St. Thomas supposes in 1, 104, 1. The illuminated body can retain light as a residual effect, without the concurrent action of an illuminating cause, just as the heated body can retain heat as a residual effect, without the concurrent action of the heating cause.

(d) Finally, Schwartz gets himself into this insoluble dilemma. Let the celestial bodies be instrumental causes subalternated to God's principal causality in conserving the being of some or all terrestrial bodies, the conservation being, of course, direct and *per se*. Let this be the meaning of St. Thomas's statement that God "established an order among things, so that some depend on others, by which they are preserved in being, though He remains the principal cause of their preservation" (I, 104, 2, ad 1).

Now if "some depend on others" be taken strictly, it means that *not all* depend on others. Hence those which do not depend on others depend directly on God for their existence, either initially or now at the moment of conservation *per se*. Hence with respect to some created things, God is the *only* cause *per se* of their conservation in being; whereas

with respect to other created things, God is merely
the principal, and not the only, cause. Now either
the created things which God *alone* conserves *per se*
are all immaterial things, or some are bodies, such
as the celestial bodies. According to Schwartz's
reading of St. Thomas, the second alternative must
be chosen in view of the passage he quotes from I,
104, 1 (quotation on his pp. 37–38); read also in
the light of his quotation on his p. 36 from I, 104,
2. If this is so, then it is not true to say, as Schwartz
says that "the conservation of things is proper to
God only in respect of the conservation of immaterial things" (his pp. 36). But if that is false, then
there is no intrinsic falsity in the statement that
"the conservation of things is proper to God both
with respect to material and immaterial things."

In short, it is not due to the very nature of material
things that they cannot be conserved in being by
the direct and *per se* action of God alone. On the
contrary, that all creatures are conserved in being
by the direct and *per se* action of God alone is precisely what St. Thomas affirms in a text which
Schwartz overlooks, namely, *S.T.*, I, 8, 1, in which
St. Thomas says that God is *directly* present to things
as an agent causing their being at every moment of
their being. Hence even if natural agents were efficient causes of being in a direct and *per se* manner,
it would be impossible for them to be instrumental
causes, for that would make God a principal cause
in this respect, which, according to I, 8, 1, God is
not.

(5) On pp. 38–39, Schwartz says that "God is not a unique cause in
the sense that He is the only cause.... Rather His uniqueness is as
a principal cause." In short, Schwartz holds that God's relation to
natural causes is the same in the sphere of being as it is in the
sphere of becoming. But this violates the fundamental truth of I,
45, 5, wherein St. Thomas argues that only God creates. But to
create is certainly to cause being. Nor can it be said that this
means that only God can initiate being; for as we have seen, the
philosopher must be able to use the word "creation" significantly
while at the same time excluding the note of an original initiation of creatures. When this note is excluded, it still remains true
that only God creates—i.e., eternally exnihilates annihilable
things. But "to create" in this restricted sense is "to cause being."
Hence it is false to say that, with respect to the causation of being,
God is not a unique cause, an efficient cause which acts without
intermediaries or instruments of any kind, for no created thing

can possibly be an instrument for God's creative action; or causation of being, even if it is without an original initiation of creatures. On the other hand, if God is a cause of becoming or motion, it must be true that, in this respect He is a principal and not a unique cause, for we know that all natural motions have natural motions as causes—except, of course, for miraculous events, in the causation of which God may be a unique cause. Hence Schwartz is utterly wrong in saying that the Divine causality is related to the operation of natural causes in the same way in both orders, i.e., that of being and that of becoming. When I say he is wrong, I mean, of course, wrong according to the authority of St. Thomas. I am not here considering what is true in reason or in fact.

(6) On p. 39, Schwartz offers as a reason for his position, that it is impossible that "God should create a creature that should not imitate its Creator." And he connects this point with a remark about an analogical understanding of God and of creatures as causes. He argues that, if no creature is an efficient cause of being, then creatures would not imitate the Divine action. His argument is false and invalid for two reasons:

(a) In the first place, if only God caused being, and if creatures only caused becoming—whether or not God also was a *causa fiendi*—there would be an analogy between Divine and creature causality; for the notion of 'cause' is only analogically common to the two notions '*causa fiendi*' and '*causa essendi*.' To demand more than this imitation of God by creature would be to demand that creatures should create in order to imitate their Creator. But obviously there is some limitation on the imitation of God by creatures. Nor is the fundamental fact of imitation violated by the fact that the analogy between Divine and creature causality is limited to the analogy between *causa essendi* and *causa fiendi*.

(b) In the second place, if Schwartz were right it would be the celestial bodies, among all creatures, which most perfectly imitated God; for according to Schwartz, these are the creatures which cause being, which conserve the being of inferior bodies in a *per se* manner. Man does not have such causal power. Therefore, among corporeal creatures man is less the image of God than the celestial bodies, so far as causal operation goes. But a thing's causal powers flow from its nature. Hence it follows that an inanimate and an irrational body by nature is, by its causal action, more imitative of God than a rational, living person. Now this is not only contrary to reason, but also to the authority of St. Thomas. Vd. I, 93, 1–9, wherein everything that St. Thomas says points to the conclusion that only man, among corporeal creatures, is the image of God; that this is due to the fact that man has a mind; that the imitation of God is found in the acts of the human soul, not the acts of the human body; that irrational creatures are not the image of God; that all creatures which are not *persons* have only a *likeness* to God, or a *trace* of Divinity, but none properly imitates God in the sense in which God's images do.

(c) In the third place, man as the image of God imitates God by his intellectual and voluntary acts, such as his free moral acts, or his artistic productions. Let us consider the latter. Man's making of a work of art imitates Divine action more than the generation of a substance which is an act of a vegetative, not an intellectual, power. But in the production of a work of art, the maker is not, according to St. Thomas, an efficient cause of the being of the thing made. Vd. I, 104, 1. The builder is only the efficient cause of the becoming of the house. Hence that creature action which most nearly imitates Divine action operates as a *causa fiendi* not as a *causa essendi.* It cannot be true, therefore, that the imitation of God is violated by the fact that no creature operates as an efficient *causa essendi.*

(7) On p. 39, Schwartz states as a conclusion he is going to prove, that it "is impossible to demonstrate God in the way Mr. Adler proposes"—namely, as a unique efficient cause required by contingent being as a caused effect. Obviously he has not so far proved that conclusion in any way. If his manner of discussion so far could have proved anything, it would have proved only that the authority of St. Thomas was against such an attempt. But even if the authority of St. Thomas were adverse, that would make no difference to the truth of the matter. Now as I have shown, Schwartz fails utterly to prove what he set out to prove, namely, that the *philosophical* authority of St. Thomas is adverse to the possibility of proving God as unique *causa essendi.*

(a) Despite these facts, Schwartz makes the following statement on p. 40: that the proposition that 'God is the unique cause of the preservation of being' (when understood in the sense intended by me) "has been shown to be false, *both according to St. Thomas's teaching and demonstratively.*" Both of Schwartz's contentions are false; *but* I have bothered to refute only one of them. No part of Schwartz's argument has any bearing *on the truth, apart from the authority of St. Thomas.* I could not show his demonstration to be false, since none was offered.

(b) Furthermore, the only way in which the impossibility of a proffered proof can be demonstrated is by considering the proof itself. But in the course of my discussion up to this point in my original article (Part II, #7–10), no proof was even offered; and as a matter of fact in the whole article I did not complete a statement of the proof.

(c) Despite this fact, Schwartz begins his consideration of my Part III, in which I do offer the proof, by pointing out that my proof depends on the truth of the proposition that God is the unique efficient cause of being. In that he is right. But the difficulty with my original statement of the proof, as I shall presently show, is that I did not know how to demonstrate the truth of that proposition. That is why I admitted that I did not know a valid proof of God's existence at the time of writing; for certainly a proof is not validated until every premise on which it depends is proved or shown to be self-evident. This premise is not self-evident, and must be proved. Nevertheless, with respect to this crucial premise in my outlined argument, Schwartz says: "This has been demonstrated to be false" (his p. 40). Since that is not so, the rest of his reasoning from this point on has no major relevance to the consideration of the proof itself.

(d) Schwartz totally misrepresents my argument when he interprets what I have done in Part II, #7–9, as a demonstrative argument for the proposition on which the proof rests, namely, that God is the unique efficient cause of being. He refers to this part as that "wherein Mr. Adler attempted to establish that God was the unique cause of preservation in being of other things" (his p. 40). As I have now shown, I did not attempt to establish the proposition as true in reason, but only as a proposition which had the authority of St. Thomas. That was all Schwartz tried to refute, albeit unsuccessfully.

(8) In summary at this point, let me say that I have now shown the following: first, that, when certain scientific errors are expunged, and his philosophical doctrine is rectified accordingly, the authority of St. Thomas favors the proposition that God is the unique efficient cause of being, the *only* efficient cause conserving being in a direct and *per se* manner; second, that Schwartz has failed to show that the main weight of St. Thomas's authority is adverse to this proposition; third, no argument advanced by Schwartz independently of the authority of St. Thomas shows that a proof which depends on this proposition is impossible; fourth, that the only arguments advanced by Schwartz to refute the proposition upon which the proposed proof rests, appeal to the authority of certain passages (in I, 104, 1, 2) which should be rejected because they depend on scientific errors about matters of fact.

(a) It is not necessary, therefore, to consider the rest of Schwartz's article (his pp. 41-45) for it has no direct bearing on the proof I am now going to propose and defend.

(b) I shall, however, mention one or two minor points that remain in Schwartz's paper, merely because they reflect further on his incapacity or unwillingness to try to understand a carefully written analysis. I will deal with these points in Section B, in the course of reviewing the argument presented in Part III of my original article.

3. Before I turn to Section B, there is one further point of criticism I wish to mention. It was made in a review by Dr. Otto Bird, in *The Commonweal* (March 12th, 1943, p. 522).

    a. Bird wrote: "It seems doubtful, to say the least, that the change in existing things can be peeled away and leave a nucleus of being remaining that is separate from change. In fact., St. Thomas says in the *De Aeternitate Mundi* that if you take change away from creatures, you have nothing left. Adler seems to find something left, and that is what he is trying to find a cause for. But that is either nothing or God,, neither of which has or needs a cause."

    b. Both reason and authority stand against what Bird here thinks.

       (1) In his *Commentary on the Metaphysics*, Book IV, #688,. St. Thomas writes: "Secundum qualitatem vel formam non oportet quod propter hoc semper omnia moveantur." What St. Thomas says in *De Aeternitate Mundi* must be understood accordingly.

       (2) The immanent principles of a thing's being—its form and matter—do not change so long as the thing exists. These principles of its being underlie its becoming and its changing. Yet these principles not only constitute the thing's being, but constitute its being as *mobile being*. Hence the being of a mobile thing is not *actually separable* from its changing. But this does not mean that no real distinction exists in the thing between its being and its changing. While it is true that you cannot take mobility or changeability away from mobile being without destroying its being, it is not true that in *ens mobile*, existence and motion are identical. Change, whether accidental or substantial, is always an incomplete actualization. But existence is a complete act. Furthermore, a motion as an act is always the act of a pre-existent potentiality. But existence is not the act of any pre-existent potentiality. Hence Bird's critical point fails because, though what he says is partly true, he cannot deny the real distinction between existence and change in changing things.

B. The Proof of God's Existence

NOTE: I shall proceed here in three stages. First, I shall briefly summarize the proof as stated in the original article, Part III, pp. 209–210. Second, I shall deal with the difficulties that I myself raised against the proof as stated (Part III, pp. 211–16); and here I shall show that none of them is insuperable. Third, I shall attempt to establish the premises on which the proof rests.

1. Original Statement of the Proof

a.   The proof was formulated in the following syllogism:

Major: IF anything exists whose continuation in existence requires the operation of an efficient cause at this very moment, THEN a being exists whose existence is uncaused.

Minor: Corporeal substances do exist.

Conclusion: THEREFORE, God does exist.

b.   The understanding of this proof, as of any proof, depends upon a definition of its terms. The definitions were as follows:

   (1) "Contingent being": *ens ab alio*, whether *ens per se* or *ens per aliud*. *Ens ab alio* is a *caused being*. A caused being is one which cannot exist except as it is caused to be. But if there were a being whose essence were identical with its existence, it would need no extrinsic cause in order to be. Such a being would be *uncaused being*. Hence a contingent being, as a caused being, is one "whose essence is not identical with its existence."

   (2) "Necessary being": *ens a se*. As we have seen, this means: uncaused being, and also "that whose essence is its existence."

   (3) "Corporeal substance": any substance is *ens per se*, but a corporeal substance is by nature corruptible. Hence we know from this fact that a corporeal substance is one whose essence is not its existence; for identity of essence and existence would be incompatible with corruptibility, not to mention accidental change. But we know corporeal substances to be both generable and corruptible, and also changeable accidentally. Hence we know that corporeal substances are contingent beings, or *ens ab alio*.

   (4) "God": necessary being or *ens a se*.

c.   Let me now discuss these definitions, summarizing what was said in the original article, but emphasizing certain points that have been overlooked by some of my readers.

   (1) There is no difficulty about the definitions given for "contingent being" or "corporeal substance."

   (2) But it may be supposed that the definitions given for the words "necessary being" and "God" beg the question. That is not so. In my original article, I showed that the conception of a necessary being does not involve the affirmation of the existence of what is conceived. Were that so, Kant would have been right in claiming that any *a posteriori* argument for God's existence, which employed "necessary being" as a nominal definition of God, surreptitiously contains an ontological argument, which invalidates it. Kant's error is shown in Part III, 2, b., at pp. 211–12.

   (3) Furthermore, my conception of "necessary being" is fundamentally negative; or to put it precisely, it is negative in so far as it is

determinate, and only positive in so far as it is indeterminate and
"analogical." Thus 'being' said of God and corporeal substances
(the only beings we know directly) is said "analogically" but when
it is said without any further qualifications it is said indeterminately. But the nominal definition of "God" contains the qualify-
ing word "necessary." Now the point is that I cannot understand
what "necessary" signifies positively, when applied to 'being.' I
can only understand "necessary" negatively, as the opposite and
negative of 'contingent' which I do understand positively when it
is applied to 'being.' Hence by 'necessary being' I understand,
first, positively and indeterminately, *that which is*; and second,
negatively and determinately, *a non-contingent mode of being*.
Hence my concept of God, expressed by this nominal definition,
does not go beyond the possibilities of my limited knowledge; for
I do know *contingent beings*; and so I can know analogically and
indeterminately that which such beings have in common with *all
beings*, understood without further qualification. And since I
know what is meant by *contingency of being*, I can understand the
qualifier "necessary" in a negative manner. A necessary being is
that which is, but not contingently.

All my natural knowledge of God is of this sort: whatever name I
apply to God with positive signification is both analogical and
indeterminate in signification; whatever name I apply to God
with negative signification is determinate and non-analogical in
signification. By means of merely positive names, I can have no
determinate knowledge of God's nature at all. And all of my negative names for God serve only as qualifiers determining the
indeterminateness of my positive names. (This theory of the
names of God will be developed in the second volume of my
three volume work on analogy.)

(4) The nominal definition "necessary being" can be used in a proof
of God's existence, in exactly the same may that the nominal definition "unmoved mover" or "uncaused cause of motion" could
be used if God could be proved from motion as an effect. The
nominal definition "unmoved mover" has both a positive and
negative note. When "mover" is said of God and natural agent
positively, it is said analogically and indeterminately. The only
movers which we know directly are all moved movers. Hence to
render this nominal definition determinate we must add the negative note "unmoved." The nominal definition "uncaused being"
which is equivalent to "necessary being" which is equivalent to
"non-contingent being" is thus seen to be constructed in the
same way as the nominal definition "unmoved mover."

(5) Hence it follows that if a proof of God is not invalidated by the
use of "unmoved mover" as the nominal definition involved, neither is a proof invalidated by the use of "uncaused being" or "necessary being" as the nominal definition involved. I do not have to

know *that* God exists to know that *if* God exists, *and if* He is a mover, He is an *unmoved* mover. I do not have to know *that* God exists in order to know that *if* God exists, He is an uncaused or necessary being. I know this because I know that I cannot use the word "God" significantly to signify a being that is in any respect contingent. It may nevertheless be true that all beings *are* in fact contingent, in *which* case I would not conclude that God is contingent, but that God does not exist.

(6) This is confirmed by the authority of St. Thomas in so far as in his Third Way (which fails as a proof), he employs "necessary being" as the nominal definition of God, just as he employs "unmoved mover" in the "first way" as a nominal definition. As St. *Thomas* says in *C.G.*, I, 12, the nominal definition we use in proving God *a posteriori* is determined by the character of the effect from which we try to infer His existence.

   (a) Dr. James Mullaney, in his discussion of my article in *The New Scholasticism* (April, 1943, Vol. XVII, No. 2) points this out (p. 177). But this fact does not mean that there can be many different proofs of God's existence because there can be many nominal definitions; or that there is some justification in this fact for St. Thomas's trying to prove God from motion as an effect.

   (b) Neither of these things is true. If God cannot be proved from motion as an effect, then the nominal definitions determined by this effect cannot be used in a proof of God's existence. If the only may in which God can be proved is from contingent being as an effect, then the only nominal definition which can be used in a proof is determined by that fact, and is 'necessary being'.

   (c) Furthermore, the fact that the several nominal definitions are co-implicative does not alter what has just been said. If a "necessary being" is a mover, it must be an "unmoved mover." If an "unmoved mover" is a being, it must be a "necessary being." And both of these nominal definitions imply and are implied by the nominal definition used in the "fourth way," i.e., "perfect being." The only nominal definitions that are not thus implied by the ones mentioned are those of the second and the fifth way: for it does not follow that a "necessary being" must be a "first cause" even if it is a cause, *unless* "first cause" does not mean a cause which is first *because* it acts through intermediate and subordinate secondary causes. If "first cause" only means "cause of the first effect which is being," then when we see that a necessary being is cause of the first effect, we will see that it is "first cause" in this sense, and this sense only.

   (d) Furthermore, it should be observed that the analytical elaboration of the notes involved in our understanding of God's nature in no may depends upon the proof of God's existence. Just as we can know, quite apart from knowing *whether* God exists, that *if* God exists, God is a necessary being; so we can know, quite apart from any proof of God's existence, that God, as a necessary being, is immutable, eternal, simple, perfect, etc. These attributes or *propria* are in no sense deduced from the proposition 'God exists,' nor is our knowledge of *what* God is, *if He is*, in any way dependent on our knowledge *that* God is, or in any way dependent on the terms used in our proof of God's existence. Thus, for example, the "first way" of St. Thomas does not prove to us *that* God is an unmoved mover, but rather, if it were a proof, it would prove *that* an unmoved mover exists. We knew before the proof started, that God is an unmoved mover, if He exists and is a mover at all. If we did not know that before the proof, we would have had no nominal definition to use in the proof. Hence we see that the notes in the conception of God's nature, which St. Thomas develops in I, QQ. 4–11, cannot be *deduced* from what is proved in Q. 2, A. 3. These questions are nothing but an analytical elaboration of co-implicative notes. There is nothing deductive about them. There is no one right ordering of the line of argument, and the appearance of deduction and unilinear ordering is entirely specious.

(e)   I mention all this to say against objectors that the proof of God as *causa essendi* in no way affects the discussion of the notes in our conception of God's nature. That discussion remains the same, however God is proved, and whether or not God can be proved. Logically, the discussion of God's nature, as we understand it, could precede as well as follow an attempt to prove God's existence, and whether it precedes or follows, it makes no difference whether that attempt is successful or unsuccessful. . . . The false supposition to the contrary is due to the false supposition that the proof of God's existence is a *process of discovery.* No demonstration is a process of discovery. The meaning of the conclusion must always be completely known prior to its demonstration. The demonstration does not even *make* the conclusion true: it merely *shows us that* the conclusion is true. . . . The psychological fact that men may come to think about God through their experience of motion and of corruptible and contingent beings, and through some understanding of the principles of cause and effect, has no bearing on the logic of demonstration. Just as they must prove *that* God is from effects which they know directly, so they must conceive *what* God is from the objects of their own experience. Both are *a posteriori* procedures, but the demonstrative process, concerning the *that* of God, proceeds from effect to cause; whereas the conceptual process, concerning the *what* of God, proceeds from experienced things by steps of analogy and negation. The two processes are obviously quite independent of one another, though both originate in experience and in our understanding of cognate objects.

(f) Finally, in this connection let me say that by its very nature an *a posteriori* demonstration cannot possibly increase our understanding of the *nature* of that which is proved to exist. In this it differs radically from a *propter quid* demonstration, which proceeds through definitions that are genuinely prior to the conclusion and which throw light on the *nature* which the concluding proposition is about. Demonstration *propter quid* proves properties which are determinate consequences of natures defined; not so in demonstration *quia*. The concluding proposition in an *a posteriori* demonstration is not about a *nature*, a *what*; it is about a *that*, attached to a *what* already nominally defined; moreover, in no real sense is the nominal definition a middle term in *a posteriori* demonstration. Strictly speaking, such demonstration always is formally accomplished in a *hypothetical* syllogism which does not have a middle term in the sense in which a *categorical* syllogism has.

d. One further point remains in connection with the original statement of the proof. It may be asked why the minor premise is "Corporeal substances do exist" instead of "Contingent beings do exist." The answer is as follows.

(1) Within our experience of cognate objects, "contingent being" can refer either to an accident or to a substance, for whether the cognate being is *per se* or *per aliud*, it is *ab alio*, i.e., contingent.

(2) But accidents do have a sufficient cause for their being in the being of the substances in which they inhere, even though this is a material cause. Furthermore, strictly speaking, they are not subsistent, and, as St. Thomas says, they are *entia entis*. They have being only through the being of the substances in which they inhere.

(3) But the being of a corporeal substance does not have a sufficient cause in either its immanent matter or form, though these are causes of its being. Because a substance is subsistent, because it is a being, having existence in its own right, not *through* the existence of another, it requires an efficient cause for the being it has. If it did not require an efficient cause, it would be an uncaused being, i.e., a necessary being; hence it would be incorruptible, which is contrary to fact.

(4) Therefore, the effect we must choose in order to prove God as *causa essendi* is that effect, known to exist, which requires an efficient, extrinsic cause. Hence corporeal substances, known by us

to exist, and known by us to be contingent in being and to require an efficient cause for their being, are the effects from which we try to infer God's existence.

2. Original Difficulties Now Surmountable

a.   In my earlier article I proposed certain difficulties, allocating them according as they occurred with respect to the minor premise, the definitions, or the major premise. Vd. Part III, pp. 210–16.

(1)   The chief difficulty about the minor premise, which needs no further discussion here, is its demonstration. It is not self-evident, as I showed on p. 210. Hence it must be demonstrated. What must be demonstrated is that the nominal definition of "corporeal substance" is a real definition, i.e., defines something that exists. This demonstration will be *a posteriori* in form. It will proceed from accidental change as the *known effect*, and it will establish the existence of a composite substance as the formal and material cause required for the explanation of accidental change. Moreover, it will have to prove that there is a plurality of such composite, corruptible substances; for accidental change cannot be explained by positing a single substance.

These are matters I shall not argue here, for they belong to another work. I shall proceed, therefore, on the assumption that the minor premise required for the proof of God's existence is demonstrable. Of course, in a perfectly complete statement of the proof of God's existence, the proof of the minor premise would have to be included. I am not now aiming at such a complete statement. That belongs to the work for which the present outline is only a rough draft.

(2)   The only problem which remains concerning the definition of God is that raised at 2, c., on p. 212. It seemed to me necessary that the nominal definition of God should imply the unity of God, "unity" in the sense that there is only one such necessary being. My reason for feeling this necessity is that I conceive the philosopher's work in demonstrating God's existence to be work carried on in the light of, but without the faith of, revealed religion. Now within the tradition of Judaism and Christianity, there is only one God. Hence the philosopher has not proved the existence of the God in which the religious believe unless the God he has proved to exist is one or unique.

(a)   This problem is not solved by the way in which God's existence is proved. It is a problem about God's nature, and can be solved quite independently of any proof of God's existence.

(b)   The solution of the problem depends on whether the note of "uniqueness" is implied by such notes as "necessity" or "simplicity."

(c) In my original article, I posed this problem more fully in 3, d. on pp. 215–16. I wrongly supposed that it might be possible for a necessary being to be composite in some may, other than the composition of essence and existence. I now see my mistake. If anything is incomposite with respect to essence and existence (which is the meaning of 'necessity'), it is incomposite in every other way (which is the meaning of 'absolute simplicity'). And if anything is totally incomposite it is positively and actually infinite, for all limitation in the being of anything arises from the way in which one principle in a composition limits another. But two infinite beings cannot exist without limiting each other, in which case they would not be infinite. Hence the note of necessity implies the note of simplicity, which implies the note of infinity in being, which implies the uniqueness of the infinite being.

(d) It follows, therefore, that if "necessary being" is used as the nominal definition of God, and if a necessary being can be proved to exist, then by the implication between the note of necessity and the note of uniqueness, which is independent of the proof, the conclusion of the proof "A necessary being exists" is equivalent to the proposition "Only one necessary being exists," and so the God in whom the religious believe is proved to exist.

(3) Thus we come to the main object of our consideration—the major premise in the original statement of the syllogism. I shall now consider the two questions which I originally raised about the major premise; whether it is self-evident, and whether it is demonstrable.

b. Whether the major premise is self-evident?

(1) In my original article (Part III, 3, b., p. 213), I saw the conditions which would have to be fulfilled for the major premise to be self-evident. A hypothetical proposition is self-evident if the consequent is seen at once to flow from the antecedent. Thus, in a way, every categorical syllogism can be formulated as a self-evident hypothetical proposition, complexly constituted by two antecedents and one consequent. 'IF A is B, and IF B is C. THEN A is C' is an hypothetical statement which is self-evidently true, whether or not the two antecedents are true, or the consequent. But if this hypothetical statement is formally true, and if the two antecedents are true in fact, then the conclusion is true in fact. Now the hypothetical major in the proof of God's existence was not self-evident, as I first stated it. This can be shown as follows.

(a) Let us state the hypothetical major briefly: "If a contingent being exists, then a necessary being exists." This is not self-evident, because, as I pointed out in the original article, the following questions remain unanswered: first, must a contingent being have a cause for its existence? and second, can a contingent being cause the existence of another contingent being? If one could answer the first question affirmatively and the second negatively, it would follow from the fact that a contingent being existed, needing a cause, which could not be another contingent being, that therefore a non contingent or necessary being is required as cause; and hence such a being exists, for its effect exists.

(b) Hence the following self-evident hypothetical proposition can be formulated:

If anything contingent exists, *and if* everything contingent must be caused to exist, *and if* nothing contingent can cause anything to exist, *then* a necessary being exists as the cause of the existence of any contingent being known by us to exist.

This complex hypothetical proposition has the formal self-evidence of a formally valid syllogism.

(2) My error in the original article consisted in my failure to see that the major premise I first stated was not formally self-evident because it was incompletely stated; and that when an adequate formulation of it is made, the problem of the proof turns upon the establishment of the three antecedent clauses from which the consequent follows. I had wrongly supposed that the hypothetical major and a single categorical minor were sufficient. Furthermore, I had wrongly supposed that *this* hypothetical major was a *premise* in the proof itself. On the contrary, when the original hypothetical major is completely stated, we see that it is a *purely formal* proposition which formulates the categorical syllogisms that constitute the proof. This leads us to see that the proof consists of these two categorical syllogisms:

First Syllogism

Major: Contingent substances must be caused to exist.

Minor: Contingent substances exist.

Conclusion: The cause required for contingent substances exists.

Second Syllogism

Minor: Nothing contingent can cause anything to exist.

Major: The cause required for contingent substances exists.

Conclusion: A non-contingent (i.e., necessary) being exists.

(*Note:* The word "cause" is always used to signify "efficient cause").

(a) Nevertheless, I was right in one fundamental insight, namely, that *a posteriori* reasoning cannot be accomplished by completely categorical syllogisms. The two categorical syllogisms just stated do not prove the conclusion, because one premise is omitted, and that one is a hypothetical proposition. If one examines the first syllogism just stated, one discovers an implicit hypothetical premise upon which the reasoning depends, namely, 'If an effect exists, its cause exists' or 'The existence of an effect *implies* the existence of a cause'. That this proposition is truly hypothetical, and cannot be reduced to a categorical judgment, is seen from the fact that there are two predications here and that these two predications are of distinct subjects. In contrast, the major and minor premises of the two aforestated syllogisms are categorical propositions.

(b) Now this hypothetical proposition 'The existence of an effect *implies* the existence of a cause' is self-evident—that is, it is known to be true from an understanding of these terms 'cause' and 'effect' and 'exists'. Furthermore, this is not *formal* self-evidence, but *real* self-evidence; by which I mean that the proposition is self-evidently known to be true of reality, not merely self-evidently known to have logical truth, as is the case with any hypothetical proposition which formulates a valid syllogism,

(c) What I have just said shows that Schwartz was both right and wrong in his criticism of my original article on the point of the self-evidence of the major premise as originally stated (Vd. Schwartz, pp. 40–42).

    (1) He was right in making a distinction between two types of self-evidence—the self-evidence of a logical formula, and the self-evidence of a proposition understood as signifying realities, or what I have here called "formal self-evidence" and "real self-evidence." And he was right in seeing that the hypothetical major, as I originally stated it, was neither formally nor really self-evident.

    (2) But he was wrong in supposing that no hypothetical proposition can be really self-evident. He says: "No proposition of the form, A implies B, or if A then B, when A and B are in the real order, can be self evident" (p. 40). But the proposition 'If the effect exists, the cause exists' or 'The existence of the effect *implies* the existence of the cause' is self-evident and its terms are in the real order. The truth of this proposition is a truth about reality, not about the logical relation of terms or propositions in the mind.

    (3) That he is wrong on this point can be shown another way. Either all hypothetical propositions are merely log-

ical formulae, or some are propositions about reality. Certainly, the second alternative is true. Now if some hypothetical propositions are propositions about reality, either they are demonstrable or self-evident. But no hypothetical proposition is demonstrable. Hence those which are true must be self-evident, i.e., *really* self-evident.

(4) The remainder of Schwartz's remarks on these pages can be ignored for the present. If they have any bearing at all, that can be better discussed after the proof is adequately formulated, as it was not in the first article.

c. Whether the major premise is demonstrable?

(1) The errors I have just pointed out in my original formulation of the proof caused other errors in that part of my first article in which I discussed the demonstrability of the major premise as then stated. (Vd. Part III, 3, c., at pp. 213–15) I was right in saying that that major premise could not be demonstrated either *propter quid* or *quia* by any direct demonstration, for such demonstration is not applicable to hypothetical propositions. Hence I was led to the conclusion that if the major premise was true, the only remaining possibility was an indirect demonstration, a *reductio ad absurdum*. I was also right in saying that when a proposition is incapable of being argued for in any way *except reductio ad absurdum*, then that proposition is self-evident. This is shown perfectly by the single case of the principle of contradiction. As Aristotle points out in *Metaphysics*, IV, there is no way of arguing the truth of this proposition except by reducing those who deny it to absurdity; and the fact that this is the *only* way of arguing for the truth of the principle of contradiction is essentially connected with the fact that the principle is self-evidently true.

(2) Now if I had been able successfully to argue by *reductio ad absurdum* for the truth of my major premise, I would have contradicted myself; for the success of such argument would have signified that the proposition thus argued for, and incapable of being argued for in any other way, is self-evident. But I had shown that this proposition was not self-evident. I did not contradict myself, however, because I did not succeed in a *reductio ad absurdum* argument for the major premise. On the contrary, I showed that a *reductio ad absurdum* argument led to the denial of the major premise.

(a) I saw that the truth of the major premise involved the truth of this proposition 'No contingent being can cause the existence of another contingent being.' Hence I proposed to deny this proposition. If the denial of this proposition had led to the affirmation of the proposition 'A necessary being exists,' then by denying the truth of a proposition involved in the major premise, I would have proved the major premise, namely, that if a contingent being exists, a necessary being exists.

(b) But this cannot be done, If one denies the proposition 'No contingent being can cause the existence of another contingent being'—which proposition, by the way, I shall show to be demonstrably, not self-evidently true—one affirms the proposition (in fact, false) that 'One contingent being can cause the existence of another.' And from this false proposition affirmed, a false conclusion follows, namely, that no necessary being is required for the existence of contingent beings, as cause of their existence. This is shown in the first article on pp. 214–15 where I show the possibility of circular causality. Though such a circle of efficient causation of being is in fact impossible, it is possible on a false assumption, namely, that one contingent being can cause the existence of another. In short, if one starts to reason from a false or impossible premise, and if one reasons correctly, one can validly reach a false or impossible conclusion. The only way to show that this conclusion is false or impossible is to show that the premise on which it rests is false or impossible.

(c) But my reasoning showed me that that premise was not self-evidently false. For if it had been, reasoning from it would have led me into contradiction, and so the *reductio ad absurdum* argument would have been successful, and I would have known that the contradictory of the false premise was self-evidently true.

(d) Hence what I learned from my attempt at *reductio ad absurdum* was this: that the proposition (No contingent being can cause the being of another) is not self-evidently true. And since the truth of my major premise involved the truth of this proposition, I also learned that that major premise is not self-evidently true. But the errors I made prevented me from seeing at the time the full consequences of this discovery. Since I "felt" that the major premise was in fact true, and that the proposition which it involved was also in fact true, I should have looked further, and tried to demonstrate the proposition 'No contingent being can cause the being of another'. Had I done this, I would have been able then to demonstrate God's existence. But at that time, I could not see how the demonstration could be made, and so I concluded the article in frankly expressed perplexity, but not in doubt.

(e) Schwartz's comments on this part of my article (his pp. 43–44) are based on a fundamental misunderstanding of what I was there trying to do. He agrees with my principle that "a proposition which can be proved *only* through *reductio* is self-evident." But he fails to see that the way in which I knew that my hypothetical major was not demonstrable was not by testing a number of proposed proofs, which is of course impossible, but rather by knowing that no really true hypothetical proposition is directly demonstrable—from the very nature of what such demonstration is. Hence in my attempted *reductio* I was not trying to *prove* that my hypothetical major was self-evident. Quite the contrary, by the failure of my *reductio*, I was trying to show that it was *not* self-evident, and it was that showing which left me in perplexity, for I "felt" the major to be true, yet it was neither demonstrable nor self-evident, which is impossible. Schwartz did not put his finger on my fundamental error here which, as I have pointed out, consisted in failing to see the really true self-evident hypothetical proposition upon which my *a posteriori* reasoning depended (i.e., 'The existence of an effect *implies* the existence of the cause'), and in failing to see that if I had fully expressed my original major premise, I would have had a formally true self-evident proposition that was nothing but a statement of the syllogisms constituting the proof. Then the only remaining problem would have been the problem of proving the categorical premises in these two syllogisms.

(f) Moreover, Schwartz misunderstands the actual process of my *reductio*. If the truth of the proposition 'If contingent beings exist, a necessary being exists' depends upon the truth of the proposition 'No contingent being can cause the being of another', then the denial of the proposition 'No contingent being can cause the existence of another' involves the denial of the proposition which depends on it for its truth. Hence by contradicting 'No contingent being causes the being of another', one also contradicts the proposition 'If contingent beings exist, a necessary being exists'. It is, therefore, logically correct to regard a *reductio ad absurdum* argument based on the denial of the proposition P, to be equivalent to a *reductio ad absurdum* argument affecting the proposition Q, if the truth of Q depends on the truth of P. This is precisely what I did, as Schwartz's own account admits. Hence his adverse remarks here are unfounded.

(g) Schwartz's final remarks (his pp. 44–45) can be briefly disposed of here. He is quite wrong in saying that "in Mr. Adler's view, ostensibly, a demonstration of God's existence must demonstrate all of God's attributes" (his p. 44). That was not my view, in the original article (my pp. 215–16); nor, as I have shown at greater length in the present paper, can it rightly be anybody's view. The discussion of the attributes of God, their co-implication and order, is entirely independent of the proof of God's existence. The question I raised in the first article was simply whether the attribute 'necessity' implied the attribute 'uniqueness'. At that time, I was not sure of the affirmative answer, as I now am. I think I can now demonstrate that "necessary being has no composition of potency and act, of matter and form, of subject and accident" though Schwartz accurately reports me as saying in the first article that I did not know this. But Schwartz is quite wrong in supposing that "when the demonstration of God's existence is understood and presupposed, the requisite demonstration of the other negative attributes can be derived from them as principles" (his p. 45). As I have already shown, even supposing the Thomistic "ways" to be valid proofs, these "ways" do not provide us with the premises from which we "deduce" or "demonstrate" the attributes of God. And Schwartz's example from geometry betrays him completely. The proof of the *existence* of an equilateral triangle in Euclid is a *construction*, which shows that the definition of an equilateral triangle is not merely nominal, but has *geometric reality*. But the properties of an equilateral triangle can be demonstrated quite apart from the proof of its geometric existence by *construction*. All the other theorems about equilateral triangles can be validly demonstrated, using only a nominal definition; if that were done, these theorems would state demonstrated truths about a *possible* geometric figure, but not about one known to be *geometrically realizable*. The existence proof by construction shows that the nominally defined figure, with all its demonstrated properties, is geometrically realizable in a space defined by the fundamental postulates which are the rules of construction.

(h) I have already answered Schwartz's remark (his p. 45) that my procedure violates the principle that if 'cause' is predicated of God and creature, it must be analogically predicated. Schwartz misunderstands this principle. It does not mean that every name of God must be said analogically of both God and creatures. Only the positive and indeterminate names are so said. All the negative names, which are determinately significant, are said of God alone, but this is not univocal predication, for a univocal predicate is a universal which is predicated in an identical determinate sense of two subjects. Thus, 'necessary being' or 'perfect being' or 'infinite being' is said of God' alone, hence these are not said univocally; whereas 'being', which is said of God and creature in an indeterminate sense, is analogically predicated. 'Necessary being' is not univocally predicated of God, though it is predicated of God alone, precisely because the term 'necessary being' involves both a positive and a negative note—the positive, indeterminate note applying to God and creature, the negative and determinate note applying to God alone. Hence though 'cause' is predicated analogically of God and creature, 'cause of being' can be predicated of God alone, and as so predicated, it is not univocal; and when our understanding of this term is examined it will be found to involve a negative as well as a positive note, which is true of every name applicable to God alone.

An adequate analysis of the names of God, and of the whole problem of what is traditionally called "analogical predication" will be presented in my forthcoming work on the theory of analogy. I need go no further into the matter here, in order to refute Schwartz's supposition that to say that God alone is an efficient cause of being is to predicate something univocally of God; for if that were so, none of the theological truths which state what is true of God alone could avoid violating the rule that anything can be said univocally of God. It is sufficient to see that that rule holds that nothing can be said univocally of God and creature, and hence the rule is not violated by the application of certain names to God alone.

d. Before turning to the validation of the proof itself, let me conclude here by pointing out two things which the original article contained that were the germinal insights leading to my discovery of the proof.

(1) One I have already mentioned, namely, that the whole argument depended upon the proposition 'No contingent being can cause the existence of another'. If this proposition is true, and if the proposition 'Contingent things need an efficient cause of their being' is true, the truth of these two propositions is equivalent to the truth of the proposition 'Being is the proper effect of God'. For by 'God' here I understand 'necessary being', and by 'necessary being' I understand 'non-contingent being'; and so it is clear that if contingent beings need a cause for their existence, and if no contingent being can cause the existence of another it must follow that *only* a non-contingent being can cause the existence of contingent beings.

(a) Let me express this formally. Let P stand for the proposition 'No contingent being can cause the existence of another'. Let Q stand for the proposition 'Contingent beings need a cause for their existence'. And let R stand for the proposition 'The existence of contingent beings can be caused only by a non-contingent (i.e., a necessary) being, i.e., by God'.

(b) Now it is evident that the propositions P and Q, taken together, are convertible with the proposition R. By "convertible" I mean that the truth of P and Q implies the truth of R, and that the truth of R implies the truth of P and Q.

Furthermore, P and Q are an analytical expansion of the truth of R.

(c) In order to prove the proposition 'Being is the proper effect of God' which is merely another verbal statement of the truth of R, we have only to prove the truth of the propositions P and Q.

(d) But the proof of R, through the proof of P and Q, does not constitute the proof of God's existence. Two more propositions are required for that. One is the proposition 'Contingent beings exist'. Let this be A. And the other is the hypothetical proposition 'If the effect exists, the required cause exists'. Let this be X. Hence to prove the proposition 'God exists'—which is Z—we must be able to affirm the following propositions: P, Q, A, and X. X is self-evident. But P and A are not self-evident. Hence these must be proved. Whether Q is self-evident is a question to be discussed presently.

(2) In the concluding pages of my first article, I expressed an insight which had since led me to the proof of the proposition P. Vd. p. 217, top paragraph. That insight was simply this: that no corporeal substance can be an efficient cause except through operations involving time and motion. But the efficient causation of being is an action apart from time and motion. Hence no corporeal substance can be the efficient cause of the existence of another corporeal substance.

(a) Unfortunately, I nullified that insight at the time by supposing that, since spiritual action can take place without time and motion, contingent incorporeal substances might be able to cause the existence of contingent corporeal, substances. Hence I found myself blocked from reaching the conclusion that 'no contingent being, corporeal or spiritual, can cause the existence of another'.

(b) This error on my part was pointed out by Dr. Mullaney in his review already referred to (*New Scholasticism*, XVII, 2). On p. 177, he says : "Had he analyzed further the notion of '*a cause of being*', the complete irrelevance of, and answer to, his unsolved problem—whether contingent, incorporeal beings could cause the existence of corporeal things—would have been perceived. Whether or not the proof he suggests is actually St. Thomas's third proof without Aquinas's obscurities is not now the point. The point is that the satisfactory formulation of his proof is in Professor Adler's hands, and he is unaware of it."

(c) Dr. Mullaney was right. I did have all the elements of the proof and was unaware of it. But in one respect Dr. Mullaney was wrong. The fulfillment of the proof does not come from analyzing further the notion '*a cause of being*', but from understanding why the difference between corporeal and spiritual substances is irrelevant to the truth that no contingent being can cause the existence of anything.

3. Statement of the Proof

a. Preliminary observations.
  (1) In order to demonstrate a conclusion, all the premises required must be known to be true. Such knowledge consists in knowing these premises as self-evident, or in knowing their demonstration.
  (2) The proposition 'God exists' follows validly as a conclusion from the following premises:

X: If an effect exists, its required cause exists.

A: Contingent (corporeal) substances exist.

P: No contingent substance can cause the existence of anything.

Q: Contingent substances require a cause for their existence.

  (3) The validity of the reasoning is known through the formal self-evidence of the following formula: "If the existence of an effect implies the existence of its required cause, *and* if anything contingent exists, *and* if everything contingent must be caused to exist, *and* if nothing contingent can cause anything to exist, then a necessary being exists as the cause of the existence of any contingent being known by us to exist."
  (4) In the foregoing formulation, and throughout all the subsequent reasoning, the word "cause" will always be used to mean *efficient cause* and never either formal or material cause.
  (5) I shall now consider each of the propositions upon which the truth of the conclusion depends. In each case, I will say whether it is self-evident or demonstrable. If it is demonstrable, I will either assume the demonstration, or give the demonstration. In giving the demonstration, I will indicate which of the premises is self-evident, and which demonstrable, but I will not give the demonstration of all the demonstrable propositions herein involved. To do that would require a statement much too extensive for the present purposes. Here my only aim is to outline the proof, and to indicate the order of its elements. If my outline is wrong, there is no point in going further. If it is right, and free from all objections or difficulties, then I shall undertake the complete statement of the proof down to the last premise. The purpose of this memorandum is to get criticism relevant to or helpful toward the proposed undertaking. Hence I shall cite the texts in St. Thomas where I think the proof of certain premises is at least indicated, if not fully developed. In doing this, I am not arguing from the authority of St. Thomas. Every text I cite is cited

because I think it contains some truth, not because St. Thomas is its author. I shall mark propositions as follows: (E) for evident to intellectual *observation*; (SE) for self-evident to the understanding; and (D) for demonstrable.

b. The proposition X, If an effect exists, its required cause exists', is self-evident.

   (1) The only problem relevant here concerns the *co-existence* of cause and effect. In the sphere of motions, we know that the actual *per se* efficient cause must be simultaneous with its actual effect; but we also know that the effected motion can continue after the causing motion has ceased. Hence though the residual effect requires a cause in the sense that the motion of which it is a residual phase must *have had* a cause simultaneous in action with its *prior* phase, it would not be true to say here that the cause of the residual effect must co-exist or be simultaneous with it. What has been said also applies to complete acts as residual effects, for when a potency has been reduced to complete act, the act endures after the efficient cause, which reduced the potency to act, ceases to operate.

   (2) But if existence, unlike motion or acts of potencies, cannot be a residual effect, then its efficient cause must be operative at every moment that existence is effected. Hence the truth that a *causa essendi* must co-exist with its effects (i.e., caused existences) and must be operative for the continuing existence of such effects will be better understood after we see that existence is not the *act* of a *potency*, but the *realization* of a *possibility*.

c. The proposition A, 'Contingent (corporeal) substances exist', is demonstrable.

   (1) I shall not give the demonstration here, but I will point out the following elements in it:

      (a) 'Accidental change occurs' (E).
      (b) 'The principles of any change are threefold: form, matter and privation' (D).
      (c) 'Motion is the act of that which is in potency in a respect in which it is in potency' (Definition).
      (d) 'The subject of change (that which changes) must be actual in some respects and potential in other respects' (D).
      (e) 'That which is composite of act and potency is composite of form and matter' (D).
      (f) 'That which is reduced from potency to act is acted on by that which is actual in a respect in which it is potential' (D).

   (2) From the foregoing elements, and from others not here mentioned, it can be proved that there exists a plurality of corporeal substances, each composite of prime matter and substantial form, and each the subject of accidental forms as well.

   (3) It remains, of course, to show that such corporeal substances are contingent in their mode of being. Once individual corporeal

substances (in the plural) are proved to exist, their generation and corruption is an *evident* fact, and from this evident fact, their corruptibility can be inferred. But if the essence of a substance were inseparable from its existence, it could not be corruptible, for such a substance could not cease to exist. The corruptibility of a substance does not imply that its essence and existence are really identical, for incorporeal substances are conceivable, and in such substances there can be a real distinction between essence and existence though there is no composition of matter and form. On the other hand, the corruptibility of a substance implies more than a composition of matter and form. It implies a real distinction between essence and existence. Since 'contingency in mode of being' is to be understood in terms of 'a real distinction between essence and existence', the evident corruptibility of corporeal substances implies the contingency of their mode of being.

d. The proposition F, 'No contingent substance can cause the existence of anything', is demonstrable. The demonstration can be outlined in the following steps.

(1) In every contingent substance, essence is really distinct from accident, including power and operation, as well as from existence (D).

(a) Every contingent substance is composite of subject and accident, and among the accidents some are operative powers and some are operations of these powers.

Vd. *S.T.*, I, 77, 1; 54, 1, 2, 3; 25, 1.

(b) In every corporeal substance, accidental change is distinct from substantial change (D). From this follows the distinction between first and second acts. But the first act of matter constitutes a thing's essence, and its second acts are its operations. Hence in corporeal substances essence and operation are distinct. Hence also the potency of which operation is the act must be distinct from the potency of which substantial form is the act. The potency of which substantial form is the act enters into the constitution of the thing's essence, but the potencies which underlie accidental forms, or second acts, are as distinct from the thing's essence, as second acts are from first act.

(2) A contingent substance cannot cause any effect by its first act, constitutive of its essence, but only through its operations which are its second acts, i.e., acts of its second potencies or powers (D).

(a) The essence of a contingent substance is that in virtue of which it *is what* it is. The operations of a contingent substance are that in virtue of which it *does* what it does.

(b) But every instance of efficient causation with which we are acquainted in the sphere of corporeal substances, involves *doing*, as well as *being*. It is not enough for a substance to *exist* in order for it to be an agent. It must also *operate*. In short, no corporeal substance efficiently causes anything by its essence, but only by the operation of its powers. In so far as it is simply, without operating, it is not an agent; it is not an efficient cause.

(c) What we know to be the case in the sphere of contingent corporeal substances, we can infer to be the case in the sphere of contingent spiritual substances, *should such exist.* We can infer this from the fact that the real distinction of essence, power and operation is connected with the fact of *contingency*, not with the fact of *materiality*.

(d) Hence although we only know that corporeal contingent substances exist (as proved in c. above), our conclusion is not limited to such substances, but holds for all substances that are contingent, i.e., in which essence and existence are really distinct. Our argument in no way depends on the existence or non-existence of spiritual substances. We know that corporeal substances, *which do exist*, exercise efficient causality through operation, not essence. And we know that *if* spiritual substances exist, and *if* they are contingent, *then* such substances also exercise efficient causality through operation, not essence.

(3) An operation cannot be the efficient cause of anything's existence, neither the existence of the agent, nor the existence of the patient.

(a) A thing's operations cannot be the cause of its own existence, for its essence and existence are prior to its own operation. Operation is a second act and an accident in anything which is contingent in being.

(b) One thing's operations cannot be the efficient cause of the existence of another. (This is meant, of course, to apply only to operations which, as acts, are distinct from the thing's essence.)

(1) In accidental change, the potency reduced to act by operation is a pre-existent potency, i.e., a potency of the matter of an already existent subject, capable of being acted upon.

(2) In substantial change, the potency reduced to act by operation is a pre-existent potency, i.e., a potency of already existent matter.

(3) Hence whatever is efficiently caused by operation is the act of a pre-existent potency. In other words, as operation (distinct from essence) is itself a change or motion, so what operation effects is also a change or motion. A reduction of potency to act in the patient of the operation is the effect caused by the reduction from potency to act in the agent of the operation. The fact that what is reduced from potency to act may, on the part of the

patient, remain in act after the operation causing the motion ceases, is a fact not here relevant.

(4) The existence of a substance is not a reduction of potency to act. Existence is not a motion or change, neither substantial nor accidental. Motion is the act of that which is in potency in the respect in which it is in potency. Existence is the realization of that which is possible *qua* possible.

(5) The proportion 'Essence: existence:: potency: act' is true, but it does not mean that *essence* can be called a potency or potential being in its own right, as matter or power are potencies or potential beings. To call an essence a "potency" is to speak metaphorically. Similarly, to call existence an "act" is to speak metaphorically, if the word "act" strictly always signifies the act of a preexistent potency. That is why I speak of an essence apart from existence as "the merely possible" and of existence, not as the "*act*" of the possible *qua* possible, but as the "*realization*" of the possible *qua* possible. The act which realizes the possible is the act of the efficient cause of an essence's existence, i.e., it is the act of an active power causing existence, not the act of a passive potency having *in itself* a real capacity for existence. It is the act of a power able to cause existence, not the act of an essence able to be caused to exist. The ability to exist *really* when caused is a possibility which has its being in the causative power. The essence pre-exists its *real* existence only in the sense that the possibility of its *real* existence is *in* the causative power whose act can *realize this possibility.*

(c) Hence it can be concluded that whatever agent exercises efficient causality through operation cannot efficiently cause existence as an effect, for existence is not the act of a pre-existent potency. But contingent beings exercise efficient causality only through their operations, all of which produce effects that are the acts of pre-existent potencies. Hence no contingent being can efficiently cause being, precisely because its essence, power, and operation are distinct. And from this it follows that if the existence of a contingent being requires a cause, then that cause must be a necessary being, i.e., a non-contingent being; and this is verified by the further fact that in a non-contingent being there is no distinction between essence, power, and operation precisely because there is no real distinction between essence and existence. Hence if a non-contingent being exercises efficient causality, it must do so through its essence which is identical with its power and operation, as it is identical with its existence. In short, two kinds of efficient causality are possible: *first,* efficient causality through operations distinct from essence; *second,* efficient causality through operation identical with essence. If a necessary being is required to cause the existence of contingent substances, it is also true that the mode of efficient causality involved is that of operation identical with essence. We do not need to know *what* such causality is in itself, for to know this positively is to know the essence of a necessary being positively, which is impossible. It is sufficient for our purposes if we know *negatively* that a non-contingent being is required as agent, and that the causality involved is *not* the sort we know, i.e., *not* through operation distinct from essence.

NOTE: The really difficult point in the foregoing reasoning concerns the distinction between the possible and the potential, and the distinction between the act by which the possible *qua* possible is *realized* and the act by which a potentiality is *actualized.* In an adequate statement of the proof of God's existence, the whole theory of the possible must be developed in terms of the distinction between *real* and *intentional* existence. The realization of the possible is not a change or a motion because it involves a shift in mode of existence (from the intentional to the real), whereas a motion involves the actualization of a *real* potency. Vd. *S. T.,* I, 46, 1, ad 1; and I, 104, 4, ad 2. Also vd. a forthcoming paper by Father Gerard Smith, 'Avicenna and the Possible'. The theory of the possible underlies the understanding of the real distinction between essence and existence.

(4) The proposition under consideration remains the same whether or not the causation of existence be conceived as involving the note of initiation. This depends upon the following reasoning.

   (a) If the causation of existence is not the act of a pre-existent potentiality, but the realization of the possible *qua* possible, then the causation of existence is *ex nihilo.* The possible, apart from existence, has no *real* being in *itself,* neither potential nor actual being. But where there is neither real potential nor real actual being, there is no real being, which is the same as real nothingness. Hence the realization of the possible *qua* possible, which is its existence, is exnihilation.

   (b) Exnihilation remains the same whether or not it involves initiation of the exnihilated.

   (c) Unless the existence of an essence (i.e., the realization of a possibility *qua* possible) is caused at every moment that it exists or is realized, it must cease to exist. The existence of an essence cannot be a residual effect, for existence is not the act of a pre-existent potency. The essence of a contingent being is not the cause of its own existence, for the words "cause of its own existence" are merely an inaccurate way of saying "uncaused existence" or "necessary being', or "that in which essence is identical with existence." Hence it follows that so long as an essence exists, so long as a possibility is realized, it requires an efficient cause of its existence.

(d) From the foregoing it follows that the efficient causation of existence remains the same whether or not the existence caused is *initiated* absolutely or, not being *initiated absolutely*, is sustained in its existence. In short, if the word "creator" is used only for such causation of existence as involves absolute initiation then the existence of contingent things does not prove the existence of a creator, for we do not know that they have ever been absolutely initiated. If, however, the word "creator" is used for exnihilation, prescinding from absolute initiation, then the existence of contingent things proves the existence of a creative cause, an exnihilating cause, for that is precisely what an efficient cause of existence is.

e. The proposition Q, 'Contingent substances require a cause for their existence', is self-evident.

(1) We know that contingency in being involves a real distinction between essence and existence. We now know also that this real distinction must be under-stood in the following manner: that the essence of a contingent substance. apart from existence is a mere possibility, i.e., it has no real being whatsoever, no existence as a real potentiality or as a real actuality. "Mere possibility" is not a mode of *real* existence; in other words, "possible existence" signifies an *intentional* mode of existence; hence the phrase "actual existence" should be used to signify *real* existence.

(2) Now by "cause of existence" we understand that act by which a mere possibility is realized. By "contingent substance" we understand that whose essence is merely possible until or unless it is realized. By this understanding of the terms, the proposition is self-evidently true.

(3) We know, furthermore, that the essence of an existent contingent substance is itself composite of real actuality and real potentiality. Hence the essence of a contingent thing apart from existence is the possibility for both real actuality and real potentiality. In the sphere of corporeal substances, this means that it is not the union of form and matter which causes the existence of the thing, for the form and matter together constitute the essence of a corporeal nature. The essence, apart from existence, is the possibility of these principles in composite union; the existence of that essence is the realization of that possibility, the realization of a possible actuality together with the realization of a possible potentiality.

(4) Hence neither the form alone, nor the matter alone, nor even the union of form and matter, can be the efficient cause of existence in a corporeal substance. The form and the matter are only the immanent principles, the formal and material causes, of the thing's *nature*. Since together or in composition, these principles constitute the thing's nature, and since such a nature is merely possible unless it exists, the existence of such a nature requires a cause to realize the possibility, a cause that lies outside the nature itself; and hence an efficient cause. To suppose the contrary is to suppose that the contingent nature is the cause of its own existence which, as we have seen, is self-contradictory, for that involves the affirmation and denial of contingency. This *reductio ad absurdum* verifies the self-evidence of the proposition that 'contingent substances require a cause for their existence.'

f. This completes my statement of the proof for God's existence. It is by no means a complete or adequate statement, for many premises are involved which have not been adequately demonstrated. This outline does, however, indicate that the fundamentals of the philosophy of nature, and almost the whole of metaphysical analysis, is logically prior to an adequate exposition of the proof of God's existence. One might almost say that the proposition 'God exists' is the last proposition in metaphysics, for though something of God's nature can be known in natural theology, what is thus known is not logically posterior to the proof of God's existence.

(1) The conclusion 'God exists' is an affirmation which rests upon a fundamental negation, namely, that no contingent being can cause existence. I mention this to indicate that we do not know God's existence from a positive knowledge of *what* God's nature is, but from an essential point of negative knowledge, namely, that God is not a contingent being.

(2) The proposition 'Being is the proper effect of God' is a premise in the proof, only in the sense that that proposition is convertible with two premises in the proof: that contingent beings require a cause for their existence; and that a non-contingent being is required as this cause. Hence the proposition 'Being is the proper effect of God', is not known by us positively, as a result of our knowledge of God's nature, but only as a result of our knowledge about contingent beings themselves—that they require a cause of being and that they cannot cause being. Hence the proof is purely *a posteriori*, reasoning, an argument from our knowledge of an effect, employing only a nominal definition of God.

(3) Our knowledge of the causation of existence is knowledge *that* it occurs, not knowledge of *what* it is. We can understand what Divine causation is, what exnihilation is, only negatively, analogically, and remotely. We do not know *how* or *why* God causes contingent things to exist. We only know *that* He does. What is

analogically common to Divine causation (of being) and natural causation (of motion) is the indeterminate meaning of 'cause'— viz., *that without which the effect would not be or happen.* What is negatively determinate about Divine causation, and peculiar to it, is this; that the causation of existence cannot be by an operation distinct from the agent's essence; or, in other words, that God causes things by his essence. Whereas natural agents cause becoming or motion by becoming or motion, God, Who is Being, causes being by His being. We can say this, but we do not understand the essence of such causation or action, for to understand that would be to understand God's essence as He understands it. Nevertheless, all of these limitations on our knowledge of God's essence and action, or of Divine causality, in no way affect the validity of a demonstration *quia*, of an *a posteriori* proof that God exists and that God is the cause required by the existence of contingent beings.

C. Supplementary Problems

Note: Between the publication of the original article in the Maritain volume of *The Thomist* and the writing of the present memorandum, I circulated a number of outlines of the proof here proposed among some of my correspondents. Although these outlines were much briefer and rougher than the present memorandum, they did contain the gist of the argument. Some of my correspondents have raised certain questions or difficulties, relevant to the elements in, or the order of, the proposed proof. These I should now like to consider briefly.

1. How do we know that God is possible, and must this not be known before we try to prove that God exists?

    a. The questioner suggests that the possibility of a "necessary being" may only be the possibility of the total nexus of contingent things, and asks, then, how we do know that the possibility of a necessary being is the possibility of a single being, distinct in being from all others, which has the properties assigned: necessity, simplicity, eternity, infinity, uniqueness, etc.?

    b. The answer is threefold.
        (1) If the nominal definition we employed in *a posteriori* inference were itself self-contradictory, it would, of course, be impossible to prove the existence of the thing defined; for the self-contradictory is the impossible, and the impossible cannot exist. Hence he who attempts to prove God must know that God is possible, in the sense indicated. The word "possible" is here used to signify "logical possibility" or a concept or notion free from self-contradiction.
        (2) The way in which we know that God is possible, in the sense indicated, prior to proving his existence, is by testing the nominal

definition for contradiction. There is no other way in which to determine that our words signify something possible, something which can exist, whether or not it does.

(3) The plurality of distinct substances is not a being, but an association or causal nexus of beings. Let us call this totality of distinct existences "the world." Now to say that the world exists is to use the word "exists" in an accidental sense. It is used in an essential sense only when it is used of that which is, by its nature, essentially one. Vd. *Metaphysics* V, 6, 7; VI, 2. But only a single being is essentially one. Hence if 'necessary being' is to be predicated essentially, it must be predicated of a single being, an essential one, not of an accidental one formed by some relation or nexus of a plurality of distinct beings. Furthermore the mode of being possessed by a plurality of beings is derived from the mode of being of its component members. Hence if all the members of the totality, or the world, are contingent, the world itself has contingent being, even though 'contingent being' is predicated accidentally of the world. Moreover, to say that the world is a necessary being is to say that the world is eternal, in the sense of never initiated. But while it is possible to say this, or the opposite, neither statement can be proved. Hence it is impossible to affirm as a known truth that the world is a necessary being. And there is nothing impossible about affirming the truth that God is a necessary being. The only problem here is to prove that a necessary being exists, the possibility of such an existence being known independently of the proof.

2. Why do contingent beings need an efficient cause for their existence; or more generally, why should there be any *causa essendi* over and above the known efficient, and other, causes which are all *causa fiendi?*

a. The questioner in this case is denying that God's existence can be proved; for he admits that God cannot be proved as *causa fiendi*, and by denying that the notion of *causa essendi* has any meaning, he is denying the possibility of a demonstration of God's existence *a posteriori*; for if motion is not an effect from which God can be proved as *causa fiendi*, and if existence is not an effect which needs a special cause, then there are no known effects from which to prove God's existence.

b. The force of the question can be understood in the following manner. Let us consider only substantial change. The generator causes the becoming of the generated. The continued existence of the generated is merely a residual effect of the generation; just as the continued actuality of the heated thing is a residual effect of the heating thing, or the continued local motion of one ball is a residual effect of the motion of another ball which has now ceased to move. In short, why does not the principle of inertia apply to first acts as well as to second acts. And if it does, is this not sufficient to account for the continued existence of a contingent substance, once a natural agent has operated as an efficient cause of its generation? If this were so, then a sufficient reason for the present existence of a corporeal substance would be given by these two factors: (1) the operation of natural agents as efficient causes of generation; and (2) the principle of inertia, by which the generated continues in actuality after generation. And if this were so, the questioner argues, then there is no need for a *causa essendi* over and above the various *causa fiendi*. Existence being merely a residual effect, it needs no additional cause to explain it.

c. The problem has already been solved by what has gone before. The solution lies in the distinction between first act, which is the act of a potency, and existence which is not the act of any potency, but rather what I have called 'the realization of the possible *qua* possible." What is a residual effect of the generative act is the endurance of the nature as such, so long as that which has the nature exists. That which is generated by a man remains actually a man so long as it exists. The generative cause is the cause of this matter becoming a man; the residual effect is the enduring humanity of this thing. But the generative cause could not have caused the existence of the generated thing, either initially or in its perpetuation. This can be shown as follows:

(1) Generation presupposes a pre-existent potentiality, i.e., it presupposes the existence of matter, which is a really existing potentiality. Hence the generative cause does not cause the existence of that the existence of which is presupposed by its action.

(2) This difficulty is not overcome by recourse to an infinite series of generators and generated things. I am not denying the possibility of an infinite series; nor am I denying that an infinite number of generators provides a sufficient *causa fiendi* for the becoming of *this thing*. What I am saying, however, is that in each act of generation, however many there be, an existence is presupposed which the generator does not cause, Hence an infinite number of generators does not account for the existence of the matter which generation presupposes, any more than one generator does. Matter is neither an actual nor a residual effect of generation or of motion. But matter is not a mere possibility. If it were, it could not be acted upon, or reduced to act. Matter is real potentiality, and as real, it is existent, i.e., it is itself the realization of a possibility. What causes the realization of this possibility? Obviously, no *causa fiendi*, for every *causa fiendi* operates upon pre-existent matter, and presupposes its reality or existence. Hence a *causa essendi* is required to cause that which is presupposed by generation, and, *a fortiori*, what is presupposed by every motion or accidental change. Every motion involves pre-existent matter which no motion causes.

(3) This does not mean that the *causa essendi* is a cause of the motion *as such*. It is rather the cause of that which underlies all motion. Thus, if one man builds a house, and another paints it, we do not say that the builder is the cause of the painting, though he is the

cause of that which underlies the painting. Though the comparison is remote, it shows us why we should not say that the *causa essendi*, the cause of matter's existence, is the cause of generation or notion. God may, of course, be both but, even so, as *causa essendi*, God is not an efficient cause of motion or generation. As *causa essendi*, God is efficient cause of the existence of *ens mobile*, and of the principles of motion which compose *ens mobile*.

(4) The foregoing shows that the proof of God's existence is not from motion as an effect, but from an effect which motion cannot cause, and that effect is one which must be caused if motion is to occur and be caused.

(5) The same sort of argument can be made in terms of the forms involved in generation or motion. The efficient *causa fiendi* is not the cause of the form *as such*, but of this form's concretion with this matter, or supervening to this matter. As matter is the principle of potentiality in the essence, so form is the principle of actuality in the essence. Neither is the principle of the essence's existence, and when the essence does exist really, both participate in that real existence, which motion cannot cause.

3. Does not this way of proving God's existence beg the question of God's existence in order to prove it; or, in other words, does not this manner of proof employ a knowledge about things which can be had only after one knows that God exists, and that God is the creator of things?

a. This questioner, unlike the previous one, holds that God's existence must be proved from motion as the effect—motion itself, not the *existence* of the principles underlying motion. Further, he holds that it is only after one knows God as prime mover, or as first or principal *causa fiendi*, that one knows, in deductive consequence, that God is also *causa essendi*. But, the questioner argues, it is only by knowing that God causes the existence of things creatively—whether or not *ab initio*—that one can know that things, God's creatures, are contingent in their mode of being, and hence need a cause for their existence. Hence to use the premise that 'contingent things exist' presupposes the knowledge that God exists, if by "contingent" we mean "that whose essence is not its existence" and hence "that which needs a cause for its existence." (Until we know that God exists and creates, the word "contingent" can only mean' *corruptible*' for us, and "necessary" *incorruptible*.) Hence it follows that a proof which argues from the existence of contingent beings, and from that fact that such beings require a cause for their existence, involves one in knowing that God exists before one has available the premises that one supposes can be used to prove His existence.

(1) There is one point of similitude between this third questioner and the second. Both are saying this: that from our knowledge of the nature and behavior of corporeal substances we cannot know that they are contingent in a sense which requires a cause for their existence. Both are saying that from our knowledge of the

nature and behavior of corporeal substances, we have no ground for positing a *causa essendi*, i.e., all the causes which need to be posited are *causa fiendi*. But there is this difference between the two questioners. The third is saying that an understanding of contingency in being, and all that that involves causally, is dependent upon a prior knowledge of God's existence, nature, and operation; whereas the second is saying that we can have no knowledge that God exists precisely because our knowledge of corporeal substances and their behavior does not require us to posit a *causa essendi*.

(2) The present questioner has some historical evidence in his favor, namely, that Aristotle, who did conceive God as creative, did not understand the contingency of things as involving more than their corruptibility. Aristotle did not see that contingency in being involved a real distinction between essence and existence, and so he saw no need for a *causa essendi* over and above all *causa fiendi*. According to this way of looking at things, Aristotle proved the existence of a prime mover, but he failed subsequently to understand that a prime mover is also a creator; and failing here to know the fact of creation—whether or not *ab initio*—he had no grounds for understanding contingency in being as in any way different from mere corruptibility.

(3) The position of this third questioner is sufficiently similar to the position taken by Schwartz (his pp. 41–42), so that an answer to the one is an answer to the other. Schwartz says that "it is patently false with respect to the human idea of contingency" to suppose "that the notion of contingent existence contains the idea of dependence in being on an existent which is absolutely necessary." To suppose this, he says, means that "God would enter into the definition of every created thing, which is not only contrary to the authority of St. Thomas, and known to be false from experience, but is contrary to reason." And he concludes by saying:

> The immediate relation between 'contingent' and 'dependence on a necessary being' is not verified for these terms as they are adequately and formally known to us. Nevertheless, in fact there is a necessary connection between these terms, inasmuch as God necessarily exists and everything else necessarily depends on Him for its existence. But this necessity is in fact, and is known as a conclusion, not as a principle of demonstration; i.e., when God is known to exist, it is known that everything else depends on Him for existence.

According to Schwartz then, the conditions of human knowledge are such that we can know that corporeal substances are contingent in their existence, over and above their corruptibility, *only after* we know that God exists, that God alone is a necessary being, and that God is the cause of the existence of all other beings which, as thus caused, are contingent in their mode of existence, whether or not they are by nature corruptible.

b. On the contrary, I hold that contingency in the mode of existence of corporeal substances can be known directly from the fact that they are corruptible by nature, and hence that the conditions of human knowledge are not opposed to our knowing the contingency of physical substances, in addition to their corruptibility, *before* we know that God exists, or that God causes the existence of the corruptible substances we know to exist. Once we know that corporeal substances are contingent beings, we can conceive the possibility of a necessary being; and from the fact that contingent beings need a cause of their existence which no contingent being can provide, we can prove that a necessary (i.e., non-contingent) being is not merely possible, but real (i.e., exists outside our minds).

(1) The historical evidence concerning Aristotle, contrasted with St. Thomas, is irrelevant. Aristotle did not prove a prime mover; nor did St. Thomas who followed Aristotle's mode of reasoning in this matter. And even if either of them had proved that a first efficient cause of motion existed, or that an unmoved mover existed, it would have been impossible to use that conclusion as a premise from which to argue that the "God" thus known to exist also caused the existence of things—*unless* one knew independently that things needed a cause for their existence, When I say "independently" here, I mean that the proposition that corporeal substances need a cause for their existence, which need is the precise point of their contingency in being, is derived from our knowledge of corporeal substances, not from our knowledge of the existence, nature, or action of God.

(2) This understanding of contingent being does not bring God into the definition of corporeal substances. On the contrary, only such an understanding of contingency excludes God from the definition of the contingency of corporeal substances; for if we could only know that a thing was contingent in being in so far as we knew that it was caused (i.e., created) by God, then the words "contingent" and "creature" would be synonymous; and in the same way that the notion of the Creator (i.e., God) enters into the notion or definition of *creature*, it would also enter into the conception or definition of *contingent being*. In short, the result which Schwartz abhors is unavoidable if one accepts his premises. But on my premises, which Schwartz rejects, that result is quite avoidable. The notion of God does not enter even remotely into the conception or definition of *contingent being*. Furthermore, even the fact that the notion of contingency entails the point that contingent beings need a cause for their existence, does not by itself imply God; for until we have proved that no contingent being can cause existence, we have not learned that a non-contingent being must be *causa essendi*. Thus we see that what Schwartz supposes is false, for there is no immediate relation between 'contingent' and 'dependence on a necessary being.'

The immediate relation is between 'contingent' and 'dependence on a *causa essendi*'. The relation between 'contingent' and 'dependence on God, or a necessary being' is *mediated* by the proposition that 'no contingent being can be *causa essendi*.' Hence the proposition 'contingent beings depend on God' is not self-evident, but is a demonstrated, or mediated, conclusion; and so it is shown that 'dependence on God' does not enter into the definition of 'contingent being.' Moreover, even the truth of the proved conclusion that 'Contingent beings depend on God' is not equivalent to the truth of the proposition 'God exists'. One further step of reasoning is required, viz., the step involving the self-evident hypothetical proposition, 'If the effect exists, its required cause exists', which is equivalent to 'If a dependent being exists, that on which it depends exists'.

(3) Furthermore, as I have already shown, our knowledge of God's nature is in no way logically posterior to our knowledge of God's existence. On the contrary, some conception of God's nature is necessarily prior to any proof of God's existence; for we must employ a nominal definition, and this definition will involve a number of implied notes which need not be made explicit. Now we can conceive the possibility of a 'necessary being' precisely because we know that the cognate objects of our experience, i.e., corporeal substances, are contingent in their being; and by negating what enters into our understanding of their contingency, we conceive God negatively and analogically. Far from our deriving our conception of the contingency of being from our knowledge of God, it is the other way around. Our initial conception of necessity in being is derived from the knowledge we have of cognate objects, such as corporeal and corruptible substances. (This is simply proved by the fact that it is only by denying of God what can be affirmed of corporeal substances—composition of matter and form, of subject and accident—that St. Thomas is able to conclude that God is a necessary being.) If we had God's knowledge of Himself and of His creative action, we could understand the essence of contingency, for then we could understand it in terms of its cause; but since we do not understand contingency in terms of its cause, we do not have a *propter quid* knowledge that corporeal things are contingent; nevertheless, we do have knowledge *that* they are, even though our understanding of *what* that contingency is must forever remain inadequate. It remains inadequate even after we know that God exists and that God creates things, for we cannot understand the *what* of creation, but only *that* it is a fact. In short, we do not and cannot reason from God as cause to contingency as effect; we can and must reason from contingency as effect to God as cause.

(4) That Aristotle failed to go beyond the distinction between corruptible and incorruptible being to a true distinction between

contingent and necessary being, is a fault in his *Metaphysics*, which may have a historical explanation of the sort the exponents of Christian philosophy give. I do not deny such an explanation. On the contrary, I affirm it, but with this limitation: that although Christian faith may have been the psychological condition prerequisite to the discovery of the distinction between contingent and necessary being, the truth of that distinction is entirely a natural truth, a truth which can be known by reason without faith, and a truth which is antecedent to the knowledge that creation is a fact. The theory of "Christian philosophy" leads some of its exponents to the false conclusion that knowing the fact of creation is prior to the understanding of contingency and necessity. It is this false conclusion which they exaggerate into a pretentious doctrine they call "existentialism," which amounts to this: that only a Christian philosopher can be an existentialist in metaphysics, for only a Christian philosopher can know the fact of creation, and apart from that fact the distinction between necessary and contingent existence cannot be known.

(a) There are two errors here. The first is that only a Christian philosopher can know the fact of creation, which is false if the proof of God's existence belongs to natural knowledge, since what is thereby proved to exist is a *causa essendi*, i.e., a creative cause. The additional point, concerning an absolute initiation of creatures, is, of course, entirely dogmatic and does not belong to philosophy at all.

(b) The second is that knowing the fact of creation is prior to knowledge of the distinction between necessary and contingent existence; or at least prior to the knowledge that corporeal substances are contingent in being. This I have already shown to be false.

(c) The understanding of creation may, however, be psychologically (though not logically) prior to the discovery of the metaphysical distinction between necessary and contingent being. The full religious dogma about the creation of the world from an absolute beginning may have been the psychological stimulus which led mediaeval thinkers to deeper levels of metaphysical analysis than Aristotle reached. The fact that the dogma of creation was the occasion for their discovery of this distinction may have even misled them, at the time, into making the false supposition that the fact of creation was logically antecedent to the validity of the distinction. Historical perspective enables us, however, to take a sounder view of the matter. We can separate the psychological factors involved in a process of discovery from the logical factors in an order of proof. We should have no difficulty in seeing that it is from the cognate objects of our experience that we learn about contingency in being, and that it is this very fact which provides the only rational basis for our seeking a creative cause, a *causa essendi*, as opposed to a *causa fiendi*. All of our natural knowledge of God is from His effects, both *that* He is and *what* He is and *how* He acts. Whatever cannot be learned from God's effects, cannot be naturally known about God. In no case is the reverse true. In no case do we understand the nature of cognate objects by understanding God as their cause; for such knowledge would presuppose adequate knowledge of God's essence and would even presume to penetrate into the mystery of God's freedom. We have *propter quid* knowledge of an effect only when we know the cause which requires the effect and understand why this cause requires this effect. We do not know God as requiring contingent being as an effect, for creatures are a consequence of God's free action. We only know God as a cause *required by*, but not *as requiring*, the existence of contingent beings. It is in this way, through knowledge *quia*, that we know the fact of creative causality. The fact is known *from* the independently known contingency in being of the corporeal substances whose nature and existence we know.

(5) I need not repeat here the arguments which I have already used against the second questioner, to show how we know that corporeal substances need a cause for their existence—without knowledge that God exists or that God created them. Those arguments apply against the third questioner, and should show him that from an understanding of existence as the realization of the possible, in distinction from generation or motion as first and second acts of pre-existent potencies, we know that the contingency of an *ens mobile*, which is signified to us by its corruptibility, goes beyond this corruptibility and consists in that real distinction between essence and existence which requires us to posit a *causa essendi*.

4. Is not this proof of God's existence a proof of God from motion, in the sense that the reasoning can proceed from motion *as an effect which could not occur without* the Divine action as a cause?

  a. While it is true that motion would not occur in the world unless God caused the existence of *mobile beings* and hence of the principles of motion, such as form and matter, or real potency and act, it does not follow from this fact that God is known by us as *causa fiendi* with respect to any natural motions with which we are acquainted. To say that motion would not occur without the Divine action as a cause is not to say that the Divine action is a *causa fiendi* of any known motion. I have already explained this point by calling attention to the distinction between a *causa fiendi* of motion, which operates by reducing a pre-existent potency to act, and a *causa essendi* of motion, which operates by causing the pre-existence of the potency which the efficient *per se* cause of every motion presupposes. (It should be added here that as *causa essendi* of motion, in the sense indicated, the Divine action does not *require* any particular motion to occur; and so God is not a *per se* efficient cause of each motion's occurrence unless He is a *causa fiendi*, as well as a *causa essendi*.)

b.   The questioner may have in mind that by regarding God as the *causa essendi* of motion, as well as of mobile beings, the Thomistic arguments from motion as the caused effect can be assimilated to the proof of God as *causa essendi*. I am not prepared to say here whether the actual wording of the Thomistic "ways" justifies such an interpretation; but whether or not it does, the basic point remains the same, namely, that God is not proved from the occurrence of any natural motion as such, but from the existential principles involved in all motions. Hence the effect under consideration is not motion, but existence. And when God is proved from this effect, the inference proceeds, not by showing the need for a first or highest principal *causa fiendi*, but by showing the need for a unique *causa essendi*.

Where These Chapters Came From

CHAPTER 1

This previously unpublished article, with the title 'A Philosopher Thinks about God', must date from about 1980. Dr. Adler refers to his interest in the existence of God since he was a student in 1921, then continuing his work on this topic for more than fifty years, and finally having published a book on the subject. This can only refer to *How to Think about God*, published in 1980, and that book title has been inserted into the text at this point.

This material was most likely presented as a lecture. Although the venue for the lecture is not listed, it's likely that Dr. Adler gave it at the Aspen Institute, where he presented programs and lectures for over forty years.

CHAPTER 2

This is the text of an interview of Mortimer J. Adler by Edward Wakin, published in *U.S. Catholic* (October 1980), pp. 26–30, under the title, 'God Exists: No Doubt about It'. The interview appeared under the following introduction:

> And so it came to pass at noon on a Sunday morning in Aspen, Colo. that a famous TV personality turned to a celebrated twentieth-century "pagan philosopher" and asked, "Do you believe in God?"
>
> Ten thousand feet high on a lovely, sun-drenched field, Mortimer Adler climaxed the third day of filming TV interviews with Bill Moyers by answering, "Yes! In fact, I think I'm ready to write a book I've been preparing all my life to write." Two years later at the age of seventy-seven, Adler has published *How to think about God: A Guide for the 20th-century Pagan*.
>
> He has always played for the highest stakes in a career as philosopher, editor, writer, teacher, and lecturer. He is the originator of the 54-volume *Great Books of the Western World*, producer of the 1771-page *Great Treasury of Western Thoughts*, and creative force behind the latest edition of *The Encyclopaedia Britannica*. Now he has taken on philosophy's highest stake: demonstrating the existence of God. As he puts it, "I am a twentieth-century pagan, nurtured in the civilization of the West, and I believe a book about God for pagans should be written by a pagan, but one who is deeply concerned with the question of God's existence and with trying to establish the reasonableness of belief in God."

CHAPTER 3

This chapter is a transcript of the *Firing Line* program, 'Firing Line: A Guide for the Twentieth-century Pagan', taped in Alexandria, Virginia, on January 14th, 1980, and originally telecast by PBS on March 24th, 1980. Host: William F. Buckley; Jr. Guest: Mortimer Adler; Examiner: Jeff Greenfield.

CHAPTER 4

Chapter 4 appeared as 'Kepler's Anguish and Hawking's Queries: Reflections on Natural Theology', in *The Great Ideas Today* (1992), Encyclopaedia Britannica, Inc., pp. 271–286.

It was accompanied by the following bio of the author:

> Owen Gingerich is senior astronomer at the Smithsonian Astrophysical Observatory in Cambridge, Massachusetts, professor of astronomy and of the history of science at Harvard University, and chairman of the university's history of science department. A leading authority on both Copernicus and Kepler, he is the editor as well of modern works, among them the twentieth-century part of the International Astronomical Union's *General History of Astronomy* (1984–), and he has written papers offering standard models of the solar atmosphere based on his own researches.
>
> His many publications include two collections of essays, *The Great Copernicus Chase* and *Eye of Heaven: Ptolemy, Copernicus, and Kepler*, both Published this year. He is a former vice president of the American Philosophical Society. Earlier articles by him appeared in *The Great Ideas Today* in 1973, 1979, and 1983.

CHAPTER 5

Chapter 5 appeared under the title 'Natural Theology, Chance, and God" in *The Great Ideas Today* (1992), Encyclopaedia Britannica, Inc., pp. 287–301. With it appeared the following bio of the author:

> Mortimer J. Adler, editor of *The Great Ideas Today*, is also chairman of the board of editors of Encyclopaedia Britannica, Inc., and editor in chief of the 1990 edition of *The Great Books of the Western World*. Dr. Adler received his Ph.D. from Columbia University and went on to teach for many years at the University of Chicago. In 1952 he founded the Institute for Philosophical Research, a center for the study of ideas of Western thought. Since 1953 he has been a trustee of the Aspen Institute, where he teaches each summer.
>
> Dr. Adler's autobiography, *Philosopher at Large*, first appeared in 1977 and will be reissued in paperback to coincide with the publication of its sequel, *A Second Look in the Rearview Mirror*. Both books are scheduled for publication in the fall of 1992.

CHAPTER 6

Chapter 6 was published in *The Great Ideas Today* (1992), Encyclopaedia Britannica, Inc., pp. 302–04, under the title, 'Response to Mortimer J. Adler'.

CHAPTER 7

Chapter 7 appeared under the title 'Adler's Cosmological Argument for the Existence of God', in *Perspectives on Science and Christian Faith*, Volume 47, #1 (March 1995), pp. 32–42. It was preceded by a note from the author:

> Fifteen years have passed since the book, *How to Think about God* by Mortimer J. Adler was published. It is a revised version of the traditional cosmological argument for the existence of God. Since then, many relevant developments in science have occurred and new philosophical critiques of cosmological arguments have appeared. In this article, I review the status of the concept of inertia, current theories of cosmology, and

arguments by J.L. Mackie and Adolf Grünbaum that consider their implications for the plausibility of Adler's argument. I conclude that, on balance, these developments enhance its plausibility.

CHAPTER 8

Chapter 8 was published as 'The Demonstration of God's Existence' in *The Thomist* (January 1943), pp. 188–218.

CHAPTER 9

Chapter 9 was published in *The Thomist* VI (April 1943), pp. 19–48, under the title, 'A Reply: The Demonstration of God's Existence'.

CHAPTER 10

Chapter 10 is the text of a mimeographed document. The title page has the following:

Rough Draft of a Second Article on the Demonstration of God's Existence
Mortimer J. Adler
June, 1943
Published as a private mimeograph

This very thorough and polished work is much more than what is usually understood by a 'rough draft'. Very few people now alive have been able to read this work, prior to the publication of this book. Dr. Adler intended to revise this draft before publication in printed form for a much wider readership, but there is no evidence to suggest that he ever did so.

THE IMPORTANCE OF PART III (CHAPTERS 8–10)

As well as Chapters 8 and 10, Dr. Adler wrote and distributed memoranda to various other individuals who had contacted him concerning his article. These memoranda were on a variety of topics, in which Dr. Adler sought detailed comments on the topics they raised, all of which were related to The Demonstration of God's Existence. It was after reviewing the responses to his memoranda that Dr. Adler wrote the material in Chapter 10.

Why are these works important? They're important for four reasons. First they show Adler carefully analyzing and correcting the errors of both Aristotle and St. Thomas. Second, they show Dr. Adler's original philosophic work in going beyond Aristotle and St. Thomas. Third, they show the evolution of Dr. Adler's philosophic thoughts and the correction of his errors. Finally, and well before his 1965 book *The Conditions of Philosophy*, in which he wrote about the necessity for carrying on public philosophy, Dr. Adler demonstrates the manner in which public philosophy should be undertaken.

KEN DZUGAN
Senior Fellow and Archivist
Center for the Study of The Great Ideas

Acknowledgments and Permissions

I make special mention of Howard Rosenbloom and the Ben and Esther Rosenbloom Foundation for their generous gift which made the publication of this book possible.

The Center is grateful for the cooperation the Adler Estate has provided in the preparation and publication of this book.

Dr. Adler donated his voluminous papers to the Special Collections Research Center located in the Regenstein Library at the University of Chicago. I deeply appreciate the co-operation of the many staff members who helped in giving me access and copies of material. This is especially true because my very numerous requests greatly exceeded their typical load of requests. Here are the names of the people whom I know touched this project in some way.

Archivists	*Page Co-ordinator*
Dan Meyer	Isabel Gonzalez
Eileen Ielmini	
Kathleen Feeney	*Student Pages*
	Alicia Caillier
Reader Services Staff	Zach DeVoe
Julia Gardner	Petra Johnson
David Pavelich	Elizabeth Keating
Christine Colburn	Alexandra Mateescu
Reina Williams	Tom Whittaker
Barbara Gilbert	Yennie Lee
	Jen Dentel

Materials located in the Special Collections Research Center and used in this book are listed below.

Adler, Mortimer J. Papers, Special Collections Research Center, University of Chicago Library

Box # 24: File Folder Name: A Philosopher Thinks about God (Contains document of same name)

I record my deep appreciation to the Center's co-founder and Director Max Weismann, for his continued help and support throughout this project and to David Ramsay Steele of Open Court for his immeasurable help in the final preparation of the manuscript.

I sincerely appreciate the donation of time and talent by Wayne Moquin in providing the index for the book.

This is my first foray into the world of book publishing. I deeply appreciate the willingness of Michael Ross of *Encyclopaedia Britannica* to answer my many questions.

I am most grateful for the legal and intellectual property advice of Michael A. Parks of Thompson Coburn LLP.

Finally my deep appreciation and loving gratitude to Miki Dzugan, my wife and best friend for over forty-five years, for her patience and support.

I wish to express my gratitude for permission to reprint material from the following sources:

'The Demonstration of God's Existence', from *The Thomist*, Volume V (January 1943), pp. 188–218.

'A Reply: The Demonstration of God's Existence', from *The Thomist*, Volume VI (April 1943), pp. 19–48.

'God Exists: No Doubt about It', Copyright 1980 *U.S. Catholic*. Reproduced by permission from the October 1980 issue of *U.S. Catholic*. Subscriptions: $22/year from 205 West Monroe, Chicago, IL 60606; Call 1-800-328-6515 for subscription information or visit <www.uscatholic.org>.

'A Guide for the 20th Century Pagan', March 24th, 1980, *Firing Line* Transcript. The copyrights in Firing Line transcripts are owned by Stanford University. They may not be published or reproduced in whole or in part without the express written permission of the Hoover Institution Archives. Please address requests for permission to Carol Leadenham, Hoover Institution Archives, Stanford, CA 94305-6010, (650) 723-3563, <leadenham@hoover.stanford.edu>.

'Kepler's Anguish and Hawking's Queries: Reflections on Natural Theology', from *The Great Ideas Today* (1992) by Encyclopaedia Britannica, Inc., pp. 271–286.

'Natural Theology, Chance, and God', from *The Great Ideas Today* (1992) by Encyclopaedia Britannica, Inc., pp. 287–301.

'Response to Mortimer J. Adler', from *The Great Ideas Today* (1992) by Encyclopaedia Britannica, Inc., pp. 302–04.

'Adler's Cosmological Argument for the Existence of God', by John Cramer, from: *Perspectives on Science and Christian Faith*, Volume 47, #1 (March 1995), pp. 32–42.

Glossary of Terms and Phrases

ab alio from, through, or in another

ab initio from the beginning

a fortiori all the more; with even more force. We're bound to accept an a fortiori claim because of our prior acceptance of a weaker application of the same reasoning. Frank can't run to the store in less than five minutes, and the restaurant is several blocks further away than the store. Thus, a fortiori, Frank can't run to the restaurant in less than five minutes.

a posteriori known only by being inferred from something else, such as facts of experience

a priori known prior to any specific facts; based on a theory rather than on experiment or experience; not needing empirical support

a se from, through, or in itself

causa efficiens efficient cause

causa essendi cause of being or existence

causa fiendi cause of becoming, change, or motion

causa movens cause of movement or change

cause per accidens an accidental cause, neither necessary nor sufficient

cause per aluid a remote cause, necessary but not sufficient

cause per se a proximate cause, necessary and sufficient

causes (according to Aristotle) 1. material cause: that *out of which* something is made. Wood is that *out of which* a table is made. 2. efficient cause: that *by which* something is made. A carpenter that *by which* a table is made. 3. formal cause: that *into which* something is made. Having four legs and a flat top is that *into which* a table is made. 4. final cause: that *for the sake of which* something is made. Eating on and writing on are that *for the sake of which* a table is made.

demonstration propter quid a demonstration a priori. It gives us knowledge both of the necessity of the fact and of the reason why the fact is true.

demonstration quia a demonstration *a posteriori*. It tells us only that the conclusion must be true if the contingent starting point is true.

deontological concerned with duties

dialectic 1. the art or practice of arriving at the truth by the exchange of logical arguments. 2. the process, especially associated with Hegel, of arriving at the truth by stating a thesis, developing a contradictory antithesis, and then arriving at a synthesis of the two.

ens a se necessary being, a thing that is completely self-sufficient

ens ab alio caused being, being from another

ens per aluid something from something, being from another

ens per se corruptible individual, corporeal substance

entia entis accidents or modes of being

ens mobile a being capable of change

essentia essence

exegesis critical examination, analysis, or exposition of a text

ex nihilo out of or from nothing, not produced from something pre-existent.

extra causas beyond reasons, beyond or outside of cause

extra nihil out of nothing, same as ex nihilo or without anything

in esse in actuality, not merely a possibility

in fieri be made, become; happen, take place

inhere to be inherent in or intrinsic to

in se in itself

insolubilia unsolvable problems

inter se between or among themselves

metaphysics the branch of philosophy dealing with the fundamental nature of being

non ab initio not from the beginning

per aluid by, in, or through another

per se by, of, or in itself

philosophia perennis perennial philosophy; philosophizing as the pursuit of truth, not dialectical display; the recognizable core of true philosophy in many different cultural traditions

prescind from withdraw one's own attention from

propria attributes, characteristics

propter quid a demonstration or argument proper quid begins from the very nature of the thing under discussion, whereas a demonstration or argument quia begins from some fact we happen to know about the thing. In medieval philosophy it was considered that only a demonstration propet quid could be truly probative.

quiddity the essence or essential quality, the 'what-ness', of a thing

quoad nos the thing as it is known

reductio ad absurdum proving a statement true by showing that its denial must lead to absurdity

reductio ad impossible the same as reductio ad absurdum

secundum quid usually, a reference to the fallacies of accident or converse accident, 'a dicto simpliciter ad dictum secundum quid' and 'a dicto secundum quid ad dictum simpliciter'.

secundum se the thing as it is.

simpliciter simply; just; without complexity; candidly

sine qua non an essential condition or element; an indispensable thing; an absolute prerequisite.

teleology the study of design or purpose in natural phenomena; the use of ultimate purpose or design to explain phenomena; belief in or perception of purposeful development toward an end, as in nature or history

transcendent surpassing others; pre-eminent or supreme; lying beyond the ordinary range of perception

Index

301